Conflict in Cyber Space

CW01498064

Adopting a multidisciplinary perspective, this book explores the key challenges associated with the proliferation of cyber capabilities.

Over the past two decades, a new man-made domain of conflict has materialized. Alongside armed conflict in the domains of land, sea, air and space, hostilities between different types of political actors are now taking place in cyber space. This volume addresses the challenges posed by cyber space hostility from theoretical, political, strategic and legal perspectives. In doing so, and in contrast to current literature, cyber security is analyzed through a multidimensional lens, as opposed to being treated solely as a military or criminal issue, for example. The individual chapters map out the different scholarly and political positions associated with various key aspects of cyber conflict and seek to answer the following questions: do existing theories provide sufficient answers to the current challenges posed by conflict in cyber space, and, if not, could alternative approaches be developed?; how do states and non-state actors make use of cyber weapons when pursuing strategic and political aims?; and, how does the advent of conflict in cyber space challenge our established legal framework? By asking important strategic questions on the theoretical, strategic, ethical and legal implications and the challenges of the proliferation of cyber-warfare capabilities, the book seeks to stimulate research into an area that has hitherto been neglected.

This book will be of much interest to students of cyber conflict and cyber warfare, war and conflict studies, international relations and security studies.

Karsten Friis is Senior Adviser and Head of the Research Group on Security and Defence at Norwegian Institute of International Affairs (NUPI), Oslo, Norway.

Jens Ringsmose is Associate Professor and Head of Department at the Department of Political Science and Public Management, University of Southern Denmark.

Routledge studies in conflict, security and technology

Series Editors: Mark Lacy, Dan Prince, Sylvia Walby and Corinne May-Chahal

Lancaster University

The *Routledge studies in conflict, technology and security* series aims to publish challenging studies that map the terrain of technology and security from a range of disciplinary perspectives, offering critical perspectives on the issues that concern publics, business and policymakers in a time of rapid and disruptive technological change.

Nonlinear Science and Warfare
Chaos, complexity and the U.S. military in the information age
Sean T. Lawson

Terrorism Online
Politics, law, technology
Edited by Lee Jarvis, Stuart Macdonald and Thomas M. Chen

Cyber Warfare
A multidisciplinary analysis
Edited by James A. Green

The Politics of Humanitarian Technology
Good intentions, unintended consequences and insecurity
Katja Lindskov Jacobsen

International Conflict and Cyberspace Superiority
Theory and practice
William D. Bryant

Conflict in Cyber Space
Theoretical, strategic and legal perspectives
Edited by Karsten Friis and Jens Ringsmose

Conflict in Cyber Space

Theoretical, strategic and legal perspectives

**Edited by Karsten Friis and
Jens Ringsmose**

LONDON AND NEW YORK

First published 2016
by Routledge
2 Park Square, Milton Park, Abingdon, Oxon OX14 4RN

and by Routledge
711 Third Avenue, New York, NY 10017

First issued in paperback 2017

Routledge is an imprint of the Taylor & Francis Group, an informa business

British Library Cataloguing-in-Publication Data
A catalogue record for this book is available from the British Library

Library of Congress Cataloging-in-Publication Data
Names: Friis, Karsten, 1968– editor. | Ringsmose, Jens, editor.
Title: Conflict in cyber space : theoretical, strategic and legal perspectives / edited by Karsten Friis and Jens Ringsmose.
Description: Abingdon, Oxon ; New York, NY : Routledge, 2016. | Series: Routledge studies in conflict, security and technology | Includes bibliographical references and index.
Identifiers: LCCN 2015041470| ISBN 9781138947788 (hardback) | ISBN 9781315669878 (ebook)
Subjects: LCSH: Cyberspace operations (Military science) | Cyberspace–Security measures. | Computer networks–Security measures. | Security, International.
Classification: LCC U163 .C6254 2016 | DDC 355.4–dc23
LC record available at http://lccn.loc.gov/2015041470

ISBN 13: 978-1-138-49795-5 (pbk)
ISBN 13: 978-1-138-94778-8 (hbk)

Typeset in Times New Roman
by Wearset Ltd, Boldon, Tyne and Wear

Contents

Contributors

Bill Boothby, Air Commodore Bill Boothby retired from the RAF Legal Branch as its Deputy Director in July 2011. His Doctorate is from the Europa Universität Viadrina in Germany. His published books are *Weapons and the Law of Armed Conflict*, *The Law of Targeting* and *Conflict Law*. He has been a member Groups of Experts that considered Direct Participation in Hostilities, that produced a Manual on the Law of Air and Missile Warfare and that produced the "Tallinn Manual on the International Law Applicable to Cyber Warfare."

Johan Eriksson is Professor of Political Science at Södertörn University and previously Head of Research at the Swedish Institute of International Affairs. His current research concerns: (1) the politics of expertise and technology, and (2) power, autonomy and territoriality in a globalized world. He has published nearly 100 texts, including seven books and numerous articles, chapters in edited volumes and research reports. His journal articles have appeared in for example *Cooperation and Conflict*, *Journal of Contingencies and Crisis Management*, *Globalizations*, *International Political Science Review*, *International Studies Perspectives*, *International Studies Review*, *Review of International Studies* and *Review of Policy Research*. Eriksson is Associate Editor of *Global Affairs*.

Karsten Friis is a Senior Adviser and Head of NUPIs Research Group on Security and Defence. He holds a *Cand. Polit.* in Political Science from the University of Oslo and a *MSc* in International Relations from London School of Economics. Friis has previously worked for the Organization for Security and Co-operation in Europe (OSCE) in Serbia, Montenegro and Kosovo, as well as for the Norwegian Armed Forces in Oslo and in Kosovo. His main area of expertise is security and defense policies, international military operations, civilian–military relations, cyber security, as well as the political developments in the Western Balkans.

Anders Henriksen, PhD, is an Associate Professor of International Law in the Faculty of Law at the University of Copenhagen and Director of the *Centre for International Law and Justice*. Professor Henriksen specializes in international law, while focusing on the regulation of interstate use of force, the laws of war, national security law and emerging technologies. He previously worked for the Danish Institute for Military Studies.

Michel Herzog is a researcher in the field of critical infrastructure protection and cyber security in the Risk and Resilience Research Group at the Center for Security Studies (CSS) at the Federal Institute of Technology (ETH) in Zurich. His main research interests are risk, incident and crisis management, especially in the field of critical infrastructure protection and cyber security. He holds a Master's degree in Political Science and Public Law from the University of Zurich.

Johan Lagerkvist is professor of Chinese language and culture at the department of Asian, Middle Eastern and Turkish Studies, Stockholm University. He is also a senior research fellow with the Swedish Institute of International Affairs. His main research interests include Chinese politics, Chinese state–society relations, digital communications and the media system, and China's evolving role in "South–South" cooperation. Johan Lagerkvist has published more than fifteen articles in international peer-reviewed journals, and more than twenty book chapters. His latest monograph is *After the Internet, Before Democracy: Competing Norms in Chinese Media and Society*, (Bern: Peter Lang, 2010).

Hans-Inge Langø is a PhD student at the Department of Government at the University of Texas at Austin. He holds an MA in International Relations from Boston University. Mr. Langø has previously worked as a junior research fellow at the Norwegian Institute of International Affairs, having spent several years researching the strategic implications of cyber security from both a national and international perspective. He also has experience working on various US foreign policy issues in Washington, DC, including providing analysis of defense spending and procurement programs to two task forces. His current research focuses on war delegation and third-party interventions in conflict.

Ryan C. Maness (PhD University of Illinois, Chicago, 2013) is a Visiting Fellow of Security and Resilience Studies in the Department of Political Science at Northeastern University. His ongoing research includes cyber conflict, post-Soviet space relations and interests, Russian foreign policy, and regional security and energy politics. Dr. Maness has published peer-reviewed articles in *Journal of Peace Research*, *Armed Forces and Society*, and *Journal of Slavic Military Studies*, as well as in *Foreign Affairs*. Maness and Valeriano have recently completed *Cyber War versus Cyber Realities* (Oxford University Press, 2015) and *Russia's Coercive Diplomacy: Cyber, Energy and Maritime Power* (Palgrave, 2015). His main focus is the continuation of an empirical cyber incident and dispute dataset and Russian energy policies in post-Soviet space.

George E. Mitchell is an assistant professor of political science and an affiliate of the public service management (MPA) and international relations (IR-MA) programs at the Powell School of the City College, New York. Specializing in NGO management and leadership, his research has appeared in journals of NGO studies, non-profit management, public administration and international relations. Before joining the Powell School he worked in the post-conflict reconstruction sector in the Middle East and was a founding Member of the Transnational NGO Initiative at the Maxwell School of Syracuse University.

Lilly Pijnenburg Muller is a Research Fellow at the University of Oxford Martin School's Global Cyber Security Capacity Centre. Prior to this she worked in the Security and Defense group at the Norwegian Institute of International Affairs (NUPI). She specializes in cyber security and cyber capacity and her research interests include global governance and public–private relations. She holds an MA in politics from the University of Glasgow.

Thomas Elkjer Nissen, MA, MSc, has worked since 2001 at the Royal Danish Defence College (RDDC) as a Military Analyst responsible for Strategic Communication (StratCom), Military Information Operations and Cyber Warfare. He conducts research and seminars as well as acts as a high level advisor within the above fields of work. In this capacity he has also published a series of books, book chapters, journal articles and research papers on the topics.

Allison Pytlak is the Policy and Advocacy Specialist for the Control Arms Coalition, a global civil society network that focuses on the Arms Trade Treaty based in New York. Previously she held advocacy and communications-related roles with global disarmament campaigns and organizations. She received a bachelor's degree in International Relations from the University of Toronto in 2004, and a Master's of International Relations from the City University of New York in 2014 where her research focus was cyber warfare. She often writes on arms control, cyber or conflict issues.

Erik Reichborn-Kjennerud is a research fellow in the Security and Defence Group at the Norwegian Institute of International Affairs and a PhD candidate at the Department of War Studies at King's College London. His research interests include military theory and strategic thinking, contemporary Western warfare, war and technology, NATO and IR theory.

Jens Ringsmose is an associate professor at the Center for War Studies and the Head of Department at the Department of Political Science and Public Management, University of Southern Denmark, where he also earned his PhD in international relations. His main research areas are NATO and strategic studies. From 2006 to 2008, he worked as a research fellow at the Danish Institute for Military Studies in Copenhagen. He has published widely, including articles in *International Politics*, *Contemporary Security Policy*, *European Security* and *Cooperation and Conflict*, on counter-insurgency, transatlantic cooperation, and Danish security and defence policy.

Kristin Bergtora Sandvik is a senior researcher at PRIO and the Director for the Norwegian Centre for Humanitarian Studies. She holds an S.J.D. from

Harvard Law School (2008). Her research takes a socio-legal approach to international law, war and humanitarian action. Her work has appeared in *Disasters*, the *International Journal of Refugee Law*, *PoLAR: Political and Legal Anthropology Review*, the *Journal of Military Ethics* and *Millennium: Journal of International Studies*. Correspondence address: PRIO PO Box 9229, Grønland NO-0134, Oslo, Norway. Email: bergtora@prio.no

Jonas Schmid is a research assistant at the Center for Security Studies (CSS) at the Federal Institute of Technology (ETH) in Zurich, where he works on cyber defense and cyber security issues. His main research interests include the functioning of security networks as well as the governance of zero-day vulnerabilities and exploits. He holds a Bachelor's degree in International Relations from the University of Geneva and a Master's degree in Comparative International Studies at the ETHZ and University of Zurich.

Brandon Valeriano is a Senior Lecturer in Global Security at the University of Glasgow in the School of Social and Political Sciences. Dr. Valeriano's research mainly explores the relationship between technology and conflict, with additional work on Latino foreign policy issues and popular culture and warfare. Dr. Valeriano has published dozens of articles and book chapters in such outlets as the *Journal of Politics*, *International Studies Quarterly*, *Journal of Peace Research* and *Foreign Affairs*. His two most recent books are *Cyber War versus Cyber Reality* (Oxford University Press, 2015) and *Russian Coercive Diplomacy* (Palgrave, 2015) with two *Foreign Affairs* pieces summarizing the work titled "The Coming Cyberpeace" and "Paper Tiger Putin." Ongoing research explores cyber coercion, external threats and video games, and arms races and arms control in cyber space.

Preface

Michael Rühle

Head, Energy Security Section, Emerging Security Challenges Division, NATO

When I was about ten years old, my parents gave me an illustrated history of World War II. The book contained all the famous photographs that captured the horrors of that war, in chronological order, from the "Blitzkrieg" to the liberation of the skeleton-like survivors of Auschwitz. Yet the one photograph that stuck in my mind above all others was taken at the very beginning of the war: Polish cavalry armed with lances were trying to defend against German tanks. Never before had I seen a picture that expressed so much military futility. This was much more than a mere "imbalance" of military power: the photograph epitomized the fatal consequences of a defense that was not prepared to cope with a new type of threat. No matter how bravely the defenders would fight, they were doomed. Twentieth-century challenges could not be met with nineteenth-century means.

Cyber means are the tanks of the twenty-first century. Threats emanating from cyber space may confront the defender with situations not unlike those that the Polish cavalry was confronted with: an inherent advantage of the attacker over the defender, as well as the attacker's use of the element of surprise. Hence, to avoid defeat, it is vitally important to fully understand the cyber domain. Generating such understanding is not easy, however. Humans, as Leonardo da Vinci said, are "creatures of eyes": they need images, but also sounds, smells and other sensations. They move across territory. They navigate through a three-dimensional world. And even though cars and planes allow them to travel much faster than by foot, their brains are still used to the walking speed of their Neanderthal ancestors. In the cyber world, however, these "physical" criteria no longer apply: things happen in nanoseconds, and often by stealth. Indeed, cyber invalidates most traditional security categories: deterrence, retaliation, attribution, the law of armed conflict, arms control—all the pillars on which traditional security has been built for decades, even centuries. And yet there is no alternative but to face the challenge.

The magnitude of the challenge

In 2008, the number of things connected to the Internet exceeded the number of people on earth. By 2020, around fifty billion mobile devices will be connected to the Internet—about seven devices per human being.[1] Put differently, fifty billion mobile devices (not counting stationary assets) will depend on an Internet that was not built with security in mind. This increase in the number of devices is outpaced by the increase and growing sophistication of malware. The annual number of attacks on software is estimated to have reached several billion. The challenge is even more serious since many vulnerabilities are unknown. Zero-day exploits, for example, are forcing software companies to frantically issue new patches. Dormant code in a software may be activated months after that software was put to work.

To some extent, the very notion of "attack" is a misnomer. In the real world, attacks are visible. In the cyber world, it is all about intrusion. Cyber is the first attack mode when it can take months before you know you have been attacked. Many companies and government agencies have learned that they had been the victim of an attack only weeks and even months after it occurred. Given the relative ease with which to use cyber assets to make illicit financial gain, it is no surprise that cyber crime is coming closer to narcotics trade in terms of financial revenue.

National security challenges

From the view of national security, cyber defense is a nightmare. Military systems are highly computerized. Accordingly, every conflict today already has a cyber dimension. As the computerization will further increase, he who manages to dominate cyber space may well emerge victorious. The a priori assumption that this will benefit the West is at best arguable. The West may have more sophisticated military and cyber capabilities, but "the rest" may be able to exploit this very sophistication to its own advantage. Unlike an opponent's weapons, which can be counted and their performance observed in exercises, evaluating an opponent's cyber capabilities involves far more guesswork. Much can be gained by probing an opponent's network—or by watching the opponent probe one's own—but the level of certainty as to the opponent's capabilities will remain far lower than in the domain of traditional military hardware.

Another stark contrast to the traditional military realm is the threshold for action. In the "real world," the attacker can estimate with some confidence where his opponent's threshold of pain might lie. There are fairly clear demarcation lines. Crossing a border, for example, or attacking an opponent's vessel are actions that are likely to trigger a violent response. But will that same opponent also react if a well-orchestrated cyber attack disables certain parts of his national energy infrastructure? Will he chose to respond robustly even if there were no casualties?

This is no trivial matter. Cyber defense is based on the new principle that you cannot stop attacks and losses but only mitigate their effects. This requires a definition of what constitutes an acceptable risk. Indeed, whether the disruption of a certain service or military capability should be treated the same way as the outright destruction of certain assets goes to the heart of the cyber challenge. Is the defender legally entitled to respond in kind? Can one even contemplate a kinetic response? And if a response is being contemplated, can the defender be certain that he is hitting the true attacker? What if the attack was carried out by non-state actors within a state? Should the government of the host country (which may well be the instigator of the attacks) be held responsible for the malicious cyber actions committed by its citizens?

This attribution challenge is another area that sets cyber apart from traditional forms of warfare. While the perpetrator of a traditional military attack is usually identifiable (and even terrorist, non-state actors usually brag about their deeds), cyber is much more ambiguous. And even if the defender is certain about the attacker's identity, and seeks to "name and shame" the perpetrator, what will be the evidence he could produce that the international community would consider convincing? Tanks and fighter jets are owned by states—and the state was seen as the actor responsible for providing security. Cyber capabilities, by contrast, are owned mostly by the private sector and even by individuals. Consequently, this raises the question of where the responsibility for security lies: the state? the company? the individual accepting the risk? the technology provider? Moreover, cyber enables individuals to cause massive damage to states—and at very little financial cost. While the strategic communities have long been worrying about Weapons of Mass Destruction in the hands of non-state actors, the "Weapon of Mass Disruption" has already reached the individual.

The term "individual," however, requires a closer look. The image of the nerdy loner sitting at home and hacking into the Pentagon's computers is a common stereotype, but the real threat comes from groups of individuals. Indeed, some cyber aggressors seem to be particularly talented at forming coalitions. And even if their motives may sometimes be benign (at least in their own view), their self-righteousness compels them to engage in actions that are hardly distinguishable from criminal activity. This should give pause to those who once hailed the arrival of the Internet simply as a new opportunity for the democratic participation of the individual in the public discourse. Cyber space has also become the empowering mechanism for the disgruntled and disenfranchised that enables them to play out their fantasies.

What does all this mean for traditional security policies? And what does it mean for alliances?

The first question that comes to mind is about deterrence. The two well-known types of deterring an opponent from committing an unwelcome action—by threatening to punish him or by denying his action any success—also apply in cyber space. However, while in the "real world" the threat of military reprisal remains the dominant form of deterrence, the emphasis in the cyber domain is likely to tilt to the denial aspect. A cyber counter-offensive may deter some prospective aggressors, but most of them will still try their luck. The focus will therefore have to be on denial—or better: resilience. Even a sophisticated concept of resilience that maintains essential services (e.g., water supply) in a degraded environment may not have a strong deterrent effect per se, yet it may convince an attacker to go after another, more promising target.

Another obvious challenge pertains to the speed of the necessary response and, consequently, the question of political control. Simply put, cyber attacks do not leave one with enough time to engage in lengthy deliberations, let alone with the opportunity to seek parliamentary approval of a response. While this challenge is already significant on the national level, it is even more severe in a multinational context. To overcome it, nations have to agree on rules of engagement, or pre-delegate authority to certain entities. This quasi-automaticity runs counter to the natural instinct of governments to retain political control over each and every aspect of their collective response; yet the slow, deliberative nature of consensus-building is unsuitable for the challenge. The consensus needs to be built before the actual event occurs.

The multinational context also reinforces the necessity for common cyber defense standards. If the attack is carried out against the weakest link of the network, a group of nations must insist that certain protective measures be taken by all of them. If this does not happen, some nations will feel that they are better off alone: those who take the risk seriously (and thus spend considerable resources on mitigating it) will not want to pay for those allies who entrust their cyber defense to chance. Lofty rhetoric of "alliance solidarity" aside, paying for your own defense while also subsidising the defense of your neighbor would be a recipe for failure.

Another consequence for national governments as well as alliances is the need for public–private partnerships. As pointed out above, most of the cyber infrastructure of modern societies is owned by the private sector. And, by the same token, it is in the private sector where most of the cyber defense expertise lies. Hence the need for governments to build new public–private partnerships. However, this is easier said than done. A discussion on cyber defense touches on state as well as business secrets. Companies may share a common interest to defend against cyber attacks, but they still remain competitors. Companies also need to balance their obligations to governments (i.e., reveal all data) with their obligations to their customers (i.e., protect your privacy from government snooping)—a tough choice. Building the "communities of trust" in which companies, let alone governments, would also frankly address their vulnerabilities, may well be among the greatest challenges in the cyber domain.

Conclusion: a new social contract

Developments in cyber space bring home a most inconvenient truth: what once was almost absolute security has become relative security. Everyone can become a victim, any time, any place. For the modern state, which in the final analysis derives its legitimacy from the fact that it is in a position to protect its citizens, this has far-reaching implications. What is needed is nothing less than a new social contract. Governments will have to admit that in the age of cyber attacks (and terrorism) they can no longer protect their citizens as comprehensively as in the past—and yet, at the same time, these citizens will have to give the state permission to use force, including offensive cyber force, earlier and perhaps more comprehensively than traditional ideas of self-defense may suggest.[2]

The implications of these changes are far-reaching indeed. Efforts to introduce a new social contract will face stiff resistance. However, inaction would ultimately be more expensive. No one has expressed this better than one of the world's richest men, Warren Buffett. The famed investor had long been thinking about the question of how major disasters would affect the insurance industry. But he had not turned his reflections into concrete action. In a letter to his shareholders, written a few weeks after the tragedy of "9/11," Buffett admitted that he had violated the "Noah rule": "predicting rain doesn't count, building arks does." This book is about building arks.

Notes

1 http://share.cisco.com/assets/images/Internet_of_Things_Infographic.jpg (accessed December 9, 2015). Other estimates are even higher.
2 I have made this point with respect to terrorism in "Sicherheit in Zeiten des Terrors" (Security in an Age of Terror), in: *Frankfurter Allgemeine Zeitung*, February 1, 2006: 6.

Introduction

Karsten Friis and Jens Ringsmose

The rapid digitalization of today's societies means that we are increasingly dependent upon a functional and stable cyber space. More and more private and public services, commerce and information flows rely on an efficient Internet, communication lines, space and geo-positioning. This dependency makes societies, governments, companies and individuals vulnerable to shut-downs, malfunction, disruptions, sabotage and criminal exploitation. The vulnerability is reinforced by the inherent weakness in many of the core functions of cyber space. It was built to be open and accessible, not secure and safe. This openness has arguably generated its enormous growth, and it has stimulated creativity and innovation on a global scale that no other commodity has. But more and more policymakers and security experts express concerns about these weaknesses. Deliberate attacks on servers, using exploitations to conduct espionage and theft are already common. Businesses lose billions of dollars annually as a result of industrial espionage, black mail and theft in cyber space.[1] States lose sensitive data of national security value. To respond to this, states and companies invest a lot in measures to achieve cyber security. Few, if any, think they ever can prevent attacks. Rather it is about reducing the risk of attack, protecting attacks from reaching the most valuable information and about swiftly returning to normal operations after an attack (resilience).

There are also a growing number of voices concerned that this development is a challenge for state security. Large-scale attacks on critical infrastructure could potentially shut down airports, cities, stock exchanges, water supply and electricity grids, it is argued (Clarke and Knake 2012). It is therefore a matter of national security. Similarly, the armed forces in most countries are increasingly digitalized. They rely on cyber space for communications, command and control, targeting, navigation and more. A potential shut-down of some of these core functions would seriously impair the ability for the military to operate. It is therefore not surprising that many states have declared cyber security a top national security issue—or that a vast number of states are developing offensive cyber capabilities. Relatedly, NATO has recently declared that a cyber attack could be regarded as conventional attack as defined in its Article 5 on collective defense.[2]

There are already some cases of what appears to be politically motivated disruptive attacks against states, such as the distributed denial of service attacks

(DDoS) against servers in Estonia in 2007 and Georgia in 2008, and of the Stuxnet worm inserted into the Iranian nuclear centrifuge in Natanz in 2010. These are frequently cited as examples of cyber attacks on states, but none had much disruptive impact on their targets. The latter stands out since it created physical (as well as digital) damage and therefore represents a watershed moment in the history of cyber attacks. The effect was nonetheless limited (Lindsay 2013), but it showed a potential for destruction that cannot be ignored by security authorities (Farwell and Rohozinski 2011). Still, both the number of such attacks as well as the effects they have had, are limited to date. Nonetheless, states continue to be targets as well as perpetrators of attacks in cyber space.

The vast majority of the cyber attacks the world is witnessing today are not of a directly disruptive nature, but rather of exploitations, espionage and theft. Rivalling states utilize cyber tools to gain access to sensitive data from each other. This can be government information, communication lines, industrial espionage, and more. It is primarily the Chinese–US mutual accusations in this respect that make the media headlines, but similar activity takes place in many other countries as well. Exploitation of zero-day vulnerabilities, or unknown holes in computer systems, is a particular concern, as it provides the attacker with a potential for both stealing information, spying on activity and ultimately disrupting or shutting down a system. A fear is that a rival state should succeed in installing several such "sleeping bombs," or botnets, which could be awakened in case of crisis and block significant parts of vital infrastructure.

This book is about these challenges. We focus primarily on the cyber security of states, and to a lesser extent on businesses or individuals, although this cannot be entirely separated.[3] As a result of the nature of the challenge, we deliberately apply the term *conflict*—as opposed to *war*. We first and foremost regard cyber weapons as a means of espionage, theft, sabotage and ultimately coercion. It cannot be ruled out that lives may be lost in the future as a result of cyber attack against for instance critical infrastructure in a country. But since this is yet to happen, and in any case is unlikely to be of huge magnitude, we do not consider war to be an appropriate term to describe cyber security challenges.[4] Nonetheless, cyber attacks could cause an escalation into conventional or violent war, something the inclusion of cyber attacks into NATO's Article 5 alludes to. Furthermore, we have already witnessed that cyber weapons are being used as an additional domain of warfare in kinetic wars, just as information warfare, electronic warfare and similar concepts and tools that already exists in most armed forces.

What is cyber space and cyber security?

Though agreeing on a definition or common vocabulary of cyber space has proven to be difficult,[5] Libicki's model of three separate but interlinked layers has become a relatively common way to describe cyber space (Libicki 2007). This consists of: the physical layer (tangible objects like servers, wires, routers, etc.); the syntactic or logical layer (software, protocols, etc.); and the semantic or cognitive layer (information and ideas). Each of these layers is associated with distinct security challenges. The physical can be destroyed or disrupted through kinetic means or through the syntactic layer, the syntactic can be harmed by malicious software (malware) and the information stored in the semantic can be stolen, altered, etc. It is important not to confuse these security challenges. Physical protection of critical infrastructure from kinetic sabotage or attacks is not cyber security. Likewise, WikiLeaks' or Edward Snowden's publication of sensitive documents from the NSA database is a breech in information security, not cyber security. However, had the same documents been stolen through an online attack on NSA's servers, it would qualify as a cyber attack.

Hence, when we speak of cyber security we are primarily focusing on how malware (viruses, Trojan horses and worms) introduced at the syntactic layer may harm the physical, syntactic or the semantic level. It is about malicious codes created to exploit holes or weaknesses in software. We may thus call the syntactic level the center of gravity in cyber security, as it is the layer which all cyber attacks must go through even though it may not be the intended target. It is the gateway to the other layers and where the cyber-security battles are being waged on a daily basis. By focusing on this basic technical nature of the problem, we also avoid having to differentiate between social categories of attacks based on intent, such as "crime," "terrorism," etc. As Dunn Cavelty puts it:

> The only way to (potentially) determine the source, nature, and scope of the incident is to investigate the incident—which means investigating the malware that caused it.
>
> (Dunn Cavelty and Balzacq 2014)

Furthermore, software is man-made and constantly evolving; new codes are written, holes are patched, and new weaknesses exploited on a non-stop basis. One cannot therefore pile up cyber weapons as one can with conventional weapons. They can be made useless overnight by software updates. In addition, today's truths about cyber security may be very different tomorrow—one can imagine for instance that spill-over from the logical to the physical layer becomes more common, thus making it a violent weapon, or that the attribution of the sources of attacks becomes less challenging than today. Both would significantly alter cyber security as we know it today (Rid and McBurney 2012).

Taken together these characteristics represent the "nature" of cyber space, and its relation to the social world. Cyber attack is about the potential for harmful penetration into the syntactic/logical level, with close to no warning time, aimed at systems and information that are of critical importance for our societies. Furthermore, the constantly evolving nature of cyber space makes the risks evolve as well, requiring a constant evolution also on security measures. In a nutshell, security cannot be provided through walls, fortresses or deterrence in its traditional form, only through constant engagement.

The aim and outline of the book

The aim of this book is to help us grasp these challenges better by looking at them from several angles. We have invited contributors to address cyber security from theoretical, political/strategic and legal perspectives. This way we shed light on several dimensions of these complex security challenges, and avoid treating it solely as for instance a military issue, criminal issue, political issue or a legal issue. It has something of all these. Something that appears as cyber crime can be politically motivated (industrial espionage against military companies), the use of cyber in warfare may challenge existing order in both legal and political domains, and framing the problem in for instance military terms may obscure an understanding of the non-military dimensions. Hence, by combining the theoretical, political and legal approaches in one volume we seek to bridge some of these divisions.

Furthermore, there is a tendency in policy circles to overblow the challenges by using apocalyptic analogies like "Pearl Harbor" or "nuclear weapons." Politicians, cyber-security professionals, lobbyist and think-tanks may deliberately use such language to attract attention and to put cyber security on the agenda. However, academic studies should take a more sober approach and critically assess what the real risks and dangers are, and how societies respond to them. This volume seeks to contribute to such a critical reading as well. Cyber security is simply too serious a matter to be wildly exaggerated.

Some of the major questions that will be addressed in this book are:

- Do our theories provide answers to important questions about conflict in cyber space? If not, could alternative approaches be developed?
- How do states and non-state actors make use of cyber weapons when pursuing strategic and political aims?
- How does the advent of conflict in cyber space challenge our established, legal categories? Are we in need of a new legal framework? Or can already existing legal norms accommodate the domain?

The first two chapters challenge the conventional theoretical approaches to cyber security and offer alternative perspectives. In Chapter 1, Hans-Inge Langø reviews the academic studies of cyber security over the last decade, categorizing them into revolutionist and traditionalist approaches, and arguing instead for what he labels an environmental approach. In Chapter 2, Karsten Friis and Erik Reichborn-Kjennerud argue in favor of utilizing risk theory rather than security theory when analyzing cyber security. By merging securitization theories and risk theories ("riskification"), they propose a theoretical approach tuned to both day-to-day incidents as well as more serious large-scale attacks.

The second part of the volume focuses on the political/strategic dimensions of cyber security: In Chapter 3, Ryan C. Maness and Brandon Valeriano explore the causal links between conflict in cyber space and conflict in the conventional domains of war. Their empirical (quantitative) analysis provides evidence to suggest that only very rarely will cyber conflicts bleed over to the traditional arenas of militarized conflict. In Chapter 4, Allison Pytlak and George E. Mitchell take a look at how cyber conflict plays out in rival dyads. Employing quantitative methods, they argue that cyber conflict is more likely to occur in rival dyads involving nuclear powers. Chapter 5 is devoted to a comparative study of Swedish and Chinese approaches to security. The contributors, Johan Eriksson and Johan Lagerqvist, argue that although there are certainly differences between how democratic and authoritarian states deal with security in cyber space, there are also important similarities. We should therefore be careful not to exaggerate propositions about "a great digital divide" between the West and the rest. In Chapter 6, Michel Herzog and Jonas Schmid examine how some states have apparently adopted contradictory approaches to managing cyber risks. On the one hand, these states purchase "zero-day exploits" on the black market to increase (short-term) cyber security, but at the same time, purchasers of zero-day exploits feed the black market for vulnerabilities and exploits thereby making the same states less secure in the long run. In Chapter 7, Lilly Pijnenburg Muller examines the current public–private cooperation to secure cyber space on both a national and international level through multi-stakeholder approaches. She explores the necessary other coordinated cooperation mechanism to govern the security of cyber space; one that can include a broader range of stakeholders and their power relations. In the second part's last chapter, Chapter 8, Thomas Nissen investigates how social network media are increasingly being weaponized as states and non-state actors employ Facebook, Twitter, etc. for traditional military purposes such as targeting, intelligence collection, propaganda, cyber operations and command and control.

The volume's third and last part, explores the major legal aspects related to the advent of cyber space as a domain of conflict. In Chapter 9, Anders Henriksen analyzes some of the existing uncertainties regarding the application of international law to cyber operations conducted in peacetime. He also links those uncertainties to the ongoing domestic efforts to develop national strategies for cyber space. In Chapter 10, one of the authors of the so-called Tallinn Manual, Bill Boothby, discusses whether—from a practical and legal perspective—the notion of cyber weapons makes sense at all. He then goes on to argue that states are legally obliged to review cyber weapons. Finally, in Chapter 11, Kristin Bergtora Sandvik offers some ideas for the further development of a critical research agenda on the role of law in the militarization of cyber space. Following existing critical scholarship on cyber security, she argues that there are ways to avoid the militarization of cyber space. Importantly, we should abstain from framing cyber conflict as a topic for the laws of armed conflict.

Notes

1 Estimates are hard to make, but the Center for and Strategic and International Studies (CSIS) and McAfee estimate it to be above $400 billion annually. See *Net Losses: Estimating the Global Cost of Cybercrime*, CSIS and McAfee, June 2014, at: www.mcafee.

com/us/resources/reports/rp-economic-impact-cybercrime2.pdf (accessed November 30, 2015).

2 See *NATO Wales Summit Declaration*, September 5, 2014, Paragraph 72: "We affirm therefore that cyber defence is part of NATO's core task of collective defence," at: www.nato.int/cps/en/natohq/official_texts_112964.htm (accessed November 30, 2015).

3 As we shall see in Chapter 9, the fact that the vast majority of cyber space infrastructure are owned by the private sector, and that literally all software development also is conducted by private enterprises, makes the state much more dependent on cooperation with the private sector than in most other forms of state security.

4 For further discussion, see for example, Thomas Rid, *Cyber War Will Not Take Place* (London: Hurst, 2013); David J. Lonsdale, *The Nature of War in the Information Age: Clausewitzian Future* (London: Frank Cass, 2004).

5 Daniel T. Kuehl's definition is often cited though. It reads:

> a global domain within the information environment whose distinctive and unique character is framed by the use of electronics and the electromagnetic spectrum to create, store, modify, exchange, and exploit information via interdependent and interconnected networks using information-communication technologies.
>
> Daniel T. Kuehl, "From Cyberspace to Cyberpower: Defining the Problem," in Franklin D. Kramer, Stuart H. Starr and Larry K. Wentz (eds), *Cyberpower and National Security* (Washington, DC: National Defense University Press, 2009), 28

References

Clarke, Richard A. and Robert Knake. 2012. *Cyber War: The Next Threat to National Security and What to Do About It*. New York: Ecco.

Farwell, James P. and Rafal Rohozinski. 2011. "Stuxnet and the Future of Cyber War." *Survival* 53 (1): 23–40.

Kuehl, Daniel T. 2009. "From Cyberspace to Cyberpower: Defining the Problem," in Franklin D. Kramer, Stuart H. Starr and Larry K. Wentz (eds), *Cyberpower and National Security*. Washington, DC: National Defense University Press.

Libicki, Martin C. 2007. *Conquest in Cyberspace: National Security and Information Warfare*. Cambridge: Cambridge University Press.

Lindsay, Jon R. 2013. "Stuxnet and the Limits of Cyberwarfare." *Security Studies* 22 (3): 365–404.

Lonsdale, David J. 2004. *The Nature of War in the Information Age: Clausewitzian Future*. London: Frank Cass.

Rid, Thomas. 2013. *Cyber War Will Not Take Place*. London: Hurst.

Rid, Thomas and Peter McBurney. 2012. "Cyber-Weapons." *RUSI Journal* 157 (1): 6–13.

1 Competing academic approaches to cyber security

Hans-Inge Langø

Introduction

Ever since science-fiction writer William Gibson coined the term "cyberspace" in his seminal novel *Neuromancer* we have waited in anticipation for how the information revolution would change society (Gibson 1984). It took a decade for the change to manifest itself in the form of the Internet, but over the past forty years information communication technology (ICT) has steadily changed the economy, civil society and also the military. The social and financial dividends of the revolution seem clearer now than they did in the 1990s, but the security implications of a society dependent on ICT for so many functions remain largely obscured. The promise of cyber wars has not (yet) been fulfilled, and both scholars and practitioners alike have struggled to define, much less agree on, what conflict in the wake of the information revolution will look like.

There is a wide range of literature on the subject, ranging from conceptualization of potential technology to operational analysis of current capabilities. However, there is severe disagreement on both the theoretical and conceptual foundations of cyber security.

At the heart of this debate is a deceptively simple question: how can actors leverage ICT to achieve political goals? For both technical and functional reasons, this technology is largely framed as a source of vulnerability, rather than a source of strength. Unlike kinetic energy, cyber weapons cannot blow up a building. Rather, they are dependent on technological vulnerabilities to be effective. In essence, the object of analysis is power, *cyber power*, and how actors can utilize their own cyber capabilities and exploit others' vulnerabilities. What this power looks like in practice is a source of contention across various epistemic communities, because we are still trying to determine rudimentary questions of how effective cyber weapons are, but also how vulnerable we are, in both a technical and political sense.

This chapter will discuss how cyber power is framed and discussed academically. The literature covering cyber security is disparate and covers a wide range of epistemic approaches and ontological subjects. However, there are some key questions common throughout, mostly concerning cyber power, and particularly coercive cyber power (Betz and Stevens 2011). In order to impose some intellectual order on the myriad texts, I have divided the literature into three schools of thought. Though the schools overlap in some ways, and sometimes in authors, they have distinct approaches to how to understand cyber power. In one way, this is also an historical, albeit brief, account of the academic field as it has developed over the past four decades or so. The three schools of thought represent eras as much as they represent epistemic communities, though as will become clear later on reality is seldom as neatly organized as one wants it to be. The typology suggested here should therefore serve only as a guide for future discussion.

The first section of this chapter will discuss the oldest school of cyber security, the Revolutionist school, which holds an expansive view of ICT and how it can change conflict. To illustrate the core ideas of this school, I present some selected central texts, showing how these ideas have influenced current thinking on cyber policy, and particularly the potential for cyber war. The next section presents the Traditionalist school. This school is largely defined by its function as a corrective to the more expansive claims of the Revolutionists, so many of its core texts and ideas have been written in response to Revolutionist thinking. The chapter will point to several weaknesses and shortcomings of both these "schools," arguing that the Revolutionists tend to see possibilities without empirics, while Traditionalists tend to see only as far as the empirics go. To overcome these shortcomings I will argue that we need to focus on the specific nature of cyber space and cyber power. To this I suggest an alternative, "environmental" approach. The last section will synthesize the few texts already published within this approach, and suggest possible ways forward.

The Revolutionists

The Revolutionist school of cyber security consists of a wide range of texts. As several of these were written in the formative years of the information revolution, they have to a certain extent defined how cyber security is understood today.[1] They shaped the thinking around this nascent technology, and as such the texts were primarily conceptual in nature. The technical details of cyber space and ICT were the launching pad for speculation and prognostication about how the technology would affect warfare and conflict. Looking back at these early texts, we can see that the Revolutionist school has two overlapping approaches to cyber security. The first, and oldest, is narrow in its approach, as it focuses on military-to-military operations and either kinetic effects or disruptive effects similar to electronic warfare. While this approach was maturing in places like the Pentagon, a second approach surfaced, one that was more holistic in examining the potential marriage of technology and organization. This second approach was part of the Revolution in Military Affairs (RMA) movement in the 1990s, and also offered glimpses of how technological change would manifest itself on a societal level. Whereas the two approaches may differ as to the subject of analysis (military versus societal structures) and purpose (capabilities concepts versus organizational concepts), both seek to identify the potential for cyber warfare in a strategic context. Moreover, the entire school of Revolutionist thinking is marked by an expansive, optimistic view of the role of technology in conflict—with some even claiming that new technology will change the very nature of war.

The idea of waging war against and through computer systems is nothing new, and we see this in the first part of the Revolutionist school. Even though most of the literature on cyber warfare has appeared in the past two decades, the vulnerabilities associated with widespread ICT integration were being discussed well before the spread of the Internet and the personal computer. In 1976, the term "information warfare" was coined in a US Department of Defense report on the potential vulnerabilities of US weapons platforms that had become reliant on computer systems.[2] If someone could manipulate or disrupt the processes controlling these platforms, that actor could keep the weapons from receiving launch commands. That would have implications for defense as well as offense: the United States could be the target of such operations, but could also exploit similar vulnerabilities in Soviet systems (Rona 1976). Pentagon analysts continued working on the concept of information warfare throughout the 1980s (Berkowitz 2003). By the time the Cold War had ended, ICT had become such an integral of society that a new term was coined, Strategic Information Warfare (SIW). A 1996 RAND report argued that the United States and a range of other countries had grown so dependent on ICT that computer network attacks (CNA) against these networks could have strategic effect (Molander *et al.* 1996). Cyber warfare was thus elevated, at least conceptually, to the same level as other forms of strategic warfare.

Scholars were now comparing cyber power to other forms of military power, with some even describing it as potential, albeit indirect, weapons of mass destruction (Clemmons and Brown 1999). The most common comparison though is between cyber power and strategic air power (Rattray 2009). In one of the most important texts on the subject, Gregory J. Rattray draws several parallels between the rise of strategic air power in the 1930s and 1940s and the possible use of cyber space as an arena for strategic warfare.[3] Rattray rejects the notion that cyber space is a virtual domain and thus the claim cyber conflict is a new phenomenon. It is all a product of physical processes, even if it is at the microscopic level. What is distinct, Rattray argues, is that SIW can be conducted in either a physically violent or a non-violent way. Even if a digital attack does not cause damage or shed blood, that does not mean it does not constitute a use of force. He refers to digital warfare as a type of microforce that can cause significant amounts of damage, despite the low level of energy expended: whereas a nuclear bomb kills many people and is terribly destructive, cyber attacks can be quite disruptive, with the potential for paralyzing economies or societal functions. However, as Rattray himself admits, the "microforce potential of digital information warfare is as yet unclear" (Rattray 2009).

Information revolution

While the concept of SIW depicted new types of military operations and targets, its focus on kinetic-like effects was largely traditional. Other scholars sought to reveal the broader implications of the information revolution underway, including, but not limited to, computer network attacks. This came with the debate on cyber security in the 1990s, when speculation about the potential for cyber power was debated through the prism of the Revolution in Military Affairs (RMA) (Gray 2005; Owens 1995).[4] ICT offered the opportunity for organizational changes in the military, in the shape of network-centric warfare, but the information revolution could also bypass the military and lead to societal conflict in cyber space. This is the second part of the Revolutionist school.

Many of these ideas were articulated by John Arquilla and David Ronfeldt. They wrote extensively about how the information revolution would revolutionize the way the military would wage war. This revolution would not be limited to new tools, the purely technological aspect, but would also encompass organizational changes enabling a more coordinated and efficient military. Arquilla and Ronfeldt indicated that, in the future, "warfare is no longer primarily a function of who puts the most capital, labor and technology on the battlefield, but of who has the best information about the battlefield" (Arquilla and Ronfeldt 1997b: 23).

Their own definition of the term cyber war is therefore quite broad. It referred to the conduct of "military operations according to information-related principles." In practical terms it would entail disrupting or destroying the opponent's ICT systems, but it could also mean maintaining informational superiority over your opponent (Arquilla and Ronfeldt 1997b: 30).

The basic idea behind Arquilla and Ronfeldt's concept, and thus its link to the RMA debate, is the translation of non-material factors into material gains. How do "we" use information and information systems to defeat an opponent when we need to do this cheaply or have no other options, due to imbalance in resources? As the authors stress, cyber war "should not be confused with past meanings of computerized, automated, robotic, or electronic warfare" (Arquilla and Ronfeldt 1997b: 30). To them, it is a broader concept that combines organization, doctrine and technology in order to transform warfare, and where information is a veritable commodity (Arquilla and Ronfeldt 1997c: 158). Informational superiority can also mean being able to manipulate the decision-making process of the opponent (Stein 1996).

Though much of what they write is speculative, Arquilla and Ronfeldt draw on historical examples such as *Blitzkrieg* and Mongol warfare to show how the information revolution might further change warfare. One of their proposals is a doctrine based on swarming: "when the dispersed nodes of a network of small (and also perhaps some large) forces can converge on an enemy from multiple directions, through either fire or maneuver." As they describe swarming, "[t]he overall aim should be *sustainable pulsing*—swarm networks must be able to coalesce rapidly and stealthily on a target, then dissever and redisperse, immediately ready to recombine for a new pulse" (Arquilla and Ronfeldt 1997d: 465). Related to this concept is the idea of a technological "Mesh," or a system of sensors, to empower the United States on the battlefield (Libicki 1994).

Whereas cyber war is fought by militaries, Arquilla and Ronfeldt also envisioned another type of conflict in cyber space, called netwar (Arquilla and Ronfeldt 1996). Such a conflict would be between states or societies, but on a lower level of conflict than cyber war. Its aim would be to affect the opposition population's beliefs or perceived knowledge about themselves or others. Netwar "may include include public diplomacy measures, propaganda and psychological campaigns, political and cultural subversion, deception of or interference with local media, infiltration of computer networks and databases, and efforts to promote a dissident or opposition movements across computer networks" (Arquilla and Ronfeldt 1997b: 28). Given both its form (asymmetrical, non-hierarchical and probably non-violent) and function (societal change), netwar can be seen as a hypothetical continuation of traditional *Kulturkampf*. Thomas Rid and Marc Hecker have come up with a related concept, "War 2.0," to describe the role of media operations and information technology in asymmetrical conflict. While it encompasses public affairs, psychological operations, public diplomacy and information operations, "War 2.0" should be seen as a subcategory of netwar.[5]

Alarmism

The group of scholars described above can be described as "Revolutionists." This does not imply uniform agreement as to the mechanics of cyber conflict, but the two groups share a fundamental view on the implications of cyber space in security—that the information revolution is, or has the potential for, changing warfare, and possibly war itself. This basic idea of a revolution in warfare has been adopted by many in the policy community, leading to what can only be described as hyperbolic predictions on the destructive potential of cyber space (Dunn Cavelty 2008; Brito and Watkins 2011; Lawson 2011; McGraw and Fick 2011; Gartzke 2013; Canabarro and Borne 2013).[6] We include some examples of this phenomenon in our discussion because much of the traditionalist critique, which will be discussed later, is specifically aimed at the alarmist rhetoric.

For quite some time policymakers, and some analysts, have warned of a potential "Cyber Pearl Harbor" or "Cyber 9/11" (Panetta 2012). Andrew F. Krepinevich has described the former as involving some sort of complex cyber attack, possibly against critical infrastructure, which

> would likely generate a similar sense of shock [as the attack on Pearl Harbor]. However, just as the attack on Pearl Harbor did not inflict a decisive blow to the United States, neither is a surprise massive cyber attack likely to do so
>
> (Krepinevich 2012: iii)

Others have gone even further in ascribing destructive qualities to cyber weapons. In his confirmation hearing, Secretary of State John F. Kerry called the challenges associated with cyber security "the 21st century nuclear weapons equivalent," while former Secretary of Defense Leon Panetta in 2012 warned that a series of cyber attacks aimed at the national critical infrastructure "would paralyze and shock the nation and create a new, profound sense of vulnerability" (Kerry 2013). This imagery is used to underscore the significant challenges and potential threats associated with cyber security (Lynn 2010: 97–108). This all adds up to a high level of uncertainty, as regards both to the threats and their potential effects.

Furthermore, policymakers, analysts and the media employ the term *cyber war* quite liberally (Arquilla and Ronfeldt 1997a; Clarke and Knake 2010; McConnell 2010; Sutter 2012). This term is frequently used as a catch-all for all kinds of extensive cyber operations and conflict, ranging from organized cyber espionage to attacks against critical national infrastructure (CNI). It is usually *not* applied in a way to describe a form of warfare; nor is it usually used to describe a stand-alone conflict in cyber space, as a narrow definition of the term would suggest. It is most commonly used to refer to an ongoing cyber conflict, but with more vivid and urgent language.

While the policymakers and analysts who use these terms rarely refer explicitly to texts from the Revolutionist school, their ideas seem strongly influenced by this school's expansive view, and particularly SIW. They share the Revolutionist idea that society is growing increasingly dependent on ICT and thus vulnerable to disruption. Furthermore, they hold that the allegedly low costs of entry into cyber space mean that more states and non-state actors are capable of committing malicious actions in cyber space as opposed to in the traditional domains of military power.[7] However, by failing to take into account the caveats on cyber power noted by Arquilla and Ronfeldt and others, these policymakers and analysts overestimate both the likelihood of such conflicts and their potential strategic effects.

The Traditionalists

The expansive claims of the Revolutionist school and the policy rhetoric have been met with skepticism and criticism by international relations scholars (Libicki 1995, 2012; Berkowski 2003; Lonsdale 2004; Denning 2009; Samaan 2010; Brito and Watkins 2011; Lawson 2011; Gartze 2013; Rid 2012; Rid and McBurney 2012; Canabarro and Borne 2013; Lindsay 2013; Valeriano and Maness 2014).[8] This trend can best be described as the "traditionalist" school of cyber security. The name does not imply backwardness or rejection of changing circumstances, but a reluctance to discard existing concepts, doctrines and policies prematurely. This school is fundamentally defined by its skepticism concerning the effects of the information revolution on international security and relations, but should also be understood as a direct reaction to the ideas put forth by Revolutionists, or more precisely, their alarmist offshoots. As such, Traditionalist literature is focused on testing the expansive claims of Revolutionist tests, with the most recent development being a growing body of political science scholarship dedicated to these questions. Some have even started doing large-scale studies of the relationship between politics and cyber security in international relations, though a lack of data means some questions are still beyond the reach of empirical analysis (Valeriano and Maness 2014). While much of this literature has only emerged in recent years as the public debate over cyber security and policy has gained momentum, critical texts date back further.

An early example of scholarly work critical to "Revolutionist" thinking on cyber security is Martin C. Libicki's *What is Information Warfare?* from 1995. Libicki argued that "Information warfare, as a separate technique of waging war, does not exist," he writes, adding: "[t]here are, instead, several distinct forms of information warfare, each laying claim to the larger concept" (Libicki 1995). One of these forms is cyber warfare, while some of the other forms show how ICT can assist other, more traditional military or covert operations.[9] Cyber warfare is the most relevant for this discussion, but also the most problematic, according to Libicki. It is "clearly the least tractable because by far the most fictitious, differing only in degree from information warfare as a whole" (Libicki 1995: 75).

Libicki concedes that the scenarios of science fiction are possible, but will not be relevant for national security anytime soon. This is the crux of the Traditionalist argument: while the theoretical potential for cyber warfare, and specifically SIW, exists, it is improbable at present and unlikely in the future. Libicki was skeptical of the utility of cyber warfare both for conceptual and empirical reasons. We see here how the potential of cyber power can depend on the object of analysis; while Libicki and others saw potential for organizational improvements as a result of the information revolution (e.g., the Mesh), the notion of network-to-network warfare should be less plausible. There have been obvious changes to cyber space in the intervening years since Libicki's book appeared, but the question is whether our empirical foundations have changed to such an extent that we can imagine plausible scenarios of cyber warfare. In recent years other scholars have picked up Libicki's mantle and sought to critique Revolutionist thinking with a better empirical grounding.

Taking the "strategic" out of SIW

The fundamental idea behind Revolutionist thinking, embodied in both the concept of SIW and cyber war, is that actions taken through cyber space can have some stand-alone, strategic effect, and may, at the final extreme, constrain conflict to cyber space alone. Several Traditionalists have criticized this particular idea. Erik Gartzke has argued that cyber attacks' lack of physical effects and the inability to conquer ground in cyber space mean that threats of cyber attacks would not be particularly effective in deterring or compelling an opponent (Gartzke 2013: 30). As such, cyber space does not have much stand-alone value. The introduction of cyber conflict entails not a narrowing of conflict, but rather a "broadening of the dimensions of warfare" (Gartzke 2013).

Others have argued that cyber attack should merely be considered as a subset of offensive operations, "a means of *denial* rather than a means of *punishment*," thus integrating it into a joint analysis of warfare in general (Samaan 2010: 16). Cyber attacks could have the disruptive effects of air strikes; though it is contested whether strategic bombing has independently caused military victory (Samaan 2010: 19). Thus, by logic, the limited coercive power of strategic bombing translates to the cyber domain (Pape 1996; Watts 1997).[10] This limitation also extends to how people respond to attacks. As Sean Lawson notes, history has shown that "both infrastructures and societies are more resilient than often assumed by policy makers" (Lawson 2011a). The implication is that even if an actor were able to launch a large-scale attack, it is questionable whether that would result in concessions or modified behavior as intended by the attacker. Electronic warfare might then serve as a better model (Samaan 2010: 20). What these criticisms have in common is that cyber space is defined less as a battlefield or environment, but more as a set of technologies or functions.[11] It is a materialistic view of cyber security, and for better or worse does not take into account the social effects of such attacks.

In addition to raising doubts about the effects of cyber attacks, traditionalists have also criticized the view that the barrier to entry is much lower in cyber space than in other domains of warfare. While it is cheaper to buy computers and develop malware than investing in traditional military capabilities like bombers and naval warships, the dichotomy is not quite that simple, according to some scholars. While the threshold might be low for simple operations, more complex ones are actually quite expensive and would still favor powerful states (Denning 2009). As Thomas Rid and Peter McBurney point out, "developing and deploying potentially destructive cyber weapons against hardened targets will require significant resources, hard-to-get and highly specific target intelligence, and time to prepare, launch and execute an attack" (Rid and McBurney 2012: 11). An analysis of Stuxnet, the most sophisticated CNO known to the public, supports this argument (Lindsay 2013).

Defining war and warfare

Related to the concept of SIW is the notion that we will see stand-alone conflict in cyber space, which is what the term cyber war actually implies. Scholars in the "Traditionalist" camp are highly critical of this notion and the theoretical underpinnings of Revolutionist thinking. Using Clausewitz's writings as a basis, we may say that *war* is a continuation of politics, a form of political violence, intended to compel the opponent to surrender or offer concessions, whereas *warfare* is the set of techniques used to wage war.[12] In the context of cyber security, this well-established definition and distinction has become muddled by a lack of conceptual clarity.

A central text in this discussion, and a key component of the traditionalist school, is a 2011 article by Thomas Rid titled "Cyber War Will Not Take Place" (Rid 2012). By applying Clausewitz's principles of war to the concept of cyber war, Rid argues that the cyber incidents we have seen do not constitute cyber war. First, the cyber attacks to date have had no possibility of causing physical violence, and therefore do not meet the criteria of violence; second, because of the difficulty attributing actions to actors, the instrumental aspect of the action cannot be proven; and third, much of what has occurred in terms of malicious actions in cyber space have been criminal acts with no clear political motivation.

Rid uses a narrow definition of the use of force, restricting it to physical violence. This is in line with Traditionalist thinking of war that holds that the introduction of technology does not fundamentally alter the nature of war. The nature of war is violent struggle, and this remains constant (Rid 2013: Ch. 6).[13]

Phillip S. Meilinger argues that this view is mistaken. While certain military historians and generals, inspired by Clausewitzian thinking, believe that the nature of war is immutable, Meilinger contends, "[they] most seriously err in equating land warfare—specifically, conventional battle as once practiced—with war. This error reflects institutional bias and downplays the role of technology" (Meilinger 2010: 26). According to him, naval blockades are evidence that technology can change war and make it less bloody (Meilinger 2010: 28).

Meilinger has an important point, but he confuses two concepts: the nature and the character of war. The former is permanent, while the latter is ever-changing. As Colin S. Gray writes, the tools of warfighting are a secondary matter of detail (Gray 2005: 33). What matters is that cyber tools are used in a political context to achieve strategic goals. This is what is meant by the permanent nature of war: it inevitably means using power to impose your will on an opponent. It does not have to involve actual bloodshed, although that is how it has been done historically. It is worth quoting at length why Gray holds that cyber conflict qualifies as cyber war:

> The answer is twofold. First, war is conducted to serve policy and a political vision that inspires policy, and policy has many instruments with which 'to impose our will on the enemy'. Cyberwar, in the particular sense of strategic, stand-alone, information warfare operations, can be seen as a reasonably distinct tool of grand strategy. A country may wage economic warfare also without using force. Coercion can take many forms. Second, cyberwar generally will be a team player to provide more or less direct support for the sharp end of the spear. Even if cyber combat has some stand-alone qualities, still it must occur in the political and strategic context of warfare. In other words, provided we are intelligent in thinking about new military instruments according to their unique natures, a traditional definition of war will not trouble us. Cyber power, and indeed space power in its current, though not future, form, cannot itself apply organized violence, or force. But so what?
>
> (Gray 2005: 293–94) [emphasis added]

While Rid sees the use of force in war as violent, instrumental and political, Gray clearly states that violence is not necessary to constitute an act of force.

"Coercion can take many forms," he writes. Fulfilling the other two criteria is hardly impossible, but Rid's article, and the cyber war debate writ large, is largely about semantics (Lawson 2011a). Perhaps the lesson then from this debate, and to Gray's point, is that instead of debating whether cyber attacks should be defined as X or Y, it might be more prudent to ask, what can cyber attacks achieve?

Some Traditionalists have tried to delineate the usefulness of cyber warfare, and thus attempt to explain the political and strategic utility of cyber space. According to Rid, there are three forms of cyber warfare—sabotage, espionage, and subversion—none of which amounts to more than "an auxiliary tool that is nice to have" (Rid 2012: 25). Others have made similar arguments. Erik Gartzke argues that cyber weapons have limited coercive potential, while Lucas Kello claims that cyber space is more conducive to destabilizing economies or societies (though he probably overstates his case on this) rather than achieving direct strategic effects (Gartzke 2013: 7–40).

Without empirical data to test these assertions, it is difficult to conclude who is right, though the Traditionalists' dismissal of CNO as an effective tool of coercion is likely overly reductive. Destructive or highly disruptive CNAs are possible and might become more frequent as the vulnerabilities and knowledge of exploiting those vulnerabilities increase. Traditionalists seem to equate large-scale CNAs implicitly with cyber war. In fact, it is possible to imagine cyber warfare aimed at critical infrastructure or command and control systems without it escalating into cyber war. Even still, beyond a certain threshold, conflict in cyber space is unlikely to remain "out there," as states will resort to other military or political tools to defend themselves or to force compliance. Considering the political context of cyber conflict is important, but that does not negate the possibility of successful CNO. Whereas Revolutionists see possibilities without empirics, Traditionalists tend to see only as far as the empirics go.

Because of the fundamentally different beliefs about the information revolution and its impact on international security, the debate over the strategic utility of cyber space is often framed as an either/or proposition. Either cyber space represents a new way of warfare, with the potential for SIW—or it is simply another tool in the toolbox. While this discussion is fruitful in forcing through conceptual clarity, it does not fully address the current use of cyber space as an arena for conflict. Understanding the granular qualities of cyber space will give a better idea of how cyber space works today and is likely to work in the near future. To achieve this, we must turn to a different approach to cyber security.

The environmentalists

There is an alternative approach to cyber security that has not been as prominent in the academic or policy debates. Whereas the Revolutionist school is defined by what might be called technological optimism and the Traditionalist school is defined by its skepticism regarding such expansive claims, this third approach is defined by its conceptual and empirical focus. I will call this the *environmental* approach to cyber security. The contributions are fragmented and do not yet constitute a "school," but this section will attempt to synthesize the various texts into a more coherent whole. Despite its flaws, this approach offers better chances of developing a systematic framework of analysis for the strategic utility of cyber space. In essence, this means that the texts seek to define and measure the inherent characteristics or features of cyber space as a distinct environment, separate from other domains and greater than the sum of its technological parts. This comprehensive approach offers the potential for a better understanding of cyber space than the often parochial or speculative approaches of the two other schools.

Cyber power

The notion of cyber power lies at the heart of the environmental school. Among the many definitions, we may note that Joseph S. Nye, Jr. defines cyber power as:

> [A] set of resources that relate to the creation, control, and communication of electronic and computer-based information—infrastructure, networks, software, human skills. This includes not only the Internet of networked computers, but also Intranets, cellular technologies, and space-based communications. Defined behaviorally, cyberpower is the ability to obtain preferred outcomes through use of the electronically interconnected information resources of the cyberdomain. Cyberpower can be used to produce preferred outcomes within cyberspace, or it can use cyberinstruments to produce preferred outcomes in other domains outside cyberspace.
>
> (Nye 2011: 123)

The first part of this definition specifies the "what" of cyber power, while the second part defines the "how." Here we are primarily interested in the latter. Nye gives a succinct definition of what cyber power means, but there are also various forms of cyber power.

David J. Betz and Tim Stevens have delineated four types: compulsory, institutional, structural and productive (Betz and Stevens 2011). Together, these four types of cyber power cover the various ways an actor can leverage cyber space for political gains. In practical terms, compulsory power would mean the ability to attack or credibly threaten an opponent into making concessions or surrendering, and this would most likely be measured by an actor's CNA capabilities and/or the opponent's vulnerabilities. Institutional power would mean an actor's ability to use international organizations to gain influence, whereas structural power defines whether the cyber-space environment is favorable to a particular actor, or not. Lastly, productive cyber power would probably refer to the ability to create norms of behavior through social interactions and discourse.

Comparativists

These conceptions of power lay the foundation for environmentalist analysis, though the focus in the literature is primarily on the compulsory and structural forms of power. The environmentalist school is not a uniform approach, and varies considerably depending on the author and the subject of analysis. Much of the early literature on cyber security attempted to draw similarities between cyber power, understood as a form of military power and other forms. This is similar to SIW and Revolutionist thinking, but is best described as an environmental approach, because it attempts to compare the inherent characteristics of cyber power vis-à-vis other forms of military power. Those characteristics are derived from the properties of the cyber-space environment. In his seminal work on SIW, Rattray undertakes a comparative study of cyber space and the rise of strategic air power in the 1930s, while other works have compared cyber power to sea power and nuclear power (Rattray 2001, 2009; Krepinevich 2012).

Such a comparative approach is intended to offer something familiar when talking about something new, but it is not without pitfalls. Comparing cyber power with some other power invariably means examining cyber power through the lens of understanding of some other form of power. And so we get descriptions of cyber space or its characteristics that are—at best—almost, but not quite, accurate. Instead of dissecting cyber space by itself, we find ourselves grasping at commonalities that can be illusory or parochial (the latter being a particular danger, due to the small amount of cases).

A clear example is the persistent comparison with strategic air power. Because cyber attacks can apparently be effectuated anywhere, with little or no warning, coupled with the focus on attacks against critical infrastructure, long-range bombers headed toward the enemy's center of gravity in order to force a surrender may seem an appropriate analogy. However, such a comparison obscures the value and character of cyber attacks. Obviously, the kinetic potential involved is vastly different, but there are other differences as well. Bombs function largely independently of their targets. Fortification or underground facilities can prevent damage, but this can be remedied by scale. Cyber weapons, on the other hand, are defined by their targets and specifically their vulnerabilities. You cannot simply make the worm bigger: each piece of malware must be specifically designed for a certain target for it to be able to exploit an existing vulnerability, and only then can it have an effect. There are many other differences as well. Cyber weapons can have highly unpredictable effects, causing cascade effects throughout systems and across sectors. In that sense, they can be more like biological viruses than bombs—but that is a discussion for another time.

Defining the space

To avoid the pitfalls of incomplete analogies, the characteristics of cyber space can be defined independently before any comparative study is undertaken (which is generally not necessary and is often perfunctory). This opens up for systematic studies of cyber space as a strategic environment, and can better distinguish between the inherent nature of cyber space and fluctuating trends. Several scholars have done so, as analyzing cyber space on its own terms forces greater conceptual clarity and avoids conflation of terms and ideas. Most of these texts do not take a comprehensive approach to cyber space (i.e., they do not try to explain everything and everyone), but taken together they offer great insight into the nature of cyber power.

Nye's work on cyber power offers a cogent discussion of what he calls "power diffusion," a consequence of the information revolution. According to Nye, "two types of power shifts are occurring in this century: power transition and power diffusion. Power transition from one dominant state to another is a familiar historical event, but power diffusion is a more novel process" (Nye 2011: 113). The latter is relevant to our discussion, as the "information revolution is changing the nature of power and increasing its diffusion" (Nye 2011: 114). Nye maintains that states will remain the dominant actor, but will face increasing competition from new actors and difficulties in controlling society (Nye 2011).

Similarly, the unique nature of cyber space means some of the traditional concepts of international security and international relations theory do not translate well into the new environment. Martin Libicki has addressed the challenges of deterrence in cyber space. Although not explicitly focusing on cyber power, his analysis is based on an environmental analysis of cyber space. Libicki questions whether "we" (the United States in his text) can hold the opponent's assets at risk, and if so, can "we" do so repeatedly. Because of the imprecise nature of cyber weapons, successful retaliation is not assured, and unforeseen effects may run the risk of escalation (Libicki 2009: 52).

The second issue is the ability to strike repeatedly. Unlike nuclear deterrence, which is singular and symmetric, "[c]yber deterrence has to be repeatable because no feasible act of cyberretaliation is likely to eliminate the offending state, lead to the government's overthrow, or even disarm the state" (Libicki 2009: 31).

While these texts deal primarily with specific phenomena, Rattray has offered a more comprehensive framework of analysis. Picking up on his earlier work on SIW, Rattray presents in a 2009 text an environmental approach to understanding cyber space and cyber power. Examining existing theories of power (land, sea, air and space), he identified four common features: technological advances, speed and scope of operations, control of key features, and national mobilization (Rattray 2009: 262). In technological advances, "[t]he rise of digital connectivity will have transformative impacts," but the increase in availability and anonymity creates new vulnerabilities to attack (Ibid.: 264–65). Not surprisingly, the speed and scope of operations in cyber space can increase with automation and increased connectedness, but this also benefits non-state actors (Rattray 2009: 266–67). When it comes to control of key features, cyber space is reliant on physical infrastructure, but also governance (Ibid.: 268–70). Rattray makes reference to naval power theory, but it is unclear how any country would be able to defend choke-points such as undersea fiber optic cables effectively.[14] Defending cyber space would also require a form of national mobilization. Rattray mentions several ways of achieving this, from harnessing the expertise of the private sector, where expertise mainly resides, to a type of whole-of-nation approach encompassing economic, diplomatic and military power (Klimburg 2010, 2011).[15]

Rattray's article is one of the most systematic analyses put to paper, but he commits one common error in discussing the strategic features or defining characteristics of cyber space: he confuses the inherent qualities of cyber space as an environment, with their security implications. This is a question of causality, as the former defines the latter. For instance, the attribution problem in cyber space is not an inherent feature, but is the result of cyber space's malleability and decentralized nature. Any systematic framework of analysis of cyber space should therefore begin with the inherent, if not permanent, features of cyber space itself, and from there draw existing or potential security implications. That would make it easier to see what is likely to be the permanent nature of cyber conflict and what is its mutable character (Langø 2013).[16]

The main strength of the environmental approach to cyber space is that it strives to provide a better understanding of the environment itself, as a whole, and not only of certain parochial or temporal issues stemming from it. Still, much work remains to be done. While none offer a complete framework, the texts discussed in this section can be synthesized into something more comprehensive and offer a way forward in the study of cyber security.

Conclusion

In recent years, Revolutionist and Traditionalist thinking on a select few issues has dominated the debate on cyber security. The possibilities of cyber war and devastating attacks on critical national infrastructure have become perhaps the most common subjects of discussion—yet the sides often seem to be talking past each other, or with a flawed understanding of the issue at hand. That said, these two schools of thought in cyber security have contributed understanding to the strategic utility of cyber space.

The Revolutionist school of cyber security is marked by an inherent optimism: not optimism in the sense that technology can solve problems, but that it will change warfare and perhaps even war itself. Twenty years after John Arquilla and David Ronfeldt's declaration that "Cyberwar is Coming," there remains little evidence to justify their claim. This is partly an issue of semantics, but we are still waiting for the full effects of the information revolution. Much of the Revolutionist literature is best seen as concept development, and not empirically based research. Nonetheless, their concepts and ideas are forward-looking and delineate the possibilities of cyber power. Similarly, Strategic Information Warfare can serve as a warning against society's increased dependence on information communication technology, even though this is a far cry from the types of attacks mentioned by the alarmists.

The Traditionalist school has served an important function as a corrective against the more expansive claims of the Revolutionists—though both make similar errors of inference. While the Revolutionists conclude too much about the impact of ICT, Traditionalists have restricted themselves to the very small number of cases, implicitly assuming that the situation is static.

However, cyber space is anything but static. Considered as an environment, it is both diffuse and malleable—neither of which qualities enables easy analysis. The Traditionalist position is thus perfectly understandable for trying to anchor something new to something old, but, as explained in this working paper, cyber space must be understood primarily on its own terms.

The environmentalist school offers the potential for a more systematic, foundational framework of analysis. The comparitivist approach has limited utility, as it may lead to conceptual confusion, but the more comprehensive approach sketched out by Gregory J. Rattray can provide a good start. Coupled with the more in-depth studies of scholars like Joseph Nye and Martin Libicki, as well as insights from computer science studies, this approach can enable a more profound understanding of both cyber space and its security implications. This is important because what might seem highly alarming today might prove to be a false alarm. Developments in cyber network defense may be able to render threats against critical infrastructure harmless, whereas new and unforeseen threats could emerge through cyber space. Whatever transpires, this field of security is in flux, and it is imperative for the literature to reflect that fact.

Notes

1 The following texts are considered to be part of the Revolutionist school. Some texts overlap with other schools, while some authors listed here, such as Martin C. Libicki and Gregory J. Rattray, moved on to other approaches with their later works. See: Thomas P. Rona, "Weapon Systems and Information War" (Office of the Secretary of Defense, July 1, 1976); Martin C. Libicki, *The Mesh and the Net: Speculations on Armed Conflict in a Time of Free Silicon* (Washington, DC: National Defense University, March 1994), at: www.dtic.mil/cgi-bin/GetTRDoc?AD=ADA278484&Location= U2&doc=GetTRDoc.pdf (accessed June 16, 2013); Roger C. Molander, Andrew Riddile and Peter A. Wilson, *Strategic Information Warfare: A New Face of War* (Santa Monica, CA: RAND Corporation, 1996), at: www.rand.org/pubs/monograph_reports/ MR661.html (accessed June 16, 2013); John Arquilla and David Ronfeldt, *The Advent of Netwar* (Santa Monica, CA: RAND Corporation, 1996), at: www.rand.org/pubs/mon-ograph_reports/MR789.html (accessed June 16, 2013); George J. Stein, *Information Attack: Information Warfare In 2025* (Montgomery, AL: US Air War College, August 1996); John Arquilla and David Ronfeldt (eds), *In Athena's Camp: Preparing for Conflict in the Information Age* (Santa Monica, CA: RAND Corporation, 1997); Buard Q. Clemmons and Gary D. Brown, "Cyberwarfare: Ways, Warriors and Weapons of Mass Destruction," *Military Review* 79: 5 (October 1999): 35–45; Gregory J. Rattray, *Strategic Warfare in Cyberspace* (Cambridge, MA: MIT Press, 2001); Colin S. Gray, *Another Bloody Century: Future Warfare* (London: Weidenfeld & Nicolson, 2005); Phillip S. Meilinger, "The Mutable Nature of War," *Air & Space Power Journal* 24: 4 (2010): 24–30; Andrew F. Krepinevich, *Cyber Warfare: A "Nuclear Option"?* (Washington, DC: Center for Strategic and Budgetary Assessments, August 24, 2012), at: www.csbaonline.org/publications/2012/08/cyber-warfare-a-nuclear-option/ (accessed

June 16, 2013); John Stone, "Cyber War Will Take Place!," *Journal of Strategic Studies* 36: 1 (2013): 101–08.

2   The concept of information warfare, as used by the author Thomas P. Rona, is more or less identical with the concept of cyber warfare, meaning the aggressive use of computer network operations to disrupt, degrade or destroy an opponent's networks.

3   Technically, Rattray's comparativist approach falls under the Environmentalist school, but will be used here to illustrate thinking on SIW. Further discussion of the merits of the comparitivist approach is presented in section on the Environmentalist school.

4   Colin S. Gray distinguishes between an information RMA and a cyber war RMA. See: Gray, *Another Bloody Century: Future Warfare*, 105. For a discussion of the intersection of information systems and organization in the military to enable greater, speed and precision, see William A. Owens, "The Emerging System of Systems," *Military Review* 75: 3 (June 1995): 15–19.

5   "Netwar" is a broader term meant to encompass whole societies, while "War 2.0" can simply mean one insurgent group, politically motivated, fighting government forces or forces intervening from the outside. "War 2.0" is a way of fighting war, but in an asymmetrical setting. See Thomas Rid and Marc Hecker, *War 2.0: Irregular Warfare in the Information Age* (Westport, CT: Prager Security International, 2009).

6   For more on the issue of threat inflation in cyber security, see Myriam Dunn Cavelty, *Cyber-Security and Threat Politics: US Efforts to Secure the Information Age* (Abingdon: Routledge, 2008); Jerry Brito and Tate Watkins, "Loving the Cyber Bomb? The Dangers of Threat Inflation in Cybersecurity Policy," *Harvard National Security Journal* 3 (1) (April 2011): 39–84; Sean Lawson, *Beyond Cyber-Doom: Cyberattack Scenarios and the Evidence of History*, Working paper (Fairfax, VA: Mercatus Center, January 2011); Gary McGraw and Nathaniel Fick, "Separating Threat from the Hype: What Washington Needs to Know about Cyber Security," in Kristin M. Lord and Travis Sharp (eds), *America's Cyber Future: Security and Prosperity in the Information Age: Volume II* (Washington, DC: Center for a New American Security, 2011), 43–53, at: www.cnas.org/files/documents/publications/CNAS_Cyber_Volume%20II_2.pdf(accessed February 8, 2012); Erik Gartzke, "The Myth of Cyberwar," *International Security* 38 (2) (Fall 2013): 41–73; Diego Rafael Canabarro and Thiago Borne, *Reflections on The Fog of (Cyber)War*, NCDG Policy Working Paper (Amherst, MA, March 1, 2013).

7   The US national security apparatus has warned that an increasing number of actors, including non-state ones, are capable of launching attacks in cyber space. See US Department of Homeland Security, "The National Strategy to Secure Cyberspace," February 2003; "Department of Defense Strategy for Operating in Cyberspace" (US Department of Defense, July 2011), at: www.defense.gov/news/d20110714cyber.pdf (accessed June 3, 2013); U.S. Department of Defense, "Sustaining U.S. Global Leadership: Priorities for 21st Century Defense," January 2012; Keith B. Alexander (Commander of United States Cyber Command), *Oversight: U.S. Strategic Command and U.S. Cyber Command* (Washington, DC, 2013).

8   For examples of Traditionalist writing, see Martin C. Libicki, *What is Information Warfare?* (Washington, DC: National Defense University, 1995); Berkowitz, *The New Face of War: How War will be Fought in the 21st Century*; David J. Lonsdale, *The Nature of War in the Information Age: Clausewitzian Future* (New York: Frank Cass, 2004); Dorothy E. Denning, "Barriers to Entry: Are They Lower for Cyber Warfare?," *IO Journal* 1: 1 (2009); Jean-Loup Samaan, "Cyber Command: The Rift in US Military Cyber-Strategy," *The RUSI Journal* 155: 6 (2010): 16–21; Brito and Watkins, "Loving the Cyber Bomb? The Dangers of Threat Inflation in Cybersecurity Policy"; Lawson, *Beyond Cyber-Doom: Cyberattack Scenarios and the Evidence of History*; Gartzke, "The Myth of Cyberwar"; Martin C. Libicki, "Cyberspace Is Not a War-Fighting Domain," *I/S: A Journal of Law and Policy for the Information Age* 8,

(2) (2012): 321–36; Thomas Rid, "Cyber War Will Not Take Place," *Journal of Strategic Studies* 35 (1) (2012): 5–32; Thomas Rid and Peter McBurney, "Cyber-Weapons," *RUSI Journal* 157 (1) (2012): 6–13; Canabarro and Borne, "Reflections on The Fog of (Cyber)War"; Jon R. Lindsay, "Stuxnet and the Limits of Cyberwarfare," *Security Studies* 22 (3) (2013): 365–404; Brandon Valeriano and Ryan C. Maness, "The dynamics of cyber conflict between rival antagonists, 2001–11," *Journal of Peace Research* 51 (3) (2014): 347–60.

9 The seven forms are: command-and-control warfare (C2W), which aims to strike at the opponent's figurative head and neck; intelligence-based warfare (IBW), which occurs when intelligence is fed directly into operations, targeting and battle-damage assessment; electronic warfare (EW), which includes the use of EMPs, jammers, and cryptography aimed at radar and communications systems; psychological warfare, which can be directed at the national will, opposing commanders, opposing troops or in a cultural conflict; hacker warfare, which includes network attacks against civilian targets, but not military ones; economic information warfare, like information blockade and information imperialism; and lastly, cyber warfare.

10 Jean-Loup Samaan refers to the works of Robert Pape and Barry D. Watts as representatives of the arguments against and for the utility of strategic bombing and coercion. See: Robert Pape, *Bombing to Win: Air Power and Coercion in War* (Ithaca, NY: Cornell University Press, 1996); Barry D. Watts, "Ignoring Reality: Problems of Theory and Evidence in Security Studies," *Security Studies* 7 (2) (1997): 115–71.

11 For the best articulation of this argument, see: Libicki, "Cyberspace Is Not a War-Fighting Domain."

12 The implication of using Clausewitz is that it gives cyber war a political context and objectives beyond the disruption or destruction of computer networks.

13 Rid later expands on his argument in his book with the same name. In it, he argues that perhaps the most potent use of cyber tools is subversion. By degrading societal functions through cyber sabotage, the attacker can undermine trust between the public and the government thus causing political change. See: Thomas Rid, *Cyber War Will Not Take Place* (Oxford: Oxford University Press, 2013), Ch. 6.

14 Here there is also the issue of stakeholding and interdependence. There are few incentives for countries to attack choke-points because the effects would not be limited to the target country, thus risking diplomatic or military backlash from third parties.

15 In an attempt to harness civil-society and private-sector resources, Estonia has established a cyber wing of its paramilitary force, the Cyber Defense League. This volunteer model might not be applicable to larger states such as the United States because of command and control issues, but this is a matter in need of further examination. Alexander Klimburg has written extensively about a whole-of-nation approach to cyber defense and offense (Alexander Klimburg, "The Whole of Nation in Cyberpower," *Georgetown Journal of International Affairs* 11 (2010): 171–79; Alexander Klimburg, "Mobilising Cyber Power," *Survival* 53 [1] [March 2011]: 41–60.)

16 The present author has drafted a more comprehensive, systematic framework of analysis for understanding compulsory cyber power. See Hans-Inge Langø, *The Limits of Compulsory Cyber Power: Assessing Ecological Potential and Restraints in the Digital Domain*, Working paper (NUPI, June 2013).

References

Alexander, Keith B., Commander of United States Cyber Command. 2013. *Oversight: U.S. Strategic Command and U.S. Cyber Command*. Washington, DC.

Arquilla, John and David Ronfeldt. 1996. *The Advent of Netwar*. Santa Monica, CA: RAND Corporation, at: www.rand.org/pubs/monograph_reports/MR789.html (Accessed June 16, 2013).

Arquilla, John and David Ronfeldt, (eds), 1997a. *In Athena's Camp: Preparing for Conflict in the Information Age*. Santa Monica, CA: RAND Corporation.

Arquilla, John and David Ronfeldt. 1997b. "Cyberwar is Coming!," in John Arquilla and David Ronfeldt (eds), *In Athena's Camp: Preparing for Conflict in the Information Age*. Santa Monica, CA: RAND Corporation, 23–60.

Arquilla, John and David Ronfeldt. 1997c. "Information, Power, and Grand Strategy: In Athena's Camp–Section 1," in John Arquilla and David Ronfeldt (eds), *In Athena's Camp: Preparing for Conflict in the Information Age*. Santa Monica, CA: RAND Corporation, 141–71.

Arquilla, John and David Ronfeldt. 1997d. "Looking Ahead: Preparing for Information-Age Conflict," in John Arquilla and David Ronfeldt (eds), *In Athena's Camp: Preparing for Conflict in the Information Age*. Santa Monica, CA: RAND Corporation, 439–501.

Berkowitz, Bruce D. 2003. *The New Face of War: How War will be Fought in the 21st Century*. New York: Free Press.

Betz, David J. and Tim Stevens. 2011. *Cyberspace and the State: Toward a Strategy for Cyber-Power*. New York: Routledge.

Brito, Jerry and Tate Watkins. 2011. "Loving the Cyber Bomb? The Dangers of Threat Inflation in Cybersecurity Policy." *Harvard National Security Journal* 3 (1) (April): 39–84.

Canabarro, Diego Rafael and Thiago Borne. 2013. "Reflections on The Fog of (Cyber) War." *NCDG Policy Working Paper* (March 1). Amherst, MA.

Clarke, Richard A. and Robert K. Knake. 2010. *Cyber War: The Next Threat to National Security and What to Do About It*. New York: Ecco.

Clemmons, Buard Q. and Gary D. Brown. 1999. "Cyberwarfare: Ways, Warriors and Weapons of Mass Destruction." *Military Review* 79 (5) (October): 35–45.

Denning, Dorothy E. 2009. "Barriers to Entry: Are They Lower for Cyber Warfare?" *IO Journal* 1 (1).

Dunn Cavelty, Myriam. 2008. *Cyber-Security and Threat Politics: US Efforts to Secure the Information Age*. Abingdon: Routledge.

Gartzke, Erik. 2013. "The Myth of Cyberwar." *International Security* 38 (2): 41–73.

Gibson, William. 1984. *Neuromancer*. New York: Ace Books.

Gray, Colin S. 2005. *Another Bloody Century: Future Warfare*. London: Weidenfeld & Nicolson.

Kello, Lucas. 2013. "The Meaning of the Cyber Revolution." *International Security* 38 (2): 7–40.

Kerry, John F. 2013. *Nomination: U.S. Senate Committee on Foreign Relations*. Washington, DC.

Klimburg, Alexander. 2010. "The Whole of Nation in Cyberpower." *Georgetown Journal of International Affairs* 11: 171–79.

Klimburg, Alexander. 2011. "Mobilising Cyber Power." *Survival* 53 (1) (March): 41–60.

Krepinevich, Andrew F. 2012. "Cyber Warfare: A 'Nuclear Option'?." Washington, DC: Center for Strategic and Budgetary Assessments. August 24, at: www.csbaonline.org/publications/2012/08/cyber-warfare-a-nuclear-option/ (accessed June 16, 2013).

Langø, Hans-Inge. 2013. "The Limits of Compulsory Cyber Power: Assessing Ecological Potential and Restraints in the Digital Domain." *NUPI Working paper* (June).

Lawson, Sean. 2011a. "Beyond Cyber-Doom: Cyberattack Scenarios and the Evidence of History." *Working paper* (January). Fairfax, VA: Mercatus Center.

Lawson, Sean. 2011b. "Cyber War and the Expanding Definition of War." *Forbes*

26 (October), at: www.forbes.com/sites/seanlawson/2011/10/26/cyber-war-and-the-expanding-definition-of-war/?feed=rss_home (accessed January 6, 2012).

Libicki, Martin C. 1994. "The Mesh and the Net: Speculations on Armed Conflict in a Time of Free Silicon." Washington, DC: National Defense University (March), at: www.dtic.mil/cgi-bin/GetTRDoc?AD=ADA278484&Location=U2&doc=GetTRDoc. pdf (accessed June 16, 2013).

Libicki, Martin C. 1995. *What Is Information Warfare?*. Washington, DC: National Defense University.

Libicki, Martin C. 2009. *Cyberdeterrence and Cyberwar*. Santa Monica, CA: RAND Corporation.

Libicki, Martin C. 2012. "Cyberspace Is Not a War-Fighting Domain." *I/S: A Journal of Law and Policy for the Information Age* 8 (2): 321–36.

Lindsay, Jon R. 2013. "Stuxnet and the Limits of Cyberwarfare." *Security Studies* 22 (3): 365–404.

Lonsdale, David J. 2004. *The Nature of War in the Information Age: Clausewitzian Future*. New York: Frank Cass.

Lynn III, William J. 2010. "Defending a New Domain." *Foreign Affairs* 89 (5) (October): 97–108.

McConnell, Mike. 2010. "Mike McConnell on how to win the cyber-war we're losing." *Washington Post*, February 28, at: www.washingtonpost.com/wp-dyn/content/article/2010/02/25/AR2010022502493.html (accessed November 20, 2012) .

McGraw, Gary and Nathaniel Fick. 2011. "Separating Threat from the Hype: What Washington Needs to Know about Cyber Security," in Kristin M. Lord and Travis Sharp (eds), *America's Cyber Future: Security and Prosperity in the Information Age: Volume II*. Washington, DC: Center for a New American Security, 43–53, at: www.cnas.org/files/documents/publications/CNAS_Cyber_Volume%20II_2.pdf (accessed February 8, 2012).

Meilinger, Phillip S. 2010. "The Mutable Nature of War." *Air & Space Power Journal* 24 (4): 24–30.

Molander, Roger C., Andrew Riddile and Peter A. Wilson. 1996. "Strategic Information Warfare: A New Face of War." Santa Monica, CA: RAND Corporation, at: www.rand. org/pubs/monograph_reports/MR661.html (accessed June 16, 2013).

Nye, Joseph S. 2011. *The Future of Power*. New York: PublicAffairs.

Owens, William A. 1995. "The Emerging System of Systems." *Military Review* 75 (3) (June): 15–19.

Panetta, Leon E. 2012. "Defending the Nation from Cyber Attack." New York, at: www. defense.gov/speeches/speech.aspx?speechid=1728 (accessed November 23, 2012).

Pape, Robert. 1996. *Bombing to Win: Air Power and Coercion in War*. Ithaca, NY: Cornell University Press.

Rattray, Gregory J. 2001. *Strategic Warfare in Cyberspace*. Cambridge, MA: MIT Press.

Rattray, Gregory J. 2009. "An Environmental Approach to Understanding Cyberpower," in Franklin D. Kramer, Stuart H. Starr and Larry K. Wentz (eds), *Cyberpower and National Security*. Washington, DC: National Defense University Press, 253–74.

Rid, Thomas. 2012. "Cyber War Will Not Take Place." *Journal of Strategic Studies* 35 (1): 5–32.

Rid, Thomas. 2013. *Cyber War Will Not Take Place*. Oxford: Oxford University Press.

Rid, Thomas and Marc Hecker. 2009. *War 2.0: Irregular Warfare in the Information Age*. Westpost, Connecticut: Prager Security International.

Rid, Thomas and Peter McBurney. 2012. "Cyber-Weapons." *RUSI Journal* 157 (1): 6–13.

Rona, Thomas P. 1976. *Weapon Systems and Information War*. Office of the Secretary of Defense, July 1.

Samaan, Jean-Loup. 2010. "Cyber Command: The Rift in US Military Cyber-Strategy." *The RUSI Journal* 155 (6): 16–21.

Stein, George J. 1996. *Information Attack: Information Warfare in 2025*. Montgomery, AL: U.S. Air War College, (August).

Stone, John. 2013. "Cyber War Will Take Place!" *Journal of Strategic Studies* 36 (1): 101–08.

Sutter, John D. 2012. "Anonymous declares 'cyberwar' on Israel." *CNN.com*, November 20, at: http://edition.cnn.com/2012/11/19/tech/web/cyber-attack-israel-anonymous/index.html (accessed November 30, 2012).

US Department of Defense. 2011. *Department of Defense Strategy for Operating in Cyberspace*. July, at: www.defense.gov/news/d20110714cyber.pdf (accessed June 3, 2013.

US Department of Defense. 2012. *Sustaining U.S. Global Leadership: Priorities for 21st Century Defense*. January.

US Department of Homeland Security. 2003. *The National Strategy to Secure Cyberspace*. February.

Valeriano, Brandon and Ryan C. Maness. 2014. "The dynamics of cyber conflict between rival antagonists, 2001–11." *Journal of Peace Research* 51 (3): 347–60.

Watts, Barry D. 1997. "Ignoring reality: Problems of theory and evidence in security studies." *Security Studies* 7 (2): 115–71.

2 From cyber threats to cyber risks

Karsten Friis and Erik Reichborn-Kjennerud

Introduction

While issues relating to cyber security have been on the security policy agenda for several decades, it is only recently that cyber space has moved to the top of national and international security agendas. As a result, discourses on cyber security have increasingly become dominated by militarized language and links between cyber space and strategic threats. The use of metaphors of war and nuclear deterrence, talk of a new Cyber Cold War, and drawing analogies to catastrophic events such as Pearl Harbor and 9/11 are all examples of this (Smith 2013; Bumiller and Shanker 2012; Lynn 2010). The debates surrounding cyber security reflect our growing dependency on cyber space and the willingness of states and non-state actors to exploit it for political, economic, military, etc. gains. This also means that cyber security is not merely a technical problem, but one that has ramifications throughout society. In addition, states, organizations and corporations have established various cyber security institutions to deal with the myriad of challenges stemming from increased dependency on cyber and the inherent vulnerabilities of cyber space.

This has led a number of scholars to examine whether cyber space has been securitized; that is, lifted out of the realm of regular politics and treated as an emergency, thus legitimizing extraordinary counter-measures (Buzan *et al.* 1998). Although they find many cases of attempted securitization, such as the hyperbolic language mentioned above, these have had limited resonance and have rarely resulted in extraordinary counter-measures. At the same time, numerous high-profile cyber attacks and empirical evidence show that cyber security is of growing importance and is being practiced on a daily basis by security professionals in various locations at the national level throughout industries and commercial entities, and by individuals. In other words, cyber security has become vital to modern societies, despite not having been securitized. Why is cyber security produced despite successful securitization? In order to overcome the apparent limitations of securitization theory, this chapter proposes an alternative analytical model, based on risk theory, in order to analyze the ongoing practice and production of cyber security.

The aim of this chapter is to contribute to the discussion on how to theorize about and how to study cyber security. We will argue that in order to develop sound theories on cyber security, we need to depart from the traditional threat-based logic of an actor's ability to realize its harmful intent, to a focus on cyber security that takes cyber space as its starting point. This calls for a focus on the material aspects of cyber space and the ongoing practices of cyber security, and not only the social process of defining something as a security problem, often associated with elite discourses. In addition, taking cyber space as the starting point means that we need to acknowledge our societal dependency on cyber space and the subsequent vulnerabilities. Cyber security will then shift away from a threat-based logic to a risk-security logic. While threat-based security deals with the direct causes of harm, risk-security centers on the conditions of possibility or constitutive causes of harm. This opens up a different logic which calls for long-term precautionary governance rather than exceptional short-term measures. Thus risk not only broadens, but transforms security, as different measures are introduced to deal with potential, hypothetical and less than existential dangers. Given the vulnerable nature of cyber space and everyday cyber-security challenges, measures to deal with cyber security are always in a state of flux.

Situating cyber security within the risk-security logic, we follow Olaf Corry's theory of "riskification" (Corry 2012) and argue that cyber space has become riskified, but not securitized. This approach also enables us to better incorporate the nature of cyber space, the material dimension, than traditionally permitted by securitization theory. In addition, it allows the incorporation of the everyday practices of cyber security into the analysis. Riskification theory thus has the potential to provide us with a better understanding and more accurate picture of cyber security.

The first section will discuss how the socio-political processes for securitizing cyber have been theorized thus far. The next section will briefly introduce risk theory, before we apply Corry's riskification model to cyber security. We will conclude with ethical reflections on the implications of applying risk theory to cyber security.

Theorising cyber-security policies: securitization

According to Myriam Dunn Cavelty, "political science literature on cyber-security [...] remains policy-oriented and does not communicate with more general international relations theory" (Dunn Cavelty 2013). The exception, she asserts, is "a limited number of scholars have used frameworks derived from Securitization Theory" (Dunn Cavelty 2012; Choucri 2012).[1] This predominantly constructivist approach to security rejects the notion that there is something like objective (in)security and focuses on the social process of defining something as security. It is never *a priori* given what and who represent a threat, to what or whom, and what to eventually do with it. In our case, where we seek to analyze the various interpretations of vulnerabilities, perceptions of dangers, the responses, policies and other attempts at creating cyber security, this theoretical approach is a good starting point.

The Copenhagen School of security studies argues that security "is the move that takes politics beyond the established rules of the game and frames the issue either as a special kind of politics or above politics" (Buzan *et al.* 1998: 23). Securitization theory defines a spectrum of possible policies, ranging from non-politicized (the state does not deal with it and it is not an issue of public debate) through politicized (the issue forms part of public policy, requiring government decisions) to securitized (an issue is presented as an existential threat, requiring emergency measures and justifying actions outside the normal bounds of political procedure). Based on a social constructivist epistemology, securitization theory is thus the placing of emphasis on the social construction of threats and the responses to these threats. Less emphasis is placed on the "nature" of the threat (such as number of warheads), as this in any case needs to be interpreted and represented by human beings in a social setting (Hansen 2011).[2]

The basic pillars of the Copenhagen School are the securitizing actor(s) conducting a "speech act," a reference object that is regarded to be under existential threat, and an audience responding to and (if the securitization is successful) accepting the securitization. The result of successful securitization is a shared recognition that extraordinary counter-measures are necessary and legitimate in order to counter the threat. However, if the audience does not accept that the referent object is under an existential threat, the securitizing move will fail. Shared acceptance of the existence of the threat, as well as of its gravity (i.e., that it is critical to the survival of the referent object) is crucial in order to understand the dynamics of securitization theory. If these conditions are missing—that is, if the audience does not recognize the threat or regards it as less imminent or grave as the securitizing actor—the securitization attempt will fail. In the case of cyber, one can therefore imagine a process where authoritative voices (cyber-security experts, government officials, etc.) call out and warn about the new dependencies and vulnerabilities following the digitization of, for instance, critical infrastructure or information. The audience, for instance the US Congress, the President and the US public, is being convinced, which may subsequently lead to the establishment of new institutions, laws and resources to counter this threat. Through the Copenhagen framework, each step in such a process may be scrutinized more closely—and critically. As there is no *a priori* link between the resources spent and the "objective" nature of the threat, securitization theory gives us an insight into *inter alia* governmental decision-making and resource allocation.

Securitization—or not?

Johan Eriksson made the first attempt to elaborate on this conceptualization of cyber security in 2001. His approach is "threat politics" which is "how and why some threat images but not others end up on the political agenda" (Eriksson 2001: 211). By combining securitization theory with framing and agenda-setting theories, he argues that cyber and IT became securitized in Sweden after the Cold War. He shows that the "military–bureaucratic security establishment" embarked upon the "new threats" at the end of the Cold War, and framed them in terms of "information warfare" and "information operations." By doing so they seized "a dominant position in the securitization of IT" (Eriksson 2001: 215). Largely inspired by the USA, Swedish security experts framed and talked about the problem in the same way as in the USA. However, the policy responses were very different. Eriksson points to "bureaucratic turf battles" taking place among the governmental agencies responsible for managing IT security. He also asserts that the "securitisation of IT is sometimes far too exaggerated. All computer problems, bugs, dada diddling, spamming and break-in attempts are hardly existential threats to a sovereign state" (Eriksson 2001: 218).

Eriksson's main approach is framing theory; he therefore elaborates less on the securitization dimension. For instance, he does not specify what the referent object is (network vulnerability or the sovereign state?), and does not explain in depth what extraordinary measures were put in place to protect the referent object. It seems clear from his analysis that the military–bureaucratic establishment—as securitizing actors—attempted to securitize cyber security. However, it is less convincing that the audience (Swedish government and society) accepted this, and that extraordinary measures were put in place. The mentioned bureaucratic turf battles indicate a classic civil service response to new intersectoral challenges. Had the stakes been higher, time of the essence, and valuable institutions under an existential threat, the government most likely would have taken action and imposed solutions. The lack of such urgency indicates that securitization actually failed in Sweden.

This is also how Bendrath, Eriksson and Giacomello describe cyber security in the USA during the Clinton years: much talk about cyber terrorism, but limited de facto responses (Bendrath *et al.* 2007). "There was not much panic politics that moved beyond democratic procedures.... The US government did talk the talk of securitization but they did not really walk the walk—not yet" (Bendrath *et al.* 2007: 67). However, Bendrath *et al.* argue that cyber security was properly securitized during the Bush years. This was done particularly in the wake of the 9/11 attacks, when specific immediate cyber-security measures were implemented. The Patriot Act and other legislation criminalized certain computer activity, the President appointed a Special Advisor on Cybersecurity, and the Office of Cybersecurity and Communications was established. One may nevertheless ask whether this represents proper securitization of cyber. The measures taken were arguably limited compared to other sectors (such as airport security), and there was no indication of existential damage to critical infrastructure or other valuable referent objects. Most importantly, however, this was hardly a securitization of cyber space itself, but rather a dimension of the general securitization linked to the "War on Terror" that followed the 9/11 attacks. The referent object here was thus the US state and society, not cyber space as such. Irrespective of their views on this particular period, the authors recognize that securitization theory does not cover the "less panicky ways" (Bendrath *et al.* 2007: 79) in which cyber threats are often framed. Instead, they argue that what they label as the "threat politics approach" is more appropriate to the study of cyber security. This approach largely builds on frame theory which "may, but do not necessarily, include an identification of existential threat and a legitimisation of extraordinary measures" (Bendrath *et al.* 2007: 80).

"Threat politics" is also Myriam Dunn Cavelty's approach, where she combines securitization theory with frame analysis and agenda-setting theory (Dunn Cavelty 2008). She tells "the story of how and why cyber threats became to be considered one of the quintessential security threats of modern times in the United States" (Dunn Cavelty 2008: 1). She states that the framing of the problem has remained largely stable since the mid-1990s: critical infrastructure protection (CIP), including the digital information security dimension, has been the focal point of US cyber-security measures for the past two decades. The focus on CIP primarily emerged in the wake of the 1995 Oklahoma City bombing; a focus not even altered by the 9/11 attacks (Dunn Cavelty 2008).[3] As cyber is predominantly a civilian and largely privately-owned domain, traditional state security approaches have been of limited relevance. As a result, Dunn Cavelty concludes that what has taken place in the USA is a "failed securitization." Although CIP is regarded as national security, "no exceptional measures are envisaged that would traditionally fall under the purview of the national security apparatus" (Dunn Cavelty 2008: 132–33). Policies are neither taken out of "normal bonds" nor are "exceptional measures" implemented. Instead she argues that we are witnessing a new logic of security where technical security merges with national security. Hence, security policy cannot be restricted to "policy for extraordinary circumstances" (Dunn Cavelty 2008). In short, her empirical research reveals shortcomings of securitization theory when applied to cyber security.

As the spectrum of potential threats is vast and fundamentally uncertain, and the list of potential malicious actors is so broad, it becomes challenging to identify key terms like "existential threat." Which referent object is under threat? In relation to CIP, it may be national key functions, but as Dunn Cavelty shows, this does not mobilize "extraordinary measures." It is more of a matter of day-to-day routine management. From an analytical perspective, it is thus difficult to say when a policy is extraordinary and when it is normal.

Lene Hansen and Helen Nissenbaum also attempt to resolve these challenges by expanding on the Copenhagen School (Hansen and Nissenbaum 2009). They seek to link securitization theory to cyber security by combining constellations of referent objects, such as "networks" and "humans." This allows a broader and inter-sectoral discursive analysis of the securitization process. They also introduce new "grammars" into the Copenhagen framework, like "technification," which highlights the role of ICT security professionals in defining the dangers and in responding to them. The important role of experts and the everyday practices in the production of security have also been highlighted in other contexts, where it is argued that security analysis should not be limited to elite discourses. Such a focus is vital to furthering our understanding of how security measures emerge bottom-up through an ongoing process of technocratic normalization by security professionals (Bigo 2002; Balzacq *et al.* 2010).

In contrast to Dunn Cavelty, and in line with Bendrath *et al.*, Hansen and Nissenbaum claim that cyber security has been successfully securitized in the USA, and list the various new institutions and strategies that have been emerged since the mid-1990s as evidence of this. Again one must ask what is "extraordinary" and what is "normal," and the diverging conclusions regarding the USA illustrate that securitization theory is unclear on this. All agree that there have been several attempts to securitize cyber, but it is unclear whether the audience has accepted them, if the referent object(s) were considered to be under existential threat, and if the measures taken were exceptional or not. As Dunn Cavelty puts it: "it remains largely unclear which audience has to accept what argument, to what degree, and for how long" (Dunn Cavelty 2008).

Hansen and Nissenbaum's main case is the cyber attacks on Estonia in 2007, when Estonian officials went far to securitize the event. However, the inability to prove that it had been orchestrated by Russia and the lack of significant damage to the Estonian society resulted in the general failure of also this securitization attempt. NATO, the EU and the USA did not recognize them as an attack on Estonian sovereignty, which could have triggered NATO's Article 5. The attacks had several effects, such as contributing to "cross-fertilization" of cyber and terrorism, highlighting politically-motivated hacking, etc., which is illuminated by Hansen and Nissenbaum's theoretical framework, and the politically important establishment of NATO's Cooperative Cyber Defence Centre of Excellence in Tallinn. However, the core of securitization theory, to demonstrate how issues are lifted out of regular politics and into a higher order politics—legitimizing extraordinary responses, was not applicable in this case.

The limits of securitization theory

All of the contributions discussed above have found it necessary to expand upon or twist securitization theory in order to make it fit cyber security. The cases of attempted securitization are found mainly through hyperbolic statements, but they have had limited resonance in various national and international audiences. Securitization has therefore failed. This begs the question: if securitization theory has limited value even for cases like Estonia, is it a useful theoretical lens for the analysis of cyber security? Given the unlikelihood that cyber attacks will cause massive death and physical destruction, can securitization *ever* be expected to be successful? Will it remain in the sphere of day-to-day management, rather than in the realm of urgent extraordinary means?

Lowering the bar for defining securitization, as in Bendrath *et al.* and Hansen and Nissenbaum, is hardly a solution. The establishment of new institutions in the USA is not enough to qualify as securitization. In our view, the term securitization should be restricted to the extreme cases when there are sudden shifts in policy, urgent responses and heated debates. The theory is highly applicable to for instance the outbreak of civil wars, as it helps provide an understanding of why neighbors suddenly turn on each other. However, it is less applicable to the less dramatic non-kinetic discourses on cyber security.

Another shortcoming in securitization theory is its relation to the material dimension of security. Claudia Aradau has argued that securitization theory has largely ignored the role of objects or "things"—due to its association with the linguistic and social constructivist turn in IR. Material factors have often been relegated to the outside realm, as simply facilitating conditions for securitization (missiles, tanks, etc.) or as remnants of mainstream positivism. She asserts that as objects have the capacity to both enable and constrain effects on what can be said and done to secure them, it is important to understand the relation between matter and meaning. Matter should not simply be understood as an end product of discourse, as the effect of performative speech acts, but should be regarded as an active factor in material–discursive processes. In this sense, it can also be seen as facilitating conditions for speech acts (Aradau 2010). Securitization theory thus has limited value in terms of illuminating how changes in the nature of cyber space (as discussed in the Introduction) impact on security discourses and practices. Without attention to the material aspects of cyber space, a proper analysis of the production of cyber security is hindered.

Furthermore, the nature of cyber space means that most of the day-to-day workings of cyber security are reactive, in the sense that the security professionals are always reacting (if they themselves are not engaged in offensive cyber operations), to new software and malware installed in the systems, patching known vulnerabilities and creating new anti-malware software.[4] This is a dynamic practice, where cyber security is constantly being co-produced by new malware and new practices to counter this malware, both constrained and enabled by the technical logic of cyber space. The nature of cyber space—and cyber security—is therefore ongoing and dynamic, and is being dealt with on a daily basis. The material or technical dimension is crucial in cyber security, but the kind of responses and counter-measures chosen are not given. Cyber security is not just a technical problem, but a practice that is co-produced by material-discursive processes.

To address these shortcomings without dismissing securitization theory altogether, we propose a framework that systematically differentiates between securitization "proper" and other, less dramatic but still serious, security challenges which also allow the analysis of the material aspects of cyber space and the practices of cyber-security experts. To do this, we need to distinguish between *threats* and *risks*. Threats and risks are both perceptions and representations of certain dangers but, as we see it, only the former can be securitized. Threats are representations of danger that imply an agent with intent and capabilities. The focus is thus outward, toward the danger, and responses typically include deterrence, defense and offense. Risk, on the other hand, has a different logic associated to it. Framing something as risk produces security practices that are about probabilities, prevention, future scenarios and management, as opposed to deterring adversaries or defending against or defeating identifiable and calculable threats.

What is risk?

Risk analysis and management of risk has been applied to almost every facet of human endeavor, from finance and fishing to epidemiology, ecology, war and welfare. In the rationalist tradition, risk analysis is an instrument that is used to enhance decision-making by estimating future danger in terms of risk. It is premised on the belief that risks can be classified, quantified and thereby predict possible futures to be managed. In recent years, however, scholars from different theoretical backgrounds and political inclinations have begun to explore the concept of risk more critically.

One can broadly lump security studies scholars within the field of risk into two camps; those who follow the work of Ulrich Beck and his risk society thesis and those who follow Michel Foucault and his work on *governmentality* (Rasmussen 2006; Coker 2002; Heng 2006; Ewald 1986; Dean 1999; Aradau and Munster 2007). The "Beckians" start off with Beck's idea of the *risk society*, a theory that describes the macro-structural changes happening in the West as the bipolar world is fading away and we are "moving from a world of enemies to one of dangers and risks" (Beck 1999: 3). Dangers are now conceptualized as risks in terms of their "probabilities and magnitude of consequences" (Heng 2006), making risks much more open to subjective interpretations than threats. In Beck's definition of a risk, they are both seen as "real" and "socially constructed," but this interpretation hinges on a distinction between risk and danger. He argues that risk arises through assessments of future dangers and becomes "real" when one sees the possibility of acting to prevent or mitigate the potential effects of danger in the future. Thus, risks only occur when one locates a danger, assesses it and then decides whether to act on it. "Risks concern the possibility of future occurrences and developments; they make present a state of the world that does not (yet) exist. Risks are always future events that may occur" (Beck 2009: 9). Risk is thus linked to interpretation and decision, while dangers are seen as "existing."

The risk-security writers that largely take Foucauldian governmentality as their starting point view risk as a tool used by certain actors (preliminary governments) to expand neo-liberal control mechanisms—rather than an inherent condition of the world. Risk, in this view, is a mode of governmentality that implies the expansion of regulatory regimes. It is a particular rationality of government that works to legitimize actions of power vis-à-vis the population. Such analyses of risk are interested in exposing "how the world and existing problematizations are made into risks [and] what effects this form of ordering entails upon populations" (Aradau and Munster 2007: 97). As such, they move away from the Beckian critique of the attempts of security elites and policymakers to control uncertainty. Instead they focus critically on control regimes that seek to govern populations through strategies portraying the future as computable, calculable and manageable.

We see that the two risk "schools" reach different conclusions as to how risks are generated and how they are dealt with. Nevertheless, they agree that security is increasingly being framed in the language of risk and that there has been a cognitive shift in how we think about security. In addition, risk-security writers agree that risk both transforms and broadens the logic of security. They are worried, albeit for different reasons, about how the logic of risk drives an expanding security agenda in which the precautionary principle and pre-emption have become guiding principles in an ever-increasing "routinization" of security. In essence, they argue that risk has become the new security, and that the changing practices and meaning of security are thus best understood through a risk framework. We will therefore next discuss how we can apply risk theorization to cyber security, while retaining the social construction elements of the Copenhagen School.

Riskification

Fortunately someone has already made such a marriage, albeit in a different sector (field) than cyber. Olaf Corry's term "*riskification*" captures the idea of a "social process of constructing something politically in terms of risks" (Corry 2012: 238). The term builds on the securitization framework, but can be placed between securitization and politicization. It is not about existential threats, but less dramatic security challenges. Corry stresses the difference between threats and risk, as discussed above. He does this by particularly highlighting how risk focuses on future scenarios and policies aimed at preventing it from materializing. From this perspective, risk tends to depersonalize danger, as it does not require an enemy to do the threatening. As risks are considered a more or less permanent feature of modern societies, they cannot be eradicated, only managed, he claims. As a result, "risk security measures will tend to be permanent features of society" (Corry 2012: 245).

Securitization theory is unable to capture security policies related to risks, as risks are neither existential nor call for radically exceptional policy responses. Corry's riskification concept helps mitigate this weakness, as it remains within the same basic parameters of securitization theory. It still requires someone to advocate security measures to be put in place, a valued reference object to protect, and an audience that accepts the need for new security measures.

A shared starting point is the constructivist epistemology position on dangers. According to Corry, nothing is inherently a threat or a risk as "different dangers can be constructed in terms of either risk or threat at different times" (Corry 2012: 246). To understand the difference between threat security policies and risk security policies, one can therefore not define the former as graver or more dangerous than the latter. Rather, Corry argues that risk security can be distinguished from threat security by three features.

First, it implies a different kind of causality. Risk makes us think of the "constitutive causes of harm," rather than the direct causes of harm (as in threats) (Corry 2012). Riskification relates to the factors that make a danger possible, such as vulnerability of societies, weak international regimes and the existence of weapons. In contrast, the threat and securitization of for instance terror is "connected to particular agents believed to exist and have malicious intent and capability to commit acts of terror" (Corry 2012). This is a more direct causation of harm than a risk, and produces a different logic for action. Furthermore, Corry argues, "(t)hinking in terms of constitutive causes draws attention to background factors and structures (material or discursive) that make certain actions or events possible" (Corry 2012). The focus on constitutive background factors thus opens for the inclusion of material factors—such as malware—into the analysis.

Second, there is a change of locus of security action: "whereas securitization involves a plan of action to *defend* a valued referent object against a threat, riskification implies a plan of action to *govern* the conditions of possibility of harm" (Corry 2012: 247). Threats cannot be governed, only defended against. The attention is therefore outward, while a risk policy looks inward. "Security thus has to take on modus operandi other than defence" (Corry 2014). It is not about deterrence, defense or fighting, but about understanding dependencies and vulnerabilities, precaution and governance. It is about reducing the chances of possible future harm through preventive policies, resilience and international governance.

Third, while securitization calls for immediate and short-term responses through extraordinary measures, riskification promotes long-term thinking, investment in governance capabilities, investment in precautionary measures and resilience. In contrast to securitization, it may open debates and increase transparency in the discourse on security (Corry 2012: 248).

To sum up, riskification is not characterized by an existential threat to a valued referent object leading to exceptional measures against external and ungovernable threatening others. Rather,

> it posits risks (understood as condition of possibly harm) to a referent object. This thus leads to programmes for permanent changes aimed at reducing vulnerability and boosting governance-capacity of the valued reference object itself.
>
> (Corry 2012)

Riskification of cyber

Armed forces worldwide are generally constrained to protecting their own information and communications technology (ICT) systems. Main responsibility for securing cyber space, on the other hand, lies with civilian and commercial agencies. This means that cyber security is mostly dealt with on a day-to-day basis by cyber-security professionals in civilian and commercial organizations rather than military "cyber warriors." In contrast to securitization theory, riskification may be a relevant tool for the analysis of these less dramatic responses and the everyday production of cyber security. This includes preparations to sustain larger attacks, while keeping the door open for escalation and securitization under particular circumstances. By applying Corry's three characteristics of riskification (constitutive causality, governance and long-term), in the following we will see how this applies to cyber security.

Constitutive causality

Cyber danger is better depicted as a constitutive rather than a direct cause of harm. The risk of cyber attacks cannot be reduced to malicious actors' intent and capabilities alone. This is partly due to the problem of attribution in cyber space (Singer and Friedman 2014) and as such it is the dependencies, vulnerabilities and resilience of own systems that largely define the probability and consequences of an attack. In other words, it is the "background factors" that make action possible that defines the dangers, not actors' intent and capabilities alone. Furthermore, in most cases cyber attacks are not regarded as an immediate threat, but an ongoing risk and a potential scenario. Risks occur through assessments of future dangers and efforts to prevent or mitigate these.

Of course, cyber attacks may occur as spillovers from political conflicts and tensions in other regions, such as Estonia in 2007 and Georgia in 2008 (O'Connell 2012) or the much-publicized cyber conflict between China and the USA (Lindsay *et al.* 2015). If a state is in the midst of such a crisis or war, the problem of attribution in cyber space is less of a mystery. In these cases, urgency is more of a concern, and securitization is a better way to characterize the processes taking place. In these cases, cyber security is simply a subset of a larger political conflict, not a security sector in and of itself.

However, the dangers stemming from a cyber attack in peacetime are better depicted as risks. It should be noted, however, that ongoing cyber operations blur the line between peace and conflict. Security policies focus on our societal dependencies and the vulnerable nature of cyber space, and aim to reduce the negative implications of a potential future attack (resilience). An analysis of today's cyber-security policies would need to capture the entire spectrum of these constitutive causes of harm; the interpretation and representation of the risks, the proposed counter-measures among various public, corporate and private actors, the international efforts and the networks between all these actors.

Thinking in terms of constitutive causes allows us to also draw attention to cyber space itself, to the digital materiality of malware, and to the vulnerabilities in our own systems. A would-be riskifying actor would need to point to the evolution of cyber space, new dependencies and vulnerabilities, and the constantly changing syntactic level. The evolution of the technical or material aspects of cyber space is thus an integral part of any risk assessment. This does not mean that there is no room for interpretation or social and political factors, but that the dynamic nature of cyber space requires an ongoing rephrasing and reassessment of the risks at hand. In other words, there is no material determinism, but an "active" material dimension which constantly plays into—and constitutes—the social dimension. Taken together, these factors constitute the risk of a cyber attack.

Governance

Riskification is about governing, not preventing, the possibility of harm. The focus on cyber security is more internal (vulnerability focus) than external (friend-enemy focus), as the locus and nature of the threat is unknown. Resilience of one's own systems is therefore key, as there are limits to what firewalls and anti-virus systems can do to protect them. Most attention is given to precautionary measures, such as patching holes in the systems, updating software, encryption and improving back-ups (Harrop and Matteson 2013–14). Cyber-defense organizations, such as computer emergency readiness teams (CERT), obviously also monitor the cyber system as a whole and look for patterns and early indicators of attacks. However, as most severe cyber attacks usually exploit unknown vulnerabilities in a system, so-called zero-day attacks (Andress and Winterfeld 2011), setting up a defense makes little sense, as they are by definition unknown. Cyber-security experts therefore never know exactly what to look for, but once malware is identified, counter-measures are put in place. Malware is therefore often labeled single-shot guns—it can only be used once. As a result, cyber security is always reactive[5] and an attack is usually only discovered long after it has been launched. Furthermore, cyber-security professionals are busy on day-to-day basis, revealing and managing the myriads of small and large attacks. They do not wait passively for an enemy to intrude, but actively scan the horizon for dangers to manage. This is cyber-security practice at its core.

The focus on internal management makes the technical cyber-security professionals the focal points of cyber security. This bottom-up and technically-heavy nature of cyber security also reinforces the point that this is management, not defense. In this respect, the inter-sectoral nature of cyber risks makes it necessary to look at governance broadly, from industry to civilian governance to the military. There is little use in mobilizing only one sector, one agency or institution to manage cyber risks of scale. Technical cooperation and shared situational awareness is a necessity in order to succeed in both the day-to-day risk management and in the event of larger attacks.

The nature of cyber makes international CERT collaboration necessary. This allows the teams to assist each other in the event of an attack and build shared situational awareness. The numerous international efforts to improve Internet governance and management indicate that cyber security is being dealt with actively on the international level, although the effectiveness can be debated There are several government and inter-governmental initiatives in the UN, the ITU,[6] the OSCE[7] and in trade organizations. There are also "I*star" organizations which deal with critical Internet resources, protocols, etc., like ICANN.[8] Finally, there are multi-stakeholder initiatives, where governments, the private sector and non-governmental actors meet, such as the Internet Governance Forum, and similar conferences (Kleinwächter 2013). These international efforts aim to reduce vulnerabilities in the system and share information, but also to generate confidence-building measures between countries with political differences or conflicting views on how to regulate the Internet. All of these national and international governance initiatives focus on governing risk, not preventing it.

The long-term perspective

Cyber security cannot be confined to the military security sector alone, which is true of much of the traditional security discourse. In particular, the private sector, telecommunications and internet providers are critical in terms of security. The myriad of actors involved in cyber security complicates the matter, as they often have diverging interests and different political aims. As such, cyber-security efforts are often aimed at "soft" measures like "awareness building," "information sharing," "confidence building" and "best practices" such as encryption, cyber hygiene, etc. in order to manage the various challenges associated with the inter-sectoral cyber space. These are long-term investments and precautionary measures aimed at reducing vulnerabilities and thereby risk, not defending against an attack. Because urgency is less of a factor in risk than in securitization, riskification allows for contemplation, debate and numerous online discussions about the various risks at hand. It is long-term security building, not driven by urgency or panic, although much of the discourse around cyber security is precisely this.

Efforts to enhance cyber security are more transparent and openly debated than in most traditional security fields. It is the technical nature that keeps much of the discourse "encrypted" for outsiders, rather than deliberate attempts to keep the processes secret. Obviously, detailed information about CERTs' and intelligence services' methodologies, or private companies' cyber-security strategies are kept secret, but the overarching discussions of principle and strategy are open and transparent. The important role of the private corporate sector and civil society like "white hat hackers" in cyber security also enhances transparency. The latter spend their days trying to worm their way into clients' computer systems to see how vulnerable they are to cyber criminals, spies and other nefarious "black hats."[9]

Edward Snowden's revelations about the NSA's cyber-security programs may arguably counter this argumentation. The secret cyber conflict taking place between the NSA and its Chinese counterpart is far from transparent and open. There is little doubt that intelligence services and numerous other global actors in cyber space operate with a high degree of secrecy. Nonetheless, this tug of war also takes the form of open debates about risks. It was for instance a private US security company, Mandiant, which revealed the location of a Chinese cyber operation's headquarters in Shanghai in 2013.[10] Furthermore, the most famous cyber attack to date, the Stuxnet worm, became publicly known, despite initially being a highly secret computer network attack (CNA). This demonstrates that even the most sophisticated and secret malware cannot be contained for ever— and eventually will leak out to the public (Lindsay 2013).

By introducing riskification and Corry's three features as an analytical category between politicization and securitization, we have opened for a more nuanced understanding of how states and societies respond to cyber security, domestically and internationally. This allows the necessary breadth in scope in terms of domains and actors, and the decoupling of the analysis from the binary logic inherent in threat politics. By doing so, we move away from a focus on enemy actors and capabilities, and the corresponding terminology of deterrence, defense, urgency, immediacy and direct causes of harm, and turn to probabilities, future scenarios, management and governance. We thus move from an outward look at the world "out there" to a more inward focus on internal dependencies, vulnerabilities, responses and resilience. Most importantly, riskification allows an analysis of the material aspects as well as the crucial role of the day-to-day cyber-security professional in the provision of cyber security. Finally, the move from threats to risk also facilitates a more critical approach toward the hyperbolic attempts to securitize cyber.

However, a focus on risk also means attention to vulnerabilities. This can have positive and negative effects. One could argue that looking at vulnerabilities instead of at external actors can result in an unhealthy focus on worst-case catastrophes—which again may lead to increased militarization of cyber space (Dunn Cavelty 2012). On the other hand, such a focus may lead to an effort to reduce vulnerabilities, thus minimizing certain risks, such as systemic failures and cyber crime. In addition, a focus on vulnerabilities rather than actors may have the benefit of cyber security not becoming a self-fulfilling prophecy of a new Cyber Cold War.

Conclusion

The inherent normative approach of the Copenhagen School is that securitization may often not be a good thing: "security should be seen as negative, as a failure to deal with issues as normal politics" (Buzan *et al.* 1998). De-securitization, in other words a return to normal politics with less dramatic features, is therefore often seen as desirable. This particularly applies to sectors like human security or environmental security, where state-centric and militarized solutions may exacerbate rather than reduce tensions (Hansen 2012). As we argued at the outset of this chapter, the same can be said about cyber security. Attempts at securitization have placed part of the cyber debate, particularly in the USA, in the military logic of friend and foe, deterrence and war. This may also have "legitimized" some of the intrusive privacy practices of the NSA, as revealed by Edward Snowden.

However, Corry warns that de-securitization may also have negative effects. In the case of climate change, it could lead to "de-riskification," thus "removing climate change away from this precautionary logic and into 'normal' politics of distribution of goods and bads" (Corry 2012: 255). This is where climate skeptics would like to see the debate; in other words, as entirely decoupled from security and heightened political attention. For others, climate change is something that requires particular attention and preparedness, as it is on a higher policy level than day-to-day politics.

In the cyber domain, few voices seek to reject the risks altogether, but the normative imperative of talking in terms of risk rather than threats de-escalates the discourse. If that were to fail, cyber security would become a domain totally dominated by security and intelligence agencies, technical experts and not least the booming "cyber-security military–industrial complex" that simultaneously cries wolf and offers solutions (Deibert 2013).

Riskification is thus an analytical tool that can be applied in order to empirically capture cyber-security efforts, the representation of the danger and the policies formulated to address it, as well as a way to conduct critical analysis aimed at unmasking securitization efforts in this field. Empirical analysis will most likely find that the riskification in certain places and at certain times begins to resemble securitization. As with climate change, such securitization of cyber can be criticized while offering an alternative security frame, so that a return to normal politics no longer is the only option.

Nonetheless, following a Foucauldian approach to risk, one may argue that risk policies are as dangerous to the freedom of society as securitization and militarization, since the former represent a more creeping and gradual change to the security and control measures of neo-liberal regimes of power that call for a permanent process with no end. The slow processes normalize security policies that would arguably have met resistance had they been put in place abruptly. From this perspective, replacing securitization with riskification may not be a positive move if the valued referent object is a free and transparent cyber space.

Applying riskification analytically therefore does not need to automatically correspond to advocating riskification of cyber security politically. That is a value judgment. Riskification as an analytical tool can be applied without taking a normative stance on these matters, but it can also be applied as a platform for critical judgments of current policies.

As we see it, applying riskification to the study of cyber security has important benefits. It allows analysts to capture processes that may be at the boundary between risk and threat, perhaps not existential, but still grave. It further allows escalation and de-escalation within the same basic analytical parameters, and can also be combined with some of the proposed "new grammars" of the Copenhagen School discussed here, such as "technification." Importantly, it allows for a deeper understanding of the intended and unintended material aspects of and the role of cyber-security professionals in production of cyber security. Furthermore, riskification does not preclude the continued use of other theoretical tools like "frame analysis" and "agenda setting-theory." It helps us escape the hyperbolic language of threats and dangers while remaining seriously committed to recognizing and understanding the risks and vulnerabilities of our networked societies. It may also serve as a normative platform for the defense of internet freedom against the growing pressure from the intelligence services and the surveillance industry toward increased control and surveillance. With a less dramatic representation of the cyber dangers, legitimate counter-measures will most likely be less intrusive and omnipotent.

Notes

1 This claim can be challenged, as other theories also have been applied. Nazli Choucri, *Cyberpolitics in International Relations* (Cambridge, MA: MIT Press, 2012), is but one example of a comprehensive theorising of cyber security in international relations which is not based on the Copenhagen framework.

2 The "nature of threats" in the Copenhagen School is widely debated. See for instance, Lene Hansen for an overview of the discussion: Lene Hansen. 2011. "The Politics of Securitization and the Muhammad Cartoon Crisis: A Post-Structuralist Perspective." *Security Dialogue* 42 (4–5).

3 However, 9/11 resulted in a return to identifying "terrorists" as the main cyber perpetrators—as opposed to "states" in the early Bush administration.

4 However, vulnerabilities that have not been exploited previously, so-called zero-day vulnerabilities, are sometimes kept as secrets by governments and sold by various entities on the black market rather than patched. See for example, www.wired.com/2014/11/what-is-a-zero-day/ (accessed December 2, 2015).

5 It should be noted that offensive computer network operations (CNO) are also part of cyber security in order to bolster emergency preparedness and in some cases prevent attacks from occurring.

6 International Telecommunication Union, at: www.itu.int/en/ITU-D/Cyber security/Pages/default.aspx (accessed December 2, 2015).

7 Organization for Security and Cooperation in Europe, at: www.osce.org/cio/126475 (accessed December 2, 2015).

8 The Internet Corporation for Assigned Names and Numbers, at: www.icann.org/ (accessed December 2, 2015).

9 "White Hats to the Rescue," *The Economist*, February 22, 2014, at: www.economist.com/news/business/21596984-law-abiding-hackers-are-helping-businesses-fight-bad-guys-white-hats-rescue (accessed December 2, 2015).

10 See http://intelreport.mandiant.com/ (accessed December 2, 2015).

References

Andress, Jason and Steve Winterfeld. 2011. *Cyber Warfare: Techniques, Tactics and Tools for Security Practitioners*. Waltham, MA: Syngress Elsevier.

Aradau, Claudia. 2010. "Security That Matters: Critical Infrastructure and Objects of Protection." [In English]. *Security Dialogue* 41 (5): 491–514.

Aradau, Claudia and Rens van Munster. 2007. "Governing Terrorism through Risk: Taking Precautions, (Un)Knowing the Future." *European Journal of International Relations* 13 (1) (March): 89–115.

Balzacq, Thierry, Tugba Basara, Didier Bigo, Emmanuel-Pierre Guittet and Christian Olsson. 2010. "Security Practices," in Robert A. Denemark (ed.), *International Studies Encyclopedia Online*. New York: Blackwell, 1–30.

Beck, Ulrich. 1999. *World Risk Society*. Malden, MA: Polity Press.

Beck, Ulrich. 2009. *World at Risk*. 2nd edition. Cambridge: Polity Press.

Bendrath, Ralph, Johan Eriksson and Giampiero Giacomello. 2007. "Cyberterrorism to Cyberwar, Back and Forth: How the United States Securitized Cyberspace," in Johan Eriksson and Giampiero Giacomello (eds), *International Relations and Security in the Digital Age*. London: Routhledge, 57–82.

Bigo, Didier. 2002. "Security and Immigration: Toward a Critique of Governmentality of Unease." *Alternatives* 27 (1): 62–92.

Bumiller, Elisabeth and Thom Shanker. 2012. "Panetta Warns of Dire Threat of Cyberattack on U.S." *New York Times*, at: www.nytimes.com/2012/10/12/world/panetta-warns-of-dire-threat-of-cyberattack.html?pagewanted=all&_r=0 (accessed December 2, 2015).

Buzan, Barry, Jaap de Wilde and Ole Wæver. 1998. *Security: A New Framework for Analysis*. Boulder, CO: Lynne Rienner.

Choucri, Nazli. 2012. *Cyberpolitics in International Relations*. Cambridge, MA: MIT Press.

Coker, Christopher. 2002. "Globalisation and Insecurity in the Twenty-First Century—Nato and the Management of Risk." *Adelphi Papers* 345. New York: Routledge.

Coker, Christopher. 2009. *War in an Age of Risk*. Cambridge: Polity Press.

Corry, Olaf. 2012. "Securitisation and 'Riskification': Second-Order Security and the Politics of Climate Change." [In English]. *Millennium-Journal of International Studies* 40 (2): 235–58.

Corry, Olaf. 2014. "From Defence to Recilience: Environmental Security Beyond Neo-Liberalism." *International Political Sociology* 8 (3): 256–74.

Dean, Mitchell. 1999. *Governmentality: Power and Rule in Modern Society*. London, Thousand Oaks, CA: Sage Publications.

Deibert, Ronald. 2013. *Black Code: Surveillance, Privacy, and the Dark Side of the Internet*. Expanded edition. Toronto: McClelland & Stewart.

Dunn Cavelty, Myriam. 2008. *Cyber-Security and Threat Politics: Us Efforts to Secure the Information Age*. London: Routledge.

Dunn Cavelty, Myriam. 2012. *The Militarisation of Cyberspace: Why Less May Be Better*. 4th International Conference on Cyber Conflict, C. Czosseck, R. Ottis and K. Ziolkowski (eds). Talinn: NATO CCD COE Publications, 141–53.

Dunn Cavelty, Myriam. 2013. "From Cyber-Bombs to Political Fallout: Threat Representations with an Impact in the Cyber-Security Discourse." *International Studies Review* 15 (1): 105–22.

Eriksson, Johan. 2001. "Cyberplagues, It, and Security: Threat Politics in the Information Age." *Journal of Contingencies and Crisis Management* 9 (4): 211–22.

Ewald, François. 1986. *L'etat Providence [the Welfare State]*. Paris: Editions Grasset.

Hansen, Lene. 2011. "The Politics of Securitization and the Muhammad Cartoon Crisis: A Post-Structuralist Perspective." [In English]. *Security Dialogue* 42 (4–5): 357–69.

Hansen, Lene. 2012. "Reconstructing Desecuritisation: The Normative-Political in the Copenhagen School and Directions for How to Apply It." *Review of International Studies* 38 (03): 525–46.

Hansen, Lene and Helen Nissenbaum. 2009. "Digital Disaster, Cyber Security, and the Copenhagen School." [In English]. *International Studies Quarterly* 53 (4): 1155–75.

Harrop, Wayne and Ashely Matteson. 2013–14. "Cyber Resilience: A Review of Critical National Infrastructure and Cyber Security Protection Measures Applied in the UK and USA." *Journal of Business Continuity & Emergency Planning* 7 (2): 149–62.

Heng, Yee-Kuang. 2006. "War as Risk Management: Strategy and Conflict in an Age of Globalised Risks." *Contemporary Security Studies*. London; New York: Routledge.

Kleinwächter, Wolfgang. 2013. "Internet Governance Outlook 2014: Good News, Bad News, No News?" *CIRLEID*, at: www.circleid.com/posts/20131231_internet_governance_outlook_2014_good_news_bad_news_no_news/ (accessed December 2, 2015).

Lindsay, John R. 2013. "Stuxnet and the Limits of Cyberwarfare." *Security Studies* 22 (3): 365–404.

Lindsay, John R., Tai Ming Cheung and Derek S. Reveron. 2015. *China and Cybersecurity: Espionage, Strategy and Politics in the Digital Domain*. New York: Oxford University Press.

Lynn III, William J. 2010. "Defending a New Domain: The Pentagon's Cyberstrategy." *Foreign Affairs* 89 (5).

O'Connell, Mary Ellen. 2012. "Cyber Security without Cyber War." *Journal of Conflict & Security Law* 17 (2): 187–209.

Rasmussen, Mikkel Vedby. 2006. *The Risk Society at War: Terror, Technology and Strategy in the Twenty-First Century*. Cambridge; New York: Cambridge University Press.

Singer, P. W. and Allan Friedman. 2014. *Cybersecurity and Cyberwar: What Everyone Needs to Know*. New York: Oxford University Press.

Smith, Gerry. 2013. "John Kerry: Foreign Hackers Are '21st Century Nuclear Weapons'." *Huffington Post*, at: www.huffingtonpost.com/2013/01/24/john-kerry-hackers_n_2544534.html (accessed December 2, 2015).

3 Cyber spillover conflicts

Transitions from cyber conflict to conventional foreign policy disputes?

Ryan C. Maness and Brandon Valeriano

Introduction

Many suggest the cyber arena is new, different and deadly. Kello (2013) argues that cyber tactics increase the range of harm in the international system. Others frequently suggest that conflicts now will originate in the cyber domain and spillover into conventional military conflicts. Our query here is the about the reality of this idea as reflected by evidence. Do cyber incidents launched by states evoke responses from their targets that involve both cyber and non-cyber means, such as economic or military repercussions? If so, is this prevalent?

In 2011, the United States government declared a cyber incident similar to an act of war, punishable with conventional military means (White House 2011; Schmitt 2013; Barlow 2013). This could be a significant step, because it allows the response to a non-physical malicious incident in cyber space to be in the physical, kinetic form. Conflict then shifts from cyber space to conventional forms. The US declaration of its willingness to act if attacked in the cyber sphere coupled with its abilities in cyber space revealed by the Snowden leaks could lead to a more dangerous and unpredictable world. Thus these new realities could represent a new direction in the way threats and actions are taken in the international sphere.

An article published by *Breaking Defense* in February 2014 lays out the director of US Cyber Command, Army General Keith Alexander's thoughts on how to respond to malicious acts in cyber space: "If it destroys government or other networks, I think it would cross that line' [that would potentially cause America to go to war.]" (Clark 2014).

More recently, on April 1, 2015, in the wake of the large-scale breach of the network of Sony Pictures by North Korea (Sanchez 2015),[1] US President Barack Obama declared that any actor found to be maliciously acting in cyber space that is deemed a threat to the national security of the United States can and will be retaliated against in the form of economic sanctions (Baker 2015). This includes and is not limited to the freezing of the individuals' or groups' assets, the barring of Americans from doing business with these individuals or groups, and blocking these individuals or groups from entering the United States (Baker 2015).

Given these fears of cyber spillover conflicts, and the added probability that responses and counter-attacks will be automated in the future, there is a great danger for cyber issues and events to dramatically alter traditional diplomatic and military interactions. Yet these fears and prognostications must be rooted in evidence and observations given that data and evidence are clearly observable in cyber space.

We can imagine many effects from the cyber domain, but the query that remains is the reality of these possible changes in direction in international affairs. The main question we ask in this chapter is whether or not cyber conflict, defined as the use of computational technologies in cyber space for malevolent and destructive purposes in order to impact, change or modify diplomatic and military interactions between entities (Valeriano and Maness 2015a), is leading to conflict escalation in other domains. Do states that launch a cyber action against an adversary risk the chance of retaliation via naval blockade, economic sanctions,or even military maneuvers? Will states that use cyber methods in their toolbox of weaponry also escalate tensions further with more conventional methods? This chapter will review the evidence we have so far and speculate about future actions given our investigation of the recent past.

Cyber-conflict terminology

Previous research has dissected the contemporary nature of cyber conflict in many ways, from cataloging all actual cyber incidents and disputes between states (Valeriano and Maness 2014, 2015a; Maness and Valeriano 2015; Healey 2013), to examining cyber espionage (Valeriano and Maness 2015a; Singer and Friedman 2014), and finally, examining the impact of cyber incidents (Maness and Valeriano 2015; Rid 2013) on the conflict-cooperation nexus of states. What has yet to be done until now is examine the nature of what we call cyber spill-over conflicts and effects.

A cyber spillover is when cyber conflicts seep and bleed into traditional arena of militarized and foreign policy conflict. In this situation, a computer network attack would lead directly or indirectly, to the escalation in conventional forms of interactions that include anything for outright attack to economic coercion. While it is dubious to claim that the cyber domain is disconnected from the physical domain given that cyber technology has to be housed somewhere, it is also true that there are very few incidents of cyber actions causing physical damage (Stuxnet, Shamoon and the Sony Hack). Our question is not about the transition from cyber to physical, but when cyber disagreements lead directly to conventional foreign policy disputes between states, thus altering how international interactions work.

We use the term "cyber conflict" instead of the more popular term "cyber warfare" as we believe that the latter term inflates the threats seen so far. The claim that is often made is that the cyber era is different and we will see drastically new dynamics evident in the international discourse. If this is true, then we would often see cyber conflicts and events transition from the digital realm to the normal international realm. This claim has been made by government officials, cyber-security experts and academics (White House 2011; Clarke and

Knake 2010: 31; Kello 2013: 32) (Bamford 2014). To quote Kello (2013: 32), "The cyber domain is a perfect breeding ground for political disorder and strategic instability. Six factors contribute to instrumental instability: offense dominance, attribution difficulties, technological volatility, poor strategic depth, and escalatory ambiguity." Thus according to Kello cyber conflict spilling over into conventional domains and being the root of escalatory crises in international politics is not only possible, but inevitable. But what is the empirical veracity of these claims? This is the goal of our work, but first we must survey the landscape of knowledge about cyber conflict to this point.

Cyber conflict and escalation

Some argue that cyber warfare has already begun, even before the information released by Snowden became public knowledge. Clarke and Knake assert,

> in anticipation of hostilities, nations are already preparing for the battlefield. They are hacking into each other's networks and infrastructures, laying in trapdoors and logic bombs ... this ongoing nature of cyber war, the blurring of peace and war, adds a dangerous new dimension of instability.
>
> Clarke and Knake (2010: 31)

Furthermore, Clark and Knake suggest there is a possibility of potentially quickly escalating crises dramatically becoming more severe under the usage of cyber tactics, given the instantaneousness at which digital interactions occur (Clarke and Knake 2010: xi).[2]

Singer and Friedman (2014: 133) also suggest that cyber conflict could change the nature of the game of international conflict and relations between states. Although this may be true, it does not mean that cyber conflict is a revolutionary new form of tactic where nation-states must calculate new strategies, as the major powers did with nuclear weapons. Cyber tactics will likely be more integrative into current tactics and strategies, in both the military and non-military international forums alike. However, the notion of outright cyber warfare and the escalatory effects it could cause are purely speculative at this point, but speculation often draws in public interest and imagination.

Cyber prognosticators such as Kello (2013) suggest that cyber weapons are going to be a threat and are no different from other forms of coercive strategies. Although no serious cyber escalations have happened at this point, for Kello (2013: 7) this does not mean that they will not in the future. As increases in cyber technology and the understanding in how to use them continue to proliferate, states will adopt them because they are easier and cheaper, as the psychological aspect of the need to demonstrate these new technologies will be impossible to resist. According to Kello, once statesmen and military strategists figure out how to best utilize these new cyber weapons in an effectively coercive manner, the cyber threat will escalate exponentially (Kello 2013: 8). While interesting as conjecture, the Internet and digital technology have been a fact of life for well over a decade and the term cyber war and netwar are near twenty-five years old at this point (Arquilla and Ronfedlt 1993).

Clarke and Knake (2010: 30–31) also take the perspective that we have yet to see the worst of what can be done with cyber tactics. What have been demonstrated thus far have been relatively benign cyber incidents. Yet for many reasons, such as the direct collateral damage effects that will happen in the civilian sphere if cyber tactics are used, their widespread usage may actually be less possible. Furthermore, we are still at a point in the cyber academic discourse where even discussing whether or not a cyber arms race is even occurring is speculative at best. There is no empirical study that quantifies the build-up of cyber weapons in terms of technologies developed and money devoted by the world's cyber-capable states.

As the era of nuclear weapons shows us, just because states have a weapon does not mean that they will use it. States must have a salient reason to enter into conflict and escalate it with their adversaries (Mansbach and Vasquez 1981). Conflict in cyber space must also happen for a reason and disagreement over issues will be at the core as to why these weapons will be used, and not just for the sake of using them. Even in the non-cyber realms, it still remains speculative if conflicts in certain areas will develop, such as the often-cited debate over whether or not war between the USA and China is inevitable (Mearsheimer and Nye 2015). It must also be noted that cyber conflict is close to thirty years old at this point and there is a history of its restrained use.

Reveron (2012b: 230) states that "just because we can imagine cyber war does not mean that it can be waged." We therefore have a lot of wiggle room in terms of theorizing and investigating questions pertaining to the future of cyber conflict. Choucri (2012) promotes Lateral Pressure theory (Choucri and North 1975) in a theoretically cohesive attempt to explain when actors will seek change in the international system applied to the digital domain. The concept is based on predictions of behavior from states with different configurations of their population, resources, and technology that will motivate them to act in the international realm. States with certain combinations of these three variables will push them to act out with adversaries in the cyber realm. Russia may act out in different ways than China or the United States based on their unique configuration. This theory and its underpinnings are an original and potentially empirically fruitful avenue for future scholars in the cyber-security field.

Sheldon (2012: 208) points out that cyber weaponry can "manipulate the strategic environment" in order to cause confusion among adversaries will make these tactics' usage all the more likely to be use alongside conventional military tools in conflicts. Choucri (2012: 4) asserts that the constraints of traversing territory and the instantaneousness of the tactic make cyber attractive for state disputes. This uniqueness will make cyber tactics even more likely in future battles, according to some.

Pollpeter (2015) looks at Chinese military and strategic writings on cyber and uncovers that China utilizes cyber tactics out of a position of weakness. They see the United States as the pre-eminent cyber power and therefore the utilization of cyber espionage tactics that China is so famous for is a necessity in order to not fall behind their more technologically advanced cyber rival. Furthermore, Chinese strategists have accused the United States of launching similar espionage campaigns, and therefore assume that the utilization of cyber tactics is now part of the normal relations range between states. For China, the concept of spillover from the cyber to the conventional arena is expected.

Empirical research conducted thus far has found that cyber conflict and its usage has been incredibly restrained, allowing for a credible counter to the prognostications evoked by many pundits. The real utility in cyber conflict seems to be much more muted than many pundits believe (Valeriano and Maness 2015a; Maness and Valeriano 2015; Healey 2013). Espionage, theft, propaganda through vandalizing websites and denial of service campaigns are the majority of cyber incidents observed thus far, and all are at a low level of severity in terms of severity and damage. When compared to military operations or even economic sanctions, these types of low-level cyber coercive measures pale in comparison. This may be a reason as to why our hypothesis about the lack of cyber spillover may have empirical backing.

Considering the strategic calculations of the development and use of cyber weapons are also important. Few seem to realize how labor intensive and expensive cyber operations are. Development of the Stuxnet worm took over three years, cost nearly $100 million, and its deployment required the synchronization of the spy agencies of the US and Israeli governments. Furthermore, the actual impact of cyber weaponry can take months to even years to be felt or even acknowledged by the target. What is the strategic utility of a cyber weapon when only a few leaders know of its existence or the actual damage of the expensive technology inflicts is very minimal? Stuxnet destroyed several of Iran's centrifuges but this only prompted the Islamic Republic to put more online and to speed up its nuclear capability ambitions. Gartzke (2013) points this out as he finds that the strategic calculations of cyber actions are quite limited. Therefore, if this is the case, why would cyber actions prompt a target state to respond with an escalatory conventional military tactic?

To sum up, we know very little about the impact of cyber actions, and we know even less about how it is connected to conventional coercive tactics utilized by states. Yet there has been much speculation as to how cyber conflict will inevitably bleed into other domains and change the strategic thinking of states. It is therefore important to find out whether or not this is actually happening. If cyber spillover is present even during these low-level and less severe cyber actions, then we must prepare for escalatory conventional conflicts if more severe cyber incidents are employed. Therefore, uncovering evidence is the key for the development of proper and considered responses to cyber actions and finding out whether or not cyber spillover is present, and cyber conflict truly is the fifth domain of conflict.

Theory of cyber restraint

Due to our theory of restraint (Valeriano and Maness 2015a: Ch. 3), we have little expectation that cyber actors will escalate digital conflicts to the conventional realm. So far, it has been found states have shown a remarkable degree of restraint in cyber space when the total macro picture of cyber actions is accounted for, from 2001–11 (Valeriano and Maness 2014). Certainly there might be isolated examples of a transition between the digital to conventional, but if cyber prognosticators are correct, we might see this process occur at a great rate, or at least 25 percent. This then leads to our first hypothesis:

> *H1: Due to restraint dynamics, cyber spillover will be rare and no more than 25 percent of cyber incidents between rival states.*

Why is there restraint in cyber space? We have outlined quite a few reasons in the past (Valeriano and Maness 2015a):

> 1) the reproducibility of the tactic, cyber weapons are not one shot weapons, they can be replicated thus they are dangerous in ways that conventional weapons are not, 2) cyber weapons are not simple to design, Stuxnet took years, the entire US intelligence apparatus (plus help from Israel and Germany), and millions of dollars and it still largely failed, 3) the chances of collateral damage (and thus blame) are high, cyber weapons are not surgical, 4) the US and now Russia (in Ukraine) have failed to use cyber weapons when engaging in enemies, if these cyber capable states refrain, why would other states engage? 5) diffusion of the conflict by dragging in third parties, the probability is high if a cyber weapons is used, others will be effected and engage either through alliances or friendship bonds;, 6) blowback, cyber weapons if used to great effect will demand repercussions, and finally, 7) fear of norm violation, no one has used cyber weapons to great effect and no one wants to be first. A taboo is developing. None of these points alone will ensure restraint, but together; they bind to create the current outcome we currently observe.

Given our expectation of restraint that will constrain behavior, if we do see an escalation from the digital to the physical, it has to be under situations of enormous importance. This is where the issue based perspective comes into play and it also outlines our general theoretical perspective regarding the likelihood of conflict (Mansbach and Vasquez 1981). In order to operationalize importance, we focus on territorial disputes which are highly salient (Hensel 2001) and war-prone (Vasquez and Valeriano 2010). To investigate this idea, we will examine the connection between territorial disputes and escalation to the physical realm. This leads us to our second hypothesis:

> *H2: Cyber spillover conflicts will only be present in territorial disputes which are highly salient to states.*

Our next task is to lay out our research design to investigate our propositions.

Research design

To test our theory, the research design in this project is straight forward. The unit of analysis is dyadic month, comparing cyber incidents that have an end date in one month and see if a militarized interstate dispute happened the following weeks, within a month period between pairs of states included in the Dyadic Cyber Incident and Dispute dataset (DCID). The dataset covers the years 2001 to 2011 and records all rival state-to-state cyber incidents. One hundred and eleven cyber incidents are included in the eleven-year period are contained in the dataset. Only events that can be directly tied to state responsibility are recorded. Non-state third-party entities such as Anonymous or the Syrian Electronic Army are not included; only state-based, government sanctioned cyber events are coded.[3] Targets must also be state-based or can be a private network that is important to a state's national security. Boeing, Google and Lockheed Martin are examples of this.[4]

The COW Militarized Interstate Disputes (MID) collection Version 4, which records cases of conflict between states "in which the threat, display or use of military force short of war by one member state is explicitly directed towards the government, official representatives, official forces, property, or territory of another state" (Jones, Bremer and Singer 1996). It uses historical and diplomatic sources to isolate and codify each isolated incident. This newest version covers MIDs from 1815 to 2010.

If an MID occurs between a pair of states within four weeks after a recorded cyber incident, then there is evidence of cyber spillover; whereas if there is an absence of an MID after the cyber event, there is a lack of such evidence. We look at all 111 cyber incidents that are able to be matched up with the available data from the MID data, which excludes the year 2011.

For connecting territorial issues to cyber actions, we sifted Huth and Allee's (2009) dataset to connect territorial claims data to ongoing cyber incidents. Territorial militarized disputes were also utilized to connect cyber actions to militarized territorial responses. For territorial militarized interstate disputes (MIDs) we combed the Correlates of War (COW) dataset and compared the start and end times of cyber conflicts with these territorial MIDs (Palmer *et al.* 2015).[5] Next we present the evidence gathered from this research endeavor.

Findings and assessment

The data analyzed in this research finds very little evidence that cyber spillover is happening thus far, refuting the claim by many that it is a game changer in international relations between states. In fact, evidence is so sparse; it is difficult to really understand why there has been such speculation about the idea that cyber conflicts will become physical.

In our dataset there are 111 cyber incidents between states from 2001 to 2011. We find that only three of these incidents are connected to further international tensions under what we might consider an MID, a use, display or threat of force (using the MID 4.0 data). We find only one incident, presented in Table 3.1 that actually precedes a militarized interstate dispute. This is the most famous case of cyber incidents preceding a militarized campaign, and was the series of deface-ments and DDoS incidents conducted by Russia against Georgia during the August 2008 five-day conflict.

This incident was minimal by cyber standards, as only a denial of service (DDoS) was employed. Russia had the ability to inflict more damage in Geor-gian cyber space, however it chose not to. Georgia retaliated with DDoS tactics against the Russian hackers, making them inoperable for a few hours, thus the damage was minimal and temporary at best. Russia refrained from the full use of cyber tactics, even in times of physical conflict against their stated enemy.

The cyber incident Russia initiated on Georgia was a DDoS method on Geor-gian government websites. DDoS methods allow cyber warriors to hijack a number of previously controllable computer terminals and direct them to access a particular network at the same time. These Russian "zombies" were directed at various Georgian government websites, including that of President Mikheil Saakishvili. These attacks left much of the Georgian population without access to information about the larger world, including the military campaign being launched in South Ossetia (Nazario 2008). This pro-Russian region became the battleground between Georgian and Russian militaries, yet much of Georgian population was left in the dark due to the flood of botnets launched in cyber space. Internet dependent media outlets were also unable to get accurate information to report to the rest of the world just exactly what was going on in the separatist enclave.

The telecommunications network VoIP, the largest mobile phone provider in Georgia, was also flooded by DDoS methods, consequently exactly during the time that the Russian and Georgian militaries were engaged (Swaine 2008). On the ground freelance journalists as well as entrenched populations witnessing the conflict could not relay the information to the outside world. South Ossetia is a remote mountainous region, and without mobile communications or internet access, the world was left in the dark. Russia made quick work of the less capable Georgian military without any credible coverage of the battles, and once most Georgian networks were back online and communications restored, the Russian military were only thirty miles from the capital of Tbilisi (Cornell and Starr 2009). With the Georgian troops having been humiliated and the military objective of keeping South Ossetia autonomous from the central Georgian gov-ernment, the Russian military pulled back to within the enclave's borders.

Georgia was able to be brought back online with the swift help from several Western allies, particularly Estonia and Poland. Estonia sent CERT teams to find the bugs and restore network, while Poland freed up bandwidth in its networks until the damaged Georgian infrastructure was brought back online. Georgia was then able to respond to the Russian cyber incidents with one of their own, with help from Estonian experts, and succeeded in infiltrating and shutting down the networks being used by the Russian hackers (Nazario 2008). Getting a taste of their own medicine for a time, these highly skilled hackers became victim to

Table 3.1 Russia–Georgia 2008: the case of cyber spillover

Initiator	Target	Name	Date of cyber incident	Date of militarized incident	Type	Target type
Russia	Georgia	Before the Gunfire	7/20/2008–8/16/2008	8/7/2008–8/12/2008	DDoS, Vandalism	Govt, non-military, Russ shuts down Georgian government websites and telecommunications to slow communication abilities in Georgia

Source: (Valeriano and Maness 2015); Correlates of War (COW) MID4 Dataset.

retaliation for a short time. The counter-DDoS attack was quickly subdued and Russian hacktivists were able to continue their cyber assault within a matter of hours.

Although it was the conventional military campaign that ultimately decided the outcome of the five-day conflict in August 2008, Russia had set a precedent not yet seen in international disputes: it used cyber technologies in tandem with a conventional military operation. Although considered for its military operations against Iraq in 2003 and Libya in 2011, the United States has publically acknowledged that it refrained from doing so, even though the tactic could have been used to give it a real strategic advantage (Hasson 2009; Schmitt and Shanker 2011).

There is also evidence that in 2013, the USA seriously considered using cyber tactics against the Assad regime when the bloody civil war in Syria began to escalate (Fung 2013). Yet the United States decided against using cyber weapons so to not to set a precedent where these tactics are utilized during a conventional military campaign. Russia, therefore, is the one that broke this potentially developing norm. Yet these particular cyber methods where there is evidence of spillover held no real strategic military value. The limited utility did succeed in confusing the Georgian government and had a psychological effect on the Georgian population. The rather primitive methods did not knock out Georgian radar, trick the Georgian infantry or shut down Georgian missile defenses. Russia also used these cyber weapons against a post-Soviet state; a region Moscow believes it can act with impunity. There is doubt that Russia would use cyber during a military campaign outside this region.

When open and unrestricted military combat existed between Russia and its perceived rival, Russia showed restraint in terms of fully unleashing its actual cyber-weapon capabilities. The series of cyber incidents employed launched in August 2008 was not a military strategy and mainly caused disruptions among the civilian population. The Russian military campaign, therefore, could have succeeded even in the absence of any cyber utilization. Perhaps its restraint from employing its full cyber arsenal against Georgia is due to the international condemnation it received in 2007 when it crippled Estonia's networks, or because it did not want to be the first of the cyber powers to match its capabilities with action in cyber space.

Lastly, claiming that the Russian cyber actions against Georgia led to its escalating into the military campaign is on shaky foundations. The cyber campaign was a matter of convenience in terms of easily confusing and instilling fear in the Georgian population, and restricted the real-time reporting of the fighting in South Ossetia. The conventional conflict was likely to have been initiated without the help of any cyber campaign.

We find evidence for three more cyber campaigns being launched within the one-month time period where militarized disputes were also present, and these are listed in Table 3.2. However the cyber incidents were preceded by the military ones, allowing for the evidence for cyber spillover pertaining to these disputes being dubious. The first two pertain to the ongoing territorial disputes

Table 3.2 Cyber incidents accompanied by militarized disputes

Initiator	Target	Name	Date of cyber incident	Date of militarized incident	Type	Target type
Japan	South Korea	Tokdo Island Dispute	3/20/2005–3/20/2005	3/8/2005–7/7/2005	Defacement	Govt, non-military, Japan defaces several South Korean government websites after South Korea sent fighter jets to warn of Japanese jets in the disputed Tokdo Islands
China	Japan	East China Sea Dispute	9/14/2010–9/17/2010	9/7/2010–present	DDoS	Govt, non-military, Chinese DDoS escalates naval tensions between China and Japan over the territorial disputes in the East China Sea
Syria	U.S.	Hama Visit	7/9/2011–7/9/2011	7/3/2011–8/4/2011	Defacement	Govt, non-military, US Ambassador Ford's visit to the Syrian city of Hama provokes defacement by Syria to the State Department. Assad's troops crackdown on Hama the next day

Source: Adapted from Valeriano and Maness 2015; Correlates of War (COW) MID4 Dataset.

over islands between Japan and its East Asian rivals. The first involves South Korea, where each country's air forces sent fighter jets into the airspace of the Tokdo Islands, a series of uninhabited rocks that each country claims as theirs. During this aerial MID, Japan defaced several South Korean government websites for a few hours on March 20, 2005, prompting condemnation from South Korea. The fly-bys continued for about four months, from early March to early July, and the cyber defacements really played no part in its continuation. It was a dispute over territory that led to this battle of wills, which was eventually stalemated because of the urging from the United States (Palmer *et al.* 2015).

The second involved Japan and China and pertained to their continuing territorial disputes in the East China Sea. The fishing waters surrounding the Senkaku Islands, claimed by both China and Japan to be in their Exclusive Economic Zones (EEZ) where the territory in this zone's economic activity is exclusively reserved for the claimant state, have been in dispute between the two Asian powers for decades. However, these tensions escalated into a near crisis stage when the arrest of a Chinese fishing captain and then extended detention for trespassing on the claimed Japanese waters by Japanese authorities led to a tit-for-tat exchange between the two countries. Japanese nationals in China were arrested for illicit behavior near Chinese military bases, Japan returned with an embargo on rare earth materials from China bound for Japanese ports, and the United States even stepped in to defend Japan's claim to the territorial waters in an attempt to de-escalate (Smith 2012). This resulted in China launching the series of DDoS incidents during the time of these tense exchanges in September of 2010.

The third incident in Table 3.2 where a militarized dispute occurred within the four-week time-frame of a cyber action occurred between the USA and Syria. In July 2011, then US Ambassador to Syria John Ford visited the city of Hama, a city that was a focal point of anti-Assad sentiment when the bloody civil war was just beginning. Seen as a slight to the regime and a move that emboldened the anti-Assad movement, the Syrian government launched several code-manipulating vandalism tactics against the US State Department's website. Propagandist images denouncing the move and the United States appeared on the website for a very short period of time. The Assad regime stepped up its military operations against the civilian population and rebel forces in Hama. Bombings and heavy artillery shelling with seemingly indiscriminate targeting intensified greatly as a result of this diplomatic move. It was here that the body count that has reached nearly half a million as of present began to intensify, and it is here that arguably the Syrian civil conflict evolved from a series of nationwide protests into one of the worst civil wars this century has seen. Hama was a hotbed of anti-Assad discontent, and Assad cracked down on this city's citizens hard in hopes to quell the unrest, yet instead he created a war that has no end in sight.

These results do not lead us to re-evaluate the nature of cyber conflicts and their precipitating influences. Instead, we feel that one needs to take a step back and re-evaluate the salience of cyber disputes as they are connected to territorial disputes. Tables 3.3 and 3.4 list all rivals involved in cyber conflict. Interestingly, fifteen out of the twenty cyber rivals in DCID are also regional rivals. Regional rivals are states that are in a proximal geographic location to each other and have territorial disputes or policy disputes pertaining to the region in question. Digging deeper, 93 percent (14 of 15) of these cyber rivals were involved in a territorial issue or dispute, or both, prior to the initiation of these cyber actions. Only Israel and Iran did not have a pressing territorial issue before a cyber incident ensued. Regarding territorial disputes, only Russia and Estonia did not escalate to a militarized crisis; where the movement of troops, naval vessels or air forces would occur.

We find little evidence for cyber spillover, where cyber incidents escalate tension between states into more conventional forms of conflict. What is interesting about the findings in Table 3.3 is that cyber conflict is overwhelmingly regional, contrary to what one may expect due to cyber tactics' instant and global reach. Like the majority of conventional disputes that evoke a response, cyber disputes are rooted in outstanding territorial disagreements (Vasquez and Henehan 2001; Senese and Vasquez 2008; Vasquez and Valeriano 2010). Cyber conflict is found to be in its proper context for regional rivals, as they are a part of the normal relations range of enemy exchanges (Azar 1972). Furthermore, the majority of these cyber disputes also involve ongoing issues that did not originate in and extend beyond cyber space.

An exception to the regional dispute presence among cyber rivals is disputes involving the United States. The USA has global military and economic interests;

Table 3.3 Cyber regional rivals and territorial issues/disputes

RivaL A	Rival B	Huth territorial issue?	COW territorial MID?
China	India	Y	Y
China	Japan	Y	Y
China	Taiwan	Y	Y
China	Vietnam	Y	Y
China	Philippines	Y	Y
North Korea	South Korea	Y	Y
North Korea	Japan	Y	Y
South Korea	Japan	Y	Y
India	Pakistan	Y	Y
India	Bangladesh	Y	Y
Israel	Iran	N	Y
Israel	Lebanon	Y	Y
Iraq	Kuwait	Y	Y
Russia	Georgia	Y	Y
Russia	Estonia	Y	N

Source: Adapted from Valeriano and Maness 2015; Huth and Allee 2009; Palmer *et al.* 2015.

Notes
75 percent (15 of 20) of cyber rivals are regional rivals.
93 percent (14 of 15) of regional cyber rivals have territorial issues.
93 percent (14 of 15) of regional cyber rivals have territorial MIDs.

Table 3.4 Cyber non-regional rivals and territorial issues/disputes

RivaL A	Rival B	Huth territorial issue?	COW territorial MID?
U.S.	China	N	Y
U.S.	Russia	N	N
U.S.	North Korea	N	Y
U.S.	Syria	N	N
U.S.	Iran	N	N

Source: Adapted from Valeriano and Maness 2015; Huth and Allee 2009; Palmer *et al.* 2015.

Notes
40 percent (2 of 5) of non-regional cyber rivals have territorial MIDs.
0 percent (0 of 5) of non-regional cyber rivals have territorial issues.

therefore the potential for non-regional animosities involving the superpower playing out in cyber space is to be expected. All of the non-regional rivals listed in Table 3.4 (5 of 20) involve the United States, implying that the only country with a true global reach is the only country evoking non-regional cyber disputes. Only two of the five cyber disputes involve a territorial dispute, which also involves disputes with third parties. One of these disputes is with China, where the territorial integrity of Taiwan was upheld by the United States. The other dispute involved South Korea and pertained to its perpetual territorial disagreements with the North. Evidence would actually suggest that we are seeing territorial disputes spillover into the cyber domain, not the other way around.

As the global superpower as well as being one of the most Internet-dependent states in the world, the United States will be an attractive target to cyber aggression. For cyber conflict, the United States, Russia and China are the states that have non-regional interests and therefore have been involved in non-regional cyber interactions. It is therefore no surprise that the global cyber interests of the USA, Russia and China are not based on the normal territorial dynamics of most cyber interactions that involve interstate rivals. Yes, for the three pre-eminent cyber powers, the actions that these states take in cyber space will shape international norms and could make cyber operations permissible.

Coercive economic cyber spillover?

In November 2014, Sony Pictures Entertainment, a US subsidiary of Sony Corporation, witnessed a major breach of data cyber incident that stole large troves of information from its secure networks. Diagnosed as a Trojan horse espionage campaign, the group claiming credit for this attack identified themselves as the "Guardians of Peace" (Griffin 2014). The group claimed that the upcoming release of the satirical movie *The Interview*, where North Korean dictator Kim Jun-Un's assassination was the underlying plot and the reason why the attacks were initiated. This led to many in the USA suspecting that the group was actually the North Korean government, later confirmed by the FBI and the State

Department (Valeriano 2014; Sanchez 2015). North Korea denied its part in the attack, although praised its efforts.

In January 2015, US President Barack Obama ordered that more economic sanctions were to be placed on North Korea's senior officials as well as the intelligence agency, the Ministry of State Security, known to be the source of many of North Korea's cyber operations (Sanger and Schmidt 2015). This was the first publicly announced retaliation of its kind to a cyber operation, and Obama promised the public that it was a "proportional response" to what had been done to a major US-based corporation (Sanger and Schmidt 2015). Later in April 2015 Obama issued an executive order that will make economic sanctions the response of choice to those choosing to launch cyber criminal or espionage activities on US government or private sector networks (Nakashima 2015).

The question that remains is whether or not this will become the norm in terms of responses to cyber operations between states. Given the fact that many of the cyber incidents witnessed so far have been relatively low in severity, are economic sanctions a more proportional response? The United States has announced that this will become their preferred retaliatory tactic when victimized in cyber space, so will the rest of the world follow the global hegemon into this possible acceptable mode of behavior? The data for economic responses to cyber operations is so sparse as of now that it is difficult making any future inferences on this matter, and we reserve these questions for future avenues of research.

Conclusion

The sparse findings of this research conducted in this chapter have possible caveats. One possibility is that cyber conflict is very new to the conflict domain and at this point it is difficult to say with certainty that cyber spillover will not become commonplace in the future. However, we do have over a ten-year collection of data that records interactions between cyber rivals, which allows us to make these inferences about how cyber actors interact. We therefore have some indication that the idea of transitions between cyber and conventional interactions are grossly overstated in the cyber security discourse.

Furthermore, future uses of a tactic such as cyber technology are often played out by how they are first utilized. That the United States, China and Russia, the three most powerful cyber actors in the international system have shown remarkable restraint in their use of cyber weaponry may mean that this restraint will become the norm for all actions in the cyber world. For example, nuclear weapons were used early in their lifetime, specifically to end a bloody world war, and were considered to be part of the military tool kit early on as well. Yet, as the destruction and long-term human suffering observed in the aftermath of the two atomic bombs dropped on Japan quickly developed, a norm against the technology's usage began to emerge. Also, as the Cold War demonstrates, the threat of using nuclear weapons has also led to dangerous and enduring foreign policy stalemates. The question that remains is whether or not these same dynamics of restraint will endure in cyber conflicts.

The ongoing conflict in Ukraine gives up some information on future uses of cyber technology in connection with combat operations. While this operation is known as an example of hybrid warfare, we see little evidence of cyber tactics being employed (Kramer 2015). The two things that are evident are attacks on telecom companies, which are not part of cyber actions, and espionage attacks on the Ukrainian military in order to steal military plans (Martin-Vegue 2015). Ukraine is likely the most pertinent and important military action by Russia for a generation but we continue to see little evidence of cyber spillover.

The cyber future remains in a state of speculation, but to this point empirical research has shown that states are restrained from the use of their full cyber capabilities, and it also shows credible evidence that cyber spillovers are close to non-existent. This must call into question the cyber revolution hypotheses, specifically that cyber weapons will be dangerously game-changing. Cyber seems to follow the same patterns of why disputes happen in the other domains, usually of a territorial and regional nature.

We do find evidence that cyber tactics are used widespread amongst territorial as well as regional rivals, where cyber is used in tandem with other forms of propaganda, threats or use of force. However, the cyber tactics utilized have been at a low severity level, and the conventional displays of animosity between the rivals have been more worrisome than anything utilized in cyber space. Furthermore, the cyber incidents that we have witnessed so far are low in severity, suggesting a paradoxical system cyber peace (Valeriano and Maness 2015b). Economic sanctions may become a more proportional response to these types of actions. While many consider these actions to be power politics statecraft and economic warfare, they are not examples of conventional warfare and unlikely to trigger the typical escalation dynamics that lead to outright war.

We are left with the more likely possibility that cyber tactics will be used as force multipliers and additives to conventional conflicts, rather than the source of conflicts in the first place. If anything, cyber conflicts occur after conventional military attacks. This seems to be the result of many technological developments. Rather than vastly changing the calculations before battles or giving states a reason to fight, instead we see technology become assimilated in the typical tactics that states use on the battlefield. Instead of suggesting that cyber tactics will change the nature and sources of conflict, we would argue cyber tactics may enhance already ongoing conflicts but are unlikely to be issues on their own that lead to war and escalation.

Notes

1 Both the FBI and US State Department have attributed the Sony Hack to the North Korean government.
2 Healey (2013: 23) notes that although cyber conflicts can be fast, they are by no means conducted "at the speed of light."
3 Organizations that initiate these types of attacks have no clear origin and many times have multiple political agendas, and as we are interested in the state-level dynamics of cyber conflict, these types cyber incidents would not be a useful addition to the DCID nor our events dataset.

4 The DCID dataset (Valeriano and Maness 2014) acknowledges the fact that attribution can be problematic, as deniability is easy for states. States that use cyber tactics against their rivals must be fairly explicit, and if attribution cannot be found, it is not included in the dataset. A state must acknowledge its part or forensics from cyber security companies must show evidence of state involvement; therefore this is a comprehensive list of cyber incidents and disputes that fits best for our model.
5 Huth and Allee look at outcomes of territorial disputes and we term them territorial issues. They look at how the disputes are settled. Palmer *et al.* (2015) look at the processes of territorial disputes, where they look at the origins of how the dispute happened in the first place. A show of first must happen for these disputes to be coded. We use both datasets for scope and breadth.

References

Arquilla, John and David Ronfeldt. 1993. "Cyberwar is Coming!" *Comparative Strategy* 12 (2): 141–65.
Azar, Edward E. 1972. "Conflict Escalation and Conflict Reduction in an International Crisis, Suez 1956." *Journal of Conflict Resolution* 16 (2): 183–201.
Baker, Peter. 2015. "Obama Expands Options for Retaliating against Foreign Hackers." *New York Times*, April 1, at: www.nytimes.com/2015/04/02/us/politics/us-expands-foreign-cyberattack-retaliation-options.html (accessed April 2, 2015).
Bamford, James. 2014. "The Most Wanted Man in the World." *Wired*, at: www.wired.com/2014/08/edward-snowden/ (accessed April 24, 2015).
Barlow, Thomas. 2013. "China Ups Ante in Cyber Warfare." *The Australian*, May 31, at: www.theaustralian.com.au/national-affairs/opinion/friendly-china-ups-ante-in-cyber-warfare/story-e6frgd0x-1226654075003 (accessed November 30, 2015).
Choucri, Nazli. 2012. *Cyberpolitics in International Relations.* Cambridge, MA: MIT Press.
Choucri, Nazli and Robert C. North. 1975. *Nations in Conflict: National Growth and International Violence.* San Francisco, CA: Freeman.
Christensen, Thomas J. 2006. "Fostering Stability or Creating a Monster? The Rise of China and U.S. Policy Toward East Asia." *International Security* 31 (1): 81–126.
Clark, Colin. 2014. "CyberCom Chief Laexander Lays Down Cyber Red Line; Destroy a Network, Risk War." *Breaking Defense*, February 27, at: http://breakingdefense.com/2014/02/cybercom-chief-alexander-lays-down-cyber-red-line-destroy-a-network-risk-war/ (accessed June 12, 2015).
Clarke, Richard A. and Robert K. Knake. 2010. *Cyber War: The Next Threat to National Security and What To Do About It.* New York: Harper Collins.
Cornell, Svante and Frederick Starr (eds). 2009. *The Guns of August 2008: Russia's War with Georgia.* New York: ME Sharpe.
Fung, Brian. 2013. "Syria could be a Crucial Proving Ground for U.S. Cyberwarriors." *Washington Post*, September 3, at: www.washingtonpost.com/blogs/the-switch/wp/2013/09/04/syria-could-be-a-crucial-proving-ground-for-u-s-cyberwarriors/ (accessed July 16, 2015).
Gartzke, Erik. 2013. "The Myth of Cyberwar: Bringing War on the Internet Back Down to Earth." *International Security* 38 (2): 41–73.
Griffin, Andrew, 2014. "Sony Hack: Who are the Guardians of Peace, and is North Korea Really behind the Attack?" *Independent*, at: www.independent.co.uk/life-style/gadgets-and-tech/news/sony-hack-who-are-the-guardians-of-peace-and-is-north-korea-really-behind-the-attack-9931282.html (accessed July 19, 2015).

Hasson, Judi. 2009. "U.S. Considered 2003 Cyber Attack on Iraq." *Fierce Government IT*, August 2, at: www.fiercegovernmentit.com/story/u-s-considered-2003-cyber-attack-iraq/2009-08-02 (accessed June 28, 2015).

Healey, Jason (ed.) 2013. *A Fierce Domain: Conflict in Cyberspace 1986–2012*. Washington, DC: Cyber Conflict Studies Association.

Hensel, Paul R. 2001. "Contentious Issues and World Politics: The Management of Territorial Claims in the Americas, 1816–1992." *International Studies Quarterly* 45 (1): 81–109.

Huth, Paul and Todd Allee. 2009. *The Democratic Peace and Territorial Conflict in the Twentieth Century*, at: http://hdl.handle.net/1902.1/10636 (accessed November 30, 2015).

Jones, Daniel M., Stuart A. Bremer and J. David Singer. 1996. "Militarized Interstate Disputes, 1816–1992: Rationale, Coding Rules, and Empirical Patterns." *Conflict Management and Peace Science* 15 (2): 163–215.

Kello, Lucas. 2013. "The Meaning of the Cyber Revolution: Perils to Theory and Statecraft." *International Security* 38 (2): 7–40.

Kramer, Franklin. 2015. "Defend the Arteries of Society: Russia, Ukraine, and the Rise of Hybrid Warfare." *US News and World Report*, June 9, at: www.usnews.com/opinion/blogs/world-report/2015/06/09/russia-ukraine-and-the-rise-of-hybrid-warfare (accessed November 30, 2015).

Lorell, Mark, Julia Lowell, Michael Kennedy and Hugh Levaux. 2000. *Cheaper, Faster, Better? Commercial Approaches to Weapons Acquisitions*. Washington. DC: RAND Corporation.

Lynch III, William J. 2010. "Defending a New Domain." *Foreign Affairs* 89 (5): 97–108.

Maness, Ryan C. and Brandon Valeriano. 2015. *The Impact of Cyber Conflict on International Interactions*. Armed Forces and Society.

Mansbach, Richard W. and John A. Vasquez. 1981. *In Search of Theory*. New York: Columbia University Press.

Martin-Vegue, Tony. 2015. "Are We Witnessing a Cyber War between Russia and Ukraine? Don't Blink, You Might Miss It." *CSO Online*, April 24, at: www.csoonline.com/article/2913743/cyber-attacks-espionage/are-we-witnessing-a-cyber-war-between-russia-and-ukraine-dont-blink-you-might-miss-it.html (accessed November 30, 2015).

Mearsheimer, John J. and Joseph S. Nye. 2015. "Mearsheimer vs. Nye on the Rise of China." *The Diplomat*, July 8, at: http://thediplomat.com/2015/07/mearsheimer-vs-nye-on-the-rise-of-china/ (accessed November 30, 2015).

Nakashima, Ellen. 2015. "U.S. Establishes Sanctions Program to Combat Cyberattacks, Cyberspying." *Washington Post*, at: www.washingtonpost.com/world/national-security/us-to-establish-sanctions-program-to-combat-cyberattacks-cyberspying/2015/03/31/7f563474-d7dc-11e4-ba28-f2a685dc7f89_story.html (accessed July 12, 2015).

Nazario, Jose. 2008. *DDoS and Security Reports: The Arbor Networks Security Blog*. Arbor Sert Website, at: http://ddos.arbornetworks.com/2008/08/georgia-ddos-attacks-a-quick-summary-of-observations/ (accessed August 5, 2012).

Palmer, Glenn, Vito D'Orazio, Michael Kenwick and Matthew Lane. Forthcoming 2015. "The MID4 Data Set: Procedures, Coding Rules, and Description." *Conflict Management and Peace Science*.

Pollpeter, Kevin. 2015. "Chinese Writings on Cyberwarfare and Coercion," in John R. Lindsay, Tai Ming Cheung and Derek S. Reveron (eds), *China and Cybersecurity: Espionage, Strategy, and Politics in the Digital Domain*. New York: Oxford University Press, 138–62.

Reveron, Derek. 2012a. "An Introduction to National Security and Cyberspace," in Derek Reveron (ed.), *Cyberspace and National Security: Threats, Opportunities, and Power in a Virtual World*. Washington DC: Georgetown University Press, 3–20.

Reveron, Derek. 2012b. "Conclusion," in Derek Reveron (ed.), *Cyberspace and National Security: Threats, Opportunities, and Power in a Virtual World*. Washington DC: Georgetown University Press, 225–230.

Richardson, Lewis Fry. 1960. *Arms and Insecurity*. Pittsburgh, PA: Boxwood.

Rid, Thomas. 2011. "Cyber War Will Not Take Place." *Journal of Strategic Studies*, 1–28.

Rid, Thomas. 2013. *Cyber War Will Not Take Place*. London: Hurst & Company.

Rid, Thomas & Peter McBurney. 2012. "Cyber Weapons." *The RUSI Journal* 157 (1): 6–13.

Sample, Susan G. 1998. "Military Buildups, War, and Realpolitik." *Journal of Conflict Resolution* 42 (2): 156–175.

Sanchez, Gabriel. 2015. "Case Study: Critical Controls that Sony Should Have Implemented." *SANS Institute*, at: www.sans.org/reading-room/whitepapers/casestudies/case-study-critical-controls-sony-implemented-36022?utm_content=buffer69ebd&utm_medium=social&utm_source=twitter.com&utm_campaign=buffer (accessed July 19, 2015).

Sanger, David E. and Michael S. Schmidt. 2015. "More Sanctions on North Korea after Sony Case." *New York Times*, at: www.nytimes.com/2015/01/03/us/in-response-to-sony-attack-us-levies-sanctions-on-10-north-koreans.html (accessed July 18, 2015).

Schmitt, Eric and Thom Shanker. 2011. "U.S. debated cyberwarfare attack in plan on Libya." *New York Times*, at: www.nytimes.com/2011/10/18/world/africa/cyber-warfare-against-libya-was-debated-by-us.html?_r=2 (accessed July 2, 2015).

Schmitt, Michael. 2013. *The Tallinn Manual on the International Law Applicable to Cyber Warfare*. NATO Cooperative Cyber Defence Center for Excellence, at: www.ccdcoe.org/249.html (accessed May 31, 2013).

Senese, Paul D. and John A. Vasquez. 2008. *The Steps to War: An Empirical Study*. Princeton, NJ: Princeton University Press.

Sheldon, John. 2012. "Toward a Theory of Cyber Power: Strategic Purpose in Peace and War," in Derek Reveron (ed.), *Cyberspace and National Security: Threats, Opportunities, and Power in a Virtual World*. Washington, DC: Georgetown University Press, 207–24.

Singer, P.W. and Allan Friedman. 2014. *Cybersecurity and Cyberwar: What Everyone Needs to Know*. Oxford: Oxford University Press.

Smith, Sheila A. 2012. *Japan and the East China Sea*. Orbis Summer 2012, at: www.cfr.org/japan/japan-east-china-sea-dispute/p28795 (accessed November 30, 2015).

Swaine, Jon. 2008. "Georgia: Russia 'Conducting Cyber War." *The Telegraph*, August 11, at: www.telegraph.co.uk/news/worldnews/europe/georgia/2539157/Georgia-Russia-l conducting-cyber-war.htm (accessed November 30, 2015).

Valeriano, Brandon. 2014. "Despite What the Cyber Skeptics Say, North Korea is Behind the Sony Hack." *Slate*. December 23, at: www.slate.com/blogs/future_tense/2014/12/23/north_korea_is_behind_the_sony_attack_don_t_listen_to_cyber_skeptics.html (accessed November 30, 2015).

Valeriano, Brandon and Ryan C. Maness. 2012a. "The Fog of Cyberwar: Why the Threat Doesn't Live Up to the Hype." *Foreign Affairs*, at: www.foreignaffairs.com/articles/138443/brandon-valeriano-and-ryan-maness/the-fog-of-cyberwar?page=show# (accessed November 30, 2015).

Valeriano, Brandon and Ryan C. Maness. 2012b. "Persistent Enemies and Cyber Security: The Future of Rivalry in an Age of Information Warfare," in Derek Reveron (ed.), *Cyberspace and National Security: Threats, Opportunity and Power in a Virtual World.* Washington, DC: Georgetown University Press, 139–158.

Valeriano, Brandon and Ryan C. Maness. 2014. "The Dynamics of Cyber Conflict between Rival Antagonists, 2001–2011." *Journal of Peace Research* 51 (3): 347–360.

Valeriano, Brandon and Ryan C. Maness. 2015a. *Cyber War versus Cyber Realities: Cyber Conflict in the International System.* New York: Oxford University Press.

Valeriano, Brandon and Ryan C. Maness. 2015b. "The Coming Cyberpeace: The Normative Argument against Cyberwarfare." *Foreign Affairs,* at: www.foreignaffairs.com/articles/2015-05-13/coming-cyberpeace (accessed November 30, 2015).

Valeriano, Brandon and John A. Vasquez. 2011. "Paths to War and Peace in a Post-American World," in Hogue, Clark and Stairs (eds), *What Lies Ahead? Debating the Prospects for a Post American World.* Toronto: University of Toronto Press.

Vasquez, John and Marie Henehan. 2001. "Territorial Disputes and the Probability of War, 1816–1992." *Journal of Peace Research* 38 (2): 123–38.

Vasquez, John A. and Brandon Valeriano. 2010. "Classification of Interstate Wars." *Journal of Politics* 72 (2): 292–309.

White House. 2011. *International Strategy for Cyberspace: Prosperity, Security, and Openness in a Networked World.* May 2011.

4 Power, rivalry and cyber conflict

An empirical analysis

Allison Pytlak and George E. Mitchell

Power, rivalry and cyber conflict: an empirical analysis

Conflict knows no boundaries. Over the last two decades interstate conflict has spilled over into a new domain—the cyber domain—an intangible space made up of networks, tools and amenities that millions rely upon to fulfill some of the most basic needs of society. The clashes that occur between states in cyber space are diverse in nature, purpose and impact. Cyber conflict comprises activities ranging from espionage to the strategic dismantling of websites and networks and has provided new opportunities for non-state actors to disrupt cyber systems. Moreover the dual-use nature of the tools of cyber conflict—so-called "cyber weapons"—and seemingly endless possibilities for their use is precisely what makes them such a terrifying specter to many. Cyber weapons, and the conflicts they engender, are dynamic, increasingly pervasive and difficult to control.

However, the actual record of cyber conflict has been far more measured than one might imagine. What is certainly clear is that for the international community to address cyber conflict meaningfully it will be necessary to have a richer understanding of the circumstances under which states engage in it. This chapter therefore seeks to identify the dyadic characteristics that appear to make cyber conflict more likely. While there is an extensive literature available about individual cyber operations, there is relatively little systematic, quantitative analysis available evaluating the possible contributors to cyber conflict. This research seeks to address this important gap.

This chapter is organized as follows. It begins by reviewing the literature relevant to cyber conflict in order to develop multiple hypotheses as to why and when rival states engage in cyber conflict. These hypotheses cover several aspects of rivalry dynamics including economic and military asymmetry, nuclear weapons possession, interconnectedness, rivalry intensity and regional and cultural factors. Building on previous research (Valeriano and Maness 2014) that has examined the scope, length and damage inflicted by cyber operations between rival states from 2001–2011, this chapter examines 97 rival dyads to understand the characteristics that predict cyber conflict, finding that nuclear weapon possession is the most significant contributor to the likelihood of cyber conflict. The remainder of this chapter explores the implications of this finding through two cases studies, one of which focuses on a rival dyad in which one country has nuclear weapons (China–Japan) and another in which both are nuclear weapons states (China–United States).

Power, cyber conflict and rivalry behavior

There is a growing literature about the role of cyber conflict in international relations (Kello 2013: 7–40), the applicability of international law (Lewis 2010) and international humanitarian law (Droege 2013), the implications for national security (Farwell and Rohozinski 2011), national boundaries (Arquilla and Ronfeldt 1993), the role of non-state actors (Mandiant Intelligence Center 2013) and public–private sector collaboration (Etzioni 2010). There are also multiple definitions and understandings applied to terms like "cyber attack," "cyber warfare," "cyber weapons" and "cyber conflict." NATO defines a "cyber attack" as "a cyber operation, whether offensive or defensive, that is reasonably expected to cause injury or death to persons or damage or destruction to objects," while New Zealand's Cyber Security Strategy defines it as "An attempt to undermine or compromise the function of a computer-based system, access information, or attempt to track the online movements of individuals without their permission" (Morgus and Maurer 2014). Other discrepancies have also been discussed in this book's introduction. We define cyber conflict as an event between states in which information and communications technology (ICT) is utilized with a malevolent or hostile purpose in order to impact, change or modify state behavior or to obtain a strategic advantage. Cyber conflict may include website defacements or vandalism, distributed denial of service (DDoS) methods, intrusions, infiltrations and advanced persistent threats (APTs). A "cyber operation" or "interaction" is a specific act within the context of a cyber conflict. These definitions are derived from Valeriano and Maness (2012).

An important element throughout the literature is the potential for cyber space to reshape the traditional power dynamics between states. While the major international relations theories offer some approaches to interpreting cyber conflict and point to some possible explanations, none seems to capture all aspects of cyber conflict in its entirely. Realism, for example, with its emphasis on the primacy of the state has been said to offer the least explanatory power because of the highly active role of non-state actors both as perpetrators and experts (Eriksson and Giampiero 2006: 229). According to some, the cyber domain only becomes relevant to realists when it is viewed as a new technological component within warfare more broadly, and as a means of the continuation or extension of other types of warfare (Eriksson and Giampiero 2006: 229). However, realism does provide some important insights. The approach that many governments are taking toward cyber conflict appears to be rooted in realism. The United States, for example, views cyber space as a "fifth domain" after air, land, sea and space (*The Economist* 2010). NATO very recently extended its collective security clause, Article V, to include cyber conflict (Ranger 2014). Cyber technology may have been developed in a civilian context, but it has rapidly become a part of military doctrine, as these two examples show. Our research focuses on state-sponsored activities and dynamics because states continue to be the basic unit of the international system. The majority of cyber conflicts exist as components of broader strategies linked to states' articulated foreign policy goals.

Balance of power theory from realism further suggests that rival dyads that exhibit a higher degree of power asymmetry may be more likely to experience conflict. Economic and militarily weak states may resort to cyber conflict as an asymmetrical tactic to harm a more powerful adversary, and dominant states may undertake cyber operations as a lower cost alternative to conventional tactics with little fear of retaliation. However, realism's focus on power and statecraft fails to take into account many other relevant aspects of cyber conflict that other perspectives emphasize.

Liberalism provides a helpful framework for explaining many of the features of cyber conflict that realism fails to address, such as transnational non-state actors, the complexity of networked economies and the changing importance of national boundaries (Eriksson and Giampiero 2006: 231). Liberalism helps to expand understanding of international relations beyond matters of security and can thus account for other facets of the cyber domain, including the growing partnership between public and private sectors as well as the merging of civilian and military interests (Eriksson and Giampiero 2006: 231). That said, relatively few liberals have engaged with the cyber issue and its implications for security. Complex interdependence emphasizes the role of economic and communications interconnectedness (Keohane and Nye 1998: 85). However, strategic information will remain highly protected and politics will likely determine the nature of communications revolution (Keohane and Nye 1998: 85). Moreover, the concept of cyber power directly captures the potential presented by cyber technology to change power differentials between states (Nye Jr. 2010). This is because the characteristics of cyber space are such that they may have a tendency to level the playing field, and therefore have the potential to create power shifts among states (Nye Jr. 2010). This shift will occur when limited opportunities open up for small states to effectively leapfrog over larger ones, which diffuses power in new ways among states and among non-state actors (Nye Jr. 2010). Cyber technology makes it more feasible for smaller states to initiate an operation against larger or more powerful opponent. While many states have engaged in some form of cyber conflict, the most prolific users of cyber technology continue to be economically developed states that also have strong militaries. This is not to say that all users fall into this group; we emphasize prolific. Much of the diplomatic debate about cyber security has therefore revolved around the concerns of these countries, while developing countries have either been silent, ignored or portrayed as troublemakers (Sheldon 2011a: 41–50). There are several issues of common concern to both developed and developing states, including a growing level of vulnerability to cyber attack (Sheldon 2011a: 41). Thus it is important to bear in mind that while the cyber-power concept addresses power diffusion, it acknowledges that this is not the same as power equalization (Sheldon 2011a: 9).

Whereas realist and liberal perspectives tend to focus on the more material aspects of international security, constructivism provides insights about the ideational components of security and the symbolism and identity-based aspects of cyber conflict. With respect to security issues, constructivist approaches usually emphasize identity and culturally related threats which tend to be downplayed in realism and liberalism (Eriksson and Giampiero 2006: 234). The theory of securitization developed by the Copenhagen School emphasizes the implications of speech acts, or political language, for political agenda-setting and political relations (Eriksson and Giampiero 2006: 234). Acts that invade privacy or other online activities can be legitimized by authorities because the threat, whether valid or not, has been securitized and framed as a threat, through clever use of language (Eriksson and Giampiero 2006: 234). The debate within the USA over the alleged North Korean hacking of Sony Pictures in December 2014 is a good example. The actual hack involved a private company and private individuals yet the language being used to describe the incident, particularly by news media, employs terms such as "attack" that frame the operation as a security threat to the state (Beauchamp 2014).

From an ideational standpoint, states may perceive the possession of cyber capabilities as a symbol of technological sophistication status in an international system increasingly reliant on information technology. A demonstrated ability to initiate cyber conflict may signify a state's technological maturity and bolster its international military prestige. Other ideational factors might also play a role in mediating the use of cyber weapons, such as a general reluctance for states that share cultural similarities to engage in conflict, whether cyber or traditional.

International relations theorists have drawn comparisons between nuclear weapons and cyber weapons (Nye Jr. 2013: 8–14). These tend to focus on exploring concepts such as deterrence, attribution and retaliation and their applicability to cyber conflict. Some observers believe that these early days of cyber conflict are reminiscent of the early days of the nuclear era, when the "rules of the road" were not yet known, yet there are obvious and very basic differences between the two (Friedman 2011). Nuclear explosions are unmistakeable and immediate, and the threat of nuclear conflict is existential, whereas cyber intrusions and actions may go unnoticed for quite some time and do not appear to pose a commensurate threat. As one expert has remarked, the destruction of cyber systems could return society to the economy of the 1990s, but a major nuclear war would return it to the Stone Age (Friedman 2011). Other comparisons have been made between cyber and biological weapons due to similarities in the challenges of attribution and verification, their dual-use nature, their value as a force multiplier in the context of military asymmetry, their attractiveness to non-state actors and questionable value as a deterrent (Koblentz and Mazanec 2013: 418–34).

Deterrence and retaliation theory might help explain why the majority of cyber operations have not been more severe, especially if they are taking place between states of roughly equal capacity. However, many have pointed out that deterrence theory does not translate perfectly into cyber space. First, the challenges of attribution are such that it is not always clear who a government may be trying to deter. Moreover, being able to successfully deter another state requires having the capacity to back up the threats or claims being made. Threats need to be made credible while not "giving anything away." Doing so would degrade a state's ability to follow through and make itself vulnerable (Gartzke 2013: 55). In the complex and secretive world of cyber technology, where there are no stockpiles to count or declare, and where technological prowess can quickly become an Achilles' heel, proving capacity is difficult.

There are numerous unanswered questions about what retaliation actually means in a cyber context and how it can be guaranteed. If the retaliation took the form of a cyber counter-attack, for example, what would that operation involve and how long would it take to develop and initiate? Would it pursue the same objective or have the same impact? Cyber technology, when used as a "weapon," takes many forms and its impact can be so specifically tailored that a standard reprisal response does not really exist in the same way that it does when one is speaking about nuclear or conventional weapons. If the retaliatory action took the form of a non-cyber operation, what justifications might be required and what standards would be applied to measure proportionality?

Rivalry between states is a matter of degree and states have a wealth of tools for advancing their foreign policy interests, including traditional combat, trade policy, nuclear deterrence and cyber operations. Most rivals have a range of hostility levels that the states involved perceive as normal and tolerable. This "normal relations range" is bound by an upper and a lower threshold (Azar 1972: 184). The upper threshold is that level of hostility above which any actions or signals exhibited by either member of the interacting dyad are regarded as unacceptable to the other, and may imply that a crisis situation has emerged. The lower critical threshold is that level of friendliness which signals between the members that some integrative shift in their relations has occurred (Azar 1972: 184).

The data on cyber conflict reveal that the vast majority of cyber interactions between states fall within a range that rivals are prepared to tolerate and that do not exceed any critical boundaries. Prior research has established that the average severity levels of the majority of cyber operations are fairly low and many are undertaken with the objective of causing disruption or annoyance, or to steal information, and not to severely disable a rival or cause any serious terrestrial damage (Valeriano and Maness 2012). Exceptions exist but this has been the prevailing norm. Each type of activity gives rise to different types of dangers. Web-based criminal activity is different from taking a website offline, or from penetrating a network to shut down a program or infrastructure. Espionage is distinct from degrading another state's military capabilities (Walt 2010). Distinguishing among the degrees of both rivalry intensity and the intensity of cyber conflict is important because it helps analysts understand how using cyber weapons fits into a state's broader foreign policy goals and strategies. As realists would note, cyber operations on their own cannot achieve either conquest or coercion, which is why they are likely to remain complementary or secondary to terrestrial force. This is largely because the damage that could be done by a cyber operation is most likely temporary. This provides the initiating state with a short-term advantage while their rival is taken off guard, but does not necessarily provide a long-term strategic advantage (Gartzke 2013: 60). Rival states may choose to initiate cyber conflict in moments of heightened tension in the rivalry or to achieve objectives that if pursued through other channels would risk escalation, as cyber tactics are not necessarily violent and often allow for plausible deniability as to the origin of attacks (Valeriano and Maness 2011).

Interconnectedness, particularly economic interdependence, may cause states to think twice about escalating the severity of their cyber interactions. For example, China and the United States are constantly engaging one another in cyber operations but also share important economic connections. Therefore any cyber operation that negatively impacted the economy of one state will harm the other (Nye Jr. 2013: 11). Interconnectedness may deter cyber conflict when the attacking nation would risk endangering itself.

Hypotheses

The prior literature and observations discussed above imply a number of hypotheses about the possible determinants of cyber activity. First, rivalry intensity is likely to be associated with cyber conflict as states turn to this sphere as a new channel to pursue their rivalry and advance their interests. The degree of dyadic rivalry should therefore increase the likelihood of cyber conflict. Second, nuclear weapons possession may increase the likelihood of cyber conflicts in rival dyads because states are unwilling to risk direct military confrontation for fear of escalation or retaliation. Third, political and economic interdependence may deter cyber conflict as interdependent states may share an interest in mutual peace and prosperity. Fourth, economic or military asymmetry between rival states may increase the likelihood of a cyber conflict because imbalances of power tend to contribute to international insecurity and make conflict more likely. Finally, cultural variables, such as civilizational differences (Huntington 2003) and regional differences may make conflict within dyads more likely generally, including cyber conflict. The following section tests these hypotheses empirically.

Data and method

Data are adapted from Valeriano and Maness' study of 126 rival dyads between 2001 and 2010. Their dataset logged 110 cyber incidents and forty-five cyber disputes, with cyber conflict occurring in twenty rival dyads.[1] There are fourteen countries within the twenty rival dyads who have initiated an incident. These countries are China, Georgia, India, Iran, Israel, Japan, Kuwait, Lebanon, North Korea, Pakistan, Russia, South Korea, Syria and the United States. There are another six countries that were victims but did not retaliate, specifically Bangladesh, Estonia, Iraq, the Philippines, Taiwan and Vietnam. The final dataset contains ninety-seven cases: twenty dyads that have been involved in cyber conflict and seventy-seven dyads that have not. As Valeriano and Maness admit, attribution can be problematic and efforts were undertaken to mitigate this as much as possible by adhering to a clear methodology.[2]

The dyads are sourced from the 2006 rivalry dataset compiled by Klein, Goertz and Diehl and operationalizes their definition of rivalry. They regard rivalries as "possessing and varying across four constituent dimensions: (1) spatial consistency, (2) duration, (3) militarized competitiveness, and (4) linked conflict" (Klein *et al.* 2006: 332). They exclude dyads that have experienced isolated conflict, and note that a rivalry relationship is one in which the military component of foreign policy is an important element and much of their foreign policy is conceived of and conducted in military terms (Klein *et al.* 2006: 334). Some have criticized this definition for overlooking the role that perception can play in interstate dynamics and placing too much emphasis on the military dimension relative to economic and cultural factors (Hensel 1998; Vasquez 1996; Bennet 1996), although military rivalries often subsume these other dimensions.

We employ logistic regression to examine the impact of five sets of variables on cyber conflict in based on the five hypotheses listed above, respectively. The dependent variable measures the presence of a cyber conflict within the dyad between 2001 and 2011 and the independent variables are measured as follows.

Rivalry intensity

To measure rivalry intensity, we employ four distinct indicator variables, each of which relates to at least one of the elements that Klein, Goertz and Diehl utilize for determining the existence of a rivalry. The first underlying variable is dichotomous and measures the *presence of a territorial dispute in the post-1945 period.* We regard a territorial dispute as evidence of linked conflict, meaning that it represents conflict over an issue of mutual concern and importance. We have defined a territorial dispute as a circumstance in which both states in the dyad lay claim to the same geographic area, whether land or sea. This may result in armed conflict or it may not escalate beyond diplomatic condemnations. Some may involve additional states as claimants. Data is sourced primarily from the CIA Field Listings of Disputes and supplemented by secondary sources where necessary (CIA n.d.). The second underlying variable is also dichotomous and measures the *presence of a trade dispute*, which we also regard as an example of linked conflict. Data are obtained from the World Trade Organization (WTO), and includes both direct disputes, in which one state is a claimant and the other a defendant, as well as indirect and third-party disputes, provided that the two states in the dyad are on opposite sides of the disagreement (WTO n.d.). The WTO cases may be open or resolved.

The third underlying variable is the *duration of the rivalry*. This variable helps to distinguish between an isolated conflict and a dispute over a single issue versus a historic and ongoing antagonism between two states. It is also one of the four elements used by Klein, Goertz and Diehl. We utilized the rivalry start and end dates that were included in their 2006 data set to calculate the duration of the rivalry in days. The counts have been rescaled to a minimum of zero and a maximum of one. Finally, the fourth underlying variable measures the *number of militarized interstate disputes (MIDs)* experienced by the dyad. MIDs are selected to substantiate the fourth of Klein, Goertz and Diehl's elements: the existence of militarized conflict. They are defined as conflicts between states that do not escalate to full-scale war involving fewer than 1,000 deaths and some application of military force. The data are taken from Version 4 of the Militarized Interstate Dispute data collection compiled by the Correlates of War Project (COW) (Faten *et al.* n.d.). The count variable has been rescaled to a minimum of zero and a maximum of one. All four underlying variables are interpreted as equally and positively contributing to the intensity of the overall rivalry. The resulting composite variable, rivalry intensity, is the mean of the four indicator variables.

Nuclear weapons possession

Nuclear states have power and clout in international relations. These states include China, France, Russia, the United Kingdom, the United States, North Korea, India, Pakistan and Israel (Arms Control Association 2014). The variable *nuclear power* indicates whether neither, one or both states in the rival dyad are believed to possess a nuclear capability.

Political and economic interconnectedness

Two separate variables are used to measure interconnectedness. *Treaty count* provides a count of the number of bilateral treaties between the two states within each dyad. Treaty data are obtained from the World Treaty Index, and include any bilateral treaty that was signed from 1945-onward. *Trade interdependence* is measured as the sum of each country's imports from the other country as a proportion of GDP. Data are obtained from the COW Trade Data Set, Version 3.0 and are measured in US dollars. The data cover the time period from 2001 to 2009 (Barbieri and Keshk n.d.). To facilitate interpretation and for convenience of display, *trade interdependence* has been rescaled to a minimum value of zero and a maximum of one.

Economic and military asymmetry

Economic asymmetry is defined as the percentage difference in GDP of the wealthier state relative to the less wealthy state. GDP data are sourced from the International Monetary Fund's Economic Outlook Database (September 2011) and are valued in current US dollars (International Monetary Fund n.d.). Military asymmetry is defined as the percentage difference in aggregate military spending of the higher spending state relative to the lower spending state. Data for military expenditures are sourced from the Stockholm International Peace Research Institute's Military Expenditure Database in US dollars at constant 2011 rates (SIPRI n.d.). To smooth the effects of transitory shocks, each variable is averaged over the time period from 2001–11.

Cultural and regional differences

There are two other variables included in the analysis that represent less well-explored facets of rivalry. *Cultural difference* indicates whether the two states within the dyad are of the same civilization type. The categories of civilizations are sourced from Henderson and Tucker (2001) and are based on Huntington's ten categories: African, Buddhist, Hindu, Islamic, Japanese, Latin American, Orthodox, Sinic, Western and Other (Henderson and Tucker 2001: 317–38). One of the learning points from examining prior research was the realization that the majority of inter-state cyber conflict takes place on a regional basis. Moreover, many of the policy instruments being developed by states in the area of cyber security are regional such as in Europe, Asia and most recently Africa. The regions include Sub-Saharan Africa, East Asia and the Pacific, Europe and Eurasia, Middle East and North Africa, South and Central Asia, the Western Hemisphere and Other. Both difference variables are coded: one if the two states in the dyad are different; and zero if otherwise.

Results and discussion

Table 4.1 reports the results of the logistic regression analysis. Three separate models are presented to assess robustness to specification. To address colinearity between economic and military asymmetry, Model 1 excludes economic asymmetry while Model 2 excludes military asymmetry. Model 3 is the full model. The results are consistent across model specifications and strongly indicate that nuclear weapons possession dramatically increases the odds of cyber conflict. The possession of a nuclear weapon by one state in a rival dyad increases the odds of a cyber conflict by a factor of about ten, while the possession of nuclear weapons by both states in a rival dyad increases the odds of cyber conflict by a factor of about eighty. Surprisingly, none of the other variables exhibits a statistically significant effect on the occurrence of cyber conflict.

The results can be interpreted with greater detail by examining the characteristics of the states within dyads that have experienced cyber conflict. Among the twenty dyads of this type, there appears to be a relationship between which country in the dyad is the nuclear weapon state and which country is the initiator of the cyber operation. Out of the original sample of seventy-nine cyber interactions that took place between rival dyads that include a nuclear weapon state and where attribution was clear, sixty-seven interactions (or 85 percent) were attributed to the nuclear weapon state. This finding might suggest that the technological sophistication and resources required to maintain a nuclear weapons program lends itself to developing cyber capabilities, that nuclear powers are status conscious and wish to obtain and exercise the most modern instruments of conflict, or that having nuclear weapons capabilities makes states more assertive in the cyber sphere and less hesitant to take action against a rival. This latter interpretation could obtain because initiating nuclear powers exhibit a reduced fear of retaliation, although it is necessary to qualify what type of retaliation.

Table 4.2 organizes the dyads that have experienced cyber conflict by the nuclear status of the dyad. It also shows how many cyber interactions occurred within the dyad according to the original data set. France and the United Kingdom are the only two nuclear weapon states that do not, according to this research, have a cyber incident attributed to them.

Table 4.1 Predictors of cyber conflict among rival dyads

	(1) Odds ratio	(1) Standard error	(2) Odds ratio	(2) Standard error	(3) Odds ratio	(3) Standard error
Rivalry intensity	4.52	7.86	5.03	8.84	6.28	11.22
Nuclear power						
One	11.80***	10.71	11.79***	10.69	10.70***	9.72
Both	81.47***	116.14	82.73***	118.16	79.91***	113.96
Treaty count	1.00	0.01	1.00	0.01	1.00	0.01
Trade interdependence	6.07	11.44	5.13	9.65	6.97	13.21
Economic asymmetry			1.00	0.00	1.01	0.01
Military asymmetry	1.00	0.00			0.99	0.01
Cultural difference	1.52	1.34	1.47	1.30	1.42	1.26
Regional difference	1.56	1.45	1.65	1.54	1.97	1.93
Constant	0.01***	0.02	0.01***	0.02	0.01***	0.02
Observations	80		79		77	
Log likelihood	−26.75		−26.81		−25.95	
Likelihood ratio χ^2	26.57***		26.00***		26.80***	
Pseudo R^2	0.33		0.33		0.34	

Table 4.2 Dyadic possession of nuclear weapons and cyber interactions

Neither is a nuclear power	Cyber interactions	One is a nuclear power	Cyber interactions	Both are nuclear powers	Cyber interactions
Iraq – Kuwait	1	North Korea* – Japan	1	US* – China*	23
South Korea – Japan	7	Russia* – Georgia	4	US* – North Korea*	3
		US* – Iran	7	China* – India*	4
		China* – Japan	7	India* – Pakistan*	13
		India* – Bangladesh	1	US* – Russia*	3
		China* – Vietnam	2		
		US* – Syria	1		
		China* – Philippines	1		
		China* – Taiwan	5		
		North Korea* – South Korea	11		
		Lebanon – Israel*	2		
		Iran – Israel*	11		
		Russia* – Estonia	4		

Note
* The state is believed to possess a nuclear weapon.

Nuclear power status and cyber conflict

The significant association between nuclear weapons possession and cyber conflict allows for a number of possible interpretations. First, states that have been involved in cyber conflict may overlap with nuclear weapons states because both technologies require a certain level of technological sophistication, resources or commitment. Consider Stuxnet, perhaps the most sophisticated and elaborate cyber operation known to date, which went well beyond disabling websites or stealing information to slowing the uranium enrichment program of Iran—a foreign policy goal of multiple governments. Yet to design and implement the operation required a well-resourced and highly-skilled team of technicians that befitted from intelligence about the target (Betz 2012: 689–711). It's possible that at least four wealthy and powerful states (Germany, Israel, the UK and the USA) colluded in its design. However, other operations have been successfully conducted at considerably less cost though (ibid.). For example, the cyber incident against Estonia in 2007 and attributed to Russian-sponsored actors was conducted using downloadable software and by individuals who mostly lacked expertise in computer programing (Sheldon 2011b: 97). These two examples demonstrate that a range of cyber possibilities exist for state and non-state actors and that greater impact comes at a higher expense. While not all nuclear weapons states are necessarily wealthy or technologically sophisticated, the experience of developing nuclear weapons might put in place the necessary infrastructure, both political and technical, that enables cyber capacity. Moreover, the level of national commitment required to develop and maintain a nuclear capability may lend itself to other domains as well, such as cyber space.

A second interpretation posits a linkage between cyber capabilities and great power status or national prestige. The possession of nuclear technology became a quintessential symbol of great power status in the latter half of the twentieth century, and proliferation continues as aspiring powers desire to assert their status in international politics (Ullman 1985: 568). But nuclear weapons technology is expensive, politically costly to develop, and normatively prohibitive to use. Cyber capabilities, as we've noted above, range in their cost and complexity and do require some technological capacity; however, they are much less expensive to develop than nuclear weapons, are not explicitly regulated or prohibited by international treaties, and do not produce similarly extreme consequences that normatively prohibit their use. As technology becomes ever more critical to the normal functioning of governments, businesses and households around the world, the ability to manipulate technology to disrupt cyber targets may increasingly become a hallmark of great power status.

Whether cyber capabilities do become a status symbol in international politics depends heavily upon how important cyber space becomes to security and military doctrine. Prestige and status in international affairs has, in recent times, typically gone hand-in-hand with modernization processes (Dore 1975: 193). The majority of governments are prioritizing cyber defense over offense, because in a networked world traditional strengths quickly become vulnerabilities. For example, the United States military is highly reliant on computer networks, more so than possibly any other state. This means that the same cyber operation could have far more devastating consequences on the United States than on China or North Korea (Singer and Friedman 2014: 151). Cyber weapons, having been developed though civilian technology, are dual-use by their nature and their prevalence in other sectors means that a greater range of actors have a stake, vulnerability and role to play in cyber space. In the future, as the virtual landscape rises in strategic importance relative to the physical landscape, the capability to successfully undertake cyber operations may become as important a signifier of national power as nuclear weapons were during the Cold War.

Nuclear power status and cyber conflict: the China–USA and Japan–China rivalries

The dynamics of the China–USA rivalry in cyber space is characterized by relatively frequent and increasing levels of antagonistic activity maintained at a fairly constant—and so far mutually tolerated—intensity level. The relationship between China and the United States could perhaps best be described as an uneasy balance of cooperation and competition, with each of those terms carrying more or less weight at different moments over the last half century. The crux of the rivalry, at least in recent years, is Chinese military and economic ascendance juxtaposed against what might be described as an irreversible relative decline in American power.

The China–USA rivalry is by far the world's most cyber-active dyad. The dyad has experienced at least five cyber disputes between 2001 and 2011 and twenty-two smaller incidents took place as parts of those larger disputes, although the majority of the cyber interactions between the China and the USA have not been very severe even if they were more frequent.

Both countries are nuclear powers, but the US arsenal vastly outnumbers the Chinese. The Americans maintain approximately 4,804 nuclear warheads, while China has around 250 warheads. China has a no-first-use policy that acts as a positive confidence-building measure, but at the same time China has been rapidly modernizing its arsenal with the objective of arming their submarine fleet (Poni Group on US–China Nuclear Dynamics 2013). China continues to be concerned about US missile defense activities in the region. Both states have indicated that kinetic attacks play a role in their cyber policies and that the ability to deter their enemies involves kinetic capabilities alongside cyber ones.

The relationship between China and Japan is significant both within the Asian region and globally. It is a rivalry with deep historic roots and one that closely interests China's primary rival, the USA. Both are among the strongest economies in the world and certainly in the Asian region, together accounting for nearly three-quarters of the region's economic activity (Calder 2006). The military dimension of their rivalry is unique, notably because of the involvement of the USA. In many ways, China is the stronger military power. China possesses nuclear weapons and have the second highest military budget in the world. Japan, on the other hand, has had a peace constitution since the end of World War II in which they renounce the right to wage war. However, Japan receives military protection from the USA, which established military bases in Japan in exchange. As a part of this relationship, Japan enjoys nuclear protection but does not possess nuclear weapons itself, nor could it develop anything for offensive use without making legislative changes to its constitution.

The cyber dynamic between China and Japan is different, reflecting the different nature of this rivalry. There are fewer (known) incidents and disputes and so far, cyber conflict has been entirely one-sided. Japan is not attributed to have initiated any hostile cyber operations against other countries and in our dataset is not responsible for any, although there have been more recent allegations from China and South Korea. Interestingly, several of the Chinese operations against the Japanese are a direct retaliation for perceived slights and affronts in the kinetic, non-cyber world. For example, there have been multiple operations that are related to a Japanese World War II memorial considered offensive by the Chinese as it includes the names of the fallen from Japan's wars. In 2001 there was an attack by hackers linked to the Honkers Union of China that targeted the servers of multiple Japanese agencies. The hackers simultaneously issued statements criticizing the visit of then-Prime Minister Koizumi to the memorial. When the Prime Minister visited the site again in 2005, Chinese hackers tried to deface Japanese government websites (Ito, Rattray and Shank 2013: 246).

In this respect, China uses cyber technology in the manner of a weapon against Japan more often than against the USA. As a rising power eager to assert great power status, China has been active in both the kinetic and cyber realms developing the advanced technologies characteristic of national security prestige in the twenty-first century. Also, China's relatively more aggressive cyber posture toward Japan, a non-nuclear state, compared with that toward the USA, a nuclear state, suggests a level of strategic pragmatism in the exercise of its cyber capabilities. As China continues to grow and to assert itself internationally, it is likely to become concomitantly more active in cyber space.

Conclusion

This research explored a series of hypotheses about cyber conflict and why rival state dyads engage in it. The results reveal that nuclear power status is associated with significantly higher odds of cyber conflict. Rivalry intensity, power asymmetry, diplomatic and economic interconnectedness, and regional and cultural differences do not appear to explain cyber conflict among rival dyads.

This finding does not necessarily imply that nuclear weapons possession causes states to take action in the cyber sphere. Both nuclear power status and cyber conflict may have a similar underlying cause in a state's latent desire to assert great power status. States desirous of great power status, in other words, may be significantly more likely to both obtain nuclear weapons and to develop and use cyber weapons. Indeed, the evidence reveals that cyber conflicts are more likely to be initiated by nuclear powers. A pair of case studies illustrate this interpretation. Chinese cyber operations against non-nuclear Japan tended to be somewhat more antagonistic or "hostile" than those conducted against the United States, even though China–USA incidents are more numerous. Several Chinese operations against Japan have taken place after a diplomatic slight from the Japanese and may reflect China's effort to reassert their pride and status.

Future scholarship could improve upon and advance this research program in a number of ways. First, while states remain key actors in international politics, a state-centric approach to understanding cyber conflict may be insufficiently broad to understand and explain the complicated network of actors involved in any interaction. A more comprehensive framework of analysis incorporating both state and non-state actors may provide additional evidence about the corre-lates of cyber conflict. Second, the challenges of attribution remain a concern in the opaque realm of cyber space, and future research could continue to refine techniques for addressing the attribution problem. While this study is built upon prior research employing a clear methodology to attribute attacks as accurately as possible, any effort to build such a database will necessarily be limited by the amount of information publicly available.

Third, the study of cyber conflict among states is a relatively new area of research and naturally there are many more hypotheses than can be examined in a single study. Future scholarship can continue to update and expand existing datasets on cyber conflict and testing additional hypotheses about the possible causes or precursors of cyber conflict. Fourth, constructivist scholars specifically may be able to more thoroughly explore the role of national identity, pride, status and prestige in states' decisions to develop cyber capabilities or to initiate cyber conflict.

Notes

1 Valeriano and Maness utilized the terms "interaction" and "dispute" rather than "cyber attack" feeling the latter to be inappropriate in that it sounds too similar to a conven-tional military attack. Cyber incidents are individual operations launched against a state that may include multiple activities or uses of a single weapon piece of software, but all as part of the same operation and conducted by the same perpetrator. Cyber disputes are specific campaigns between two states using cyber tactics during a particular time period and can contain one to several incidents, often including an initial engagement and responses.

2 When attribution was in serious doubt, they did not include the incident or dispute in their dataset. They have also not included incidents or disputes involving anonymous hackers or operatives, seeking instead instances that are clear and explicit. They have considered the context of any alleged incident including the history of relations between the two states involved, noting that many incidents and disputes listed were corroborated with multiple news articles, blogs or reports. This thesis does not have the capacity to review the incidents and disputes they have listed to ensure their accuracy in the event of any new information being released subsequent to the conclusion of their research and will work from the information contained there.

References

Arms Control Association. 2014. "Nuclear Weapons: Who Has What at a Glance," at: www.armscontrol.org/factsheets/Nuclearweaponswhohaswhat (accessed November 10, 2014).

Arquilla, John and David Ronfeldt. 1993. "Cyber War Is Coming!" *Comparative Strategy* 12 (2): 145–65.

Azar, Edward E. 1972. "Conflict Escalation and Conflict Reduction in an International Crisis: Suez, 1956." *The Journal of Conflict Resolution* 16 (2): 183–201.

Barbieri, Katherine and Omar Keshk. n.d. *Correlates of War Project Trade Data Set Codebook, Version 3.0*, at: www.correlatesofwar.org/ (accessed May 4, 2014).

Beauchamp, Zack. 2014. "The Sony Hack isn't Cyberwar—and the US Can't Really Punish North Korea for It." *Vox*, December 19, 2014, at: www.vox.com/2014/12/19/7417363/sony-hack-cyberwar (accessed December 20, 2014).

Bennet, D. Scott. 1996. "Security, Bargaining, and the End of Interstate Rivalry." *International Studies Quarterly* 40 (2): 157–83.

Betz, David. 2012. "Cyberpower in Strategic Affairs: Neither Unthinkable nor Blessed." *Journal of Strategic Studies* 35 (5): 689–711.

Calder, Kent E. 2006. "China and Japan's Simmering Rivalry." *Foreign Affairs*, at: www.cfr.org/japan/china-japans-simmering-rivalry/p10146 (accessed November 29, 2014).

CIA. n.d. "The World Factbook: Field Listing on International Disputes," at: www.cia.gov/library/publications/the-world-factbook/fields/2070.html (accessed November 14, 2014).

Dore, R.P. 1975. "The Prestige Factor in International Affairs." *International Affairs* 51 (2): 190–207.

Droege, Cordula. 2013. "Get off My Cloud: Cyber Warfare, International Humanitarian Law, and the Protection of Civilians." *International Review of the Red Cross*, June 5, 94 (886): 533–78.

The Economist. 2010. "War in the Fifth Domain." *The Economist*, July 1, at: www.economist.com/node/16478792 (accessed August 2, 2014).

Eriksson, Johan and Giacomello Giampiero. 2006. "The Information Revolution, Security, and International Relations: (IR) Relevant Theory?" *International Political Science Review/Revue Internationale de Science Politique* 27 (3), at: www.jstor.org/stable/20445053 (accessed May 4, 2014) .

Etzioni, Amitai. 2013. "Cyberwar and the Private Sector." *The National Interest*, March 5, at: http://nationalinterest.org/commentary/cyberwar-the-private-sector-8160 (accessed December 18, 2014).

Farwell, James P. and Rafal Rohozinski. 2011. "Stuxnet and the Future of Cyber War." *Survival* 53 (1): 23–40. doi:10.1080/00396338.2011.555586.

Faten, Ghosn, Glenn Palmer and Stuart Bremer. n.d. "The MID3 Data Set, 1993–2001: Procedures, Coding Rules, and Descriptions." *Conflict Management and Peace Science* 2116: 133–54.

Friedman, Jonah. 2011. "Cyber Weapons vs Nuclear Weapons." *Center for Strategic and International Studies*, July 26., at: https://csis.org/blog/cyber-weapons-vs-nuclear-weapons (accessed December 2, 2014).

Gartzke, Erik. 2013. "The Myth of Cyberwar: Bringing War in Cyberspace Back Down to Earth." *International Security* 38 (2): 41–73. doi:10.1162/ISEC_a_00136.

Henderson, Errol A. and Richard Tucker. 2001. "Clear and Present Strangers: The Clash of Civilizations and International Conflict." *International Studies Quarterly* 45: 317–38.

Hensel, Paul R. 1998. "Interstate Rivalry and the Study of Militarized Conflict." *New Directions in the Study of International Conflict, Crises, and War*: 162–204.

Huntington, Samuel P. 2003. "The Clash of Civilizations." *Foreign Affairs* (Summer).

International Monetary Fund. n.d. *International Monetary Fund*. World Economic Outlook Database, at: www.imf.org/external/ns/cs.aspx?id=28 (accessed November 14, 2014).

Ito, Yurie, Greg Rattray and Sean Shank. 2013. "Japan's Cyber Security History," in Jason Healy (ed.), *A Fierce Domain: Conflict in Cyberspace*, 233–50.

Kello, Lucas. 2013. "The Meaning of the Cyber Revolution: Perils to Theory and Statecraft." *International Security* 38 (2): 7–40. doi:10.1162/ISEC_a_00138.

Keohane, Robert O. and Joseph S. Nye Jr. 1998. "Power and Interdependence in the Information Age." *Foreign Affairs* (September/October): 81–94.

Klein, James P., Gary Goertz and Paul F. Diehl. 2006. "The New Rivalry Dataset: Procedures and Patterns." *Journal of Peace Research* 43 (3): 331–48.

Koblentz, Gregory D. and Brian M. Mazanec. 2013. "Viral Warfare: The Security Implications of Cyber and Biological Weapons." *Comparative Strategy* 32 (5): 418–34. doi: 10.1080/01495933.2013.821845.

Lewis, James A. 2010. "A Note on the Laws of War in Cyberspace." *Center for International and Strategic Studies* (April).

Mandiant Intelligence Center. 2013. *APT1: Exposing One of China's Cyber Espionage Units*. February 18.

Morgus, Robert, and Tim Maurer. 2014. "Compilation of Existing Cybersecurity and Information Security Related Definitions." *New America Foundation* (October).

Nye Jr., J.S. 2010. *Cyber Power*. DTIC Document, at: http://oai.dtic.mil/oai/oai?verb=get Record&metadataPrefix=html&identifier=ADA522626 (accessed May 4, 2014).

Nye Jr., J.S.. 2013. "From Bombs to Bytes: Can Our Nuclear History Inform Our Cyber Future?" *Bulletin of the Atomic Scientists* 69 (5): 8–14. doi: 10.1177/0096340213501338.

Poni Group on U.S.–China Nuclear Dynamics. 2013. *Nuclear Weapons and U.S.–China Relations: A Way Forward*. Centre for Strategic and International Studies, March.

Ranger, Steve. 2014. *NATO Updates Policy: Offers Members Article 5 Protection Against Cyber Attacks*. Atlantic Council, June 30, at: www.atlanticcouncil.org/blogs/nato-source/nato-updates-policy-offers-members-article-5-protection-against-cyber-attacks (accessed December 18, 2014).

Sheldon, John B. 2011a. "Achieving Mutual Comprehension." *Disarmament Forum Four*: 41–50.

Sheldon, John B. 2011b. *Deciphering Cyberpower: Strategic Purpose in Peace and War*. DTIC Document, at: http://oai.dtic.mil/oai/oai?verb=getRecord&metadataPrefix=html &identifier=ADA544498 (accessed September 27, 2014).

Singer, Peter and Allan Friedman. 2014. *Cybersecurity and Cyberwar: What Everyone Needs to Know*. New York: Oxford University Press.

SIPRI Military Expenditure Database, 1988–2013. n.d. Stockholm International Peace Research Institute, at: http://milexdata.sipri.org/files/?file=SIPRI+military+expenditure +database+1988-2013.xlsx (accessed November 14, 2014).

Ullman, Richard H. 1985. "Denuclearizing International Politics." *Ethics, Special Issue: Symposium on Ethics and Nuclear Deterrence* 95 (3): 567–88.

Valeriano, Brandon and Ryan C. Maness. 2011. "Persistent Enemies and Cyberwar: Rivalry Relations in an Age of Information Warfare." Paper presented at the annual meeting for the Western Political Science Association, SSRN, at: http://ssrn.com/ abstract=1766692 (accessed July 26, 2014).

Valeriano, Brandon and Ryan C. Maness. 2012. "The Fog of Cyberwar." *Foreign Affairs*, November 21, at: www.foreignaffairs.com/articles/138443/brandon-valeriano-and-ryan-maness/the-fog-of-cyberwar (accessed May 3, 2014).

Valeriano, Brandon and Ryan C. Maness. 2014. "The Dynamics of Cyber Conflict between Rival Antagonists, 2001–11." *Journal of Peace Research* 51 (3): 347–60. doi: 10.1177/0022343313518940.

Valeriano, Brandon, and Matthew Powers. 2014. "Complex Interstate Rivals." *Foreign Policy Analysis*.

Vasquez, John A. 1996. "Distinguishing Rivals That Go to War from Those That Do Not: A Quantitative Comparative Case Study of the Two Paths to War." *International Studies Quarterly* 40 (4): 531–58.

Walt, Stephen. 2010. "Is the Cyber Threat Overblown?" *Foreign Policy*, March 30, at: www.foreignpolicy.com/posts/2010/03/30/is_the_cyber_threat_overblown (accessed August 2, 2014).

World Trade Organization. n.d. *Dispute Gateway*, at: www.wto.org/english/tratop_e/dispu_e/dispu_e.htm#disputes (accessed December 4, 2014).

5 Cyber security in Sweden and China

Going on the attack?

Johan Eriksson and Johan Lagerkvist

Introduction

In recent years Western pundits and politicians have played up the specter of a new digital divide, between opposing democratic and authoritarian information orders, by at times even labeled an Internet cold war 2.0. The term digital divide originally explained unequal access to the Internet and digital information resources inside and between countries (Norris 2001). The new digital divide was not about unequal access to the Internet and digital information resources. It was political in nature due to different conceptions of liberties, freedom of expression, and how information flows should be governed nationally and internationally. Most notably, former US Secretary of State, Hillary Clinton, in her by now well-known talk in Washington DC on January 21, 2010, emphasized that an "information curtain" had descended between free and closed nations of the world (Clinton 2010). Clinton, invoked and echoed Winston Churchill's famous words on the iron curtain that came to divide Europe for more than fifty years when she in Washington DC said: "an information curtain now separates the free from the unfree."

Two years later, the International Telecommunication Union's (ITU) World Conference on International Communications (WCIT-12) meeting, which negotiated a revision to the 1988 international telecommunications regulations (ITR), broke down on vague wordings on Internet governance in the final resolution on December 14, 2012. Subsequently, *The Economist* magazine ran the headline "A digital cold war?" (Dubai 2012). However, the leaks by Edward Snowden in June 2013 radically changed the nature of the debate on Internet freedom and Internet security, although black-and-white dichotomies between the "free world" and the "unfree world" remain remarkably persistent, even after Snowden, a former employee with a contractor of the National Security Agency of the United States, revealed the enormous extent of surveillance and monitoring of individual citizens worldwide and in the USA. As statements by US congressmen about Chinese spyware infiltrating the mobile phones of Hong Kong activists illustrate, hypocrisy and myth making about "good" and "evil" surveillance is very much alive (Farrell and Finnemore 2013). Internet governance issues, however, are not black-and-white uncomplicated issues on either side of the imagined cyber curtain separating the free from the unfree (cf. Stalla-Bourdin *et al.* 2014).

Russia, China and Iran are autocratic but not totalitarian countries. They showcase complex authoritarian–capitalist settings, which in the cases of Russia and Iran entail constrained but, nevertheless, electoral politics. Unlike totalitarian North Korea, these countries are not isolated from the rest of the world, but are deeply involved in social and economic globalization. And in China, interestingly, the state cannot fully trust private commercial companies to fully comply with the party-state's intent to censor and monitor citizens' communication over social networks.

The remainder of this chapter discusses Swedish and Chinese cyber-security strategy, focusing on threat perceptions, cyber-security methods and organization. Why compare Sweden and China? The main reason is that while both have relatively advanced information societies and cyber-security measures, they represent on the one hand a parliamentary democracy, and on the other an autocratic political system. While many other democracies and autocracies could have been chosen, Sweden and China are particularly interesting given their difference in size and position in the global system. Also, while the USA is a leading cyber power, and thus in a sense a major geopolitical counterpart of China, we are not here analyzing the balance of cyber power, but are mainly interested in differences and similarities between democracy and autocracy concerning cyber security. And while US cyber-security policies have been extensively discussed elsewhere (Mueller and Kuehn 2013; Dunn Cavelty 2008), there is hardly any studies on Swedish cyber security (for exceptions, see Eriksson 2001a, 2001b, 2004). Moreover, our particular expertise on Swedish and Chinese cyber politics is a pragmatic reason for studying these rather than any other countries.

It should also be made clear that we conceive of cyber security in a broad sense. Cyber security, as we understand it, includes defensive measures against cyber attacks such as firewalls and CERT (Computer Emergency Response Team) functions, offensive measures such as computer hacking and denial of service attacks, and cyber surveillance and cyber espionage (Andreasson 2012; Dunn Cavelty 2008).

Threat perceptions

Swedish threat perceptions

In Swedish analyses and debates on cyber security, the focus is almost entirely on threats perceived to originate from "abroad." While cyber adversaries are not always mentioned explicitly, the fear of particularly Russian and Chinese cyber-offensive capability is clear, as is the fear of non-state cyber terrorism and transnationally organized cyber crime. Indeed, during 2014 and 2015, when military tensions increased in the Baltic Sea area, Swedish authorities became more outspoken than before on cyber threats mainly emerging from Russia. Admittedly, it is often emphasized how cyber culprits do not stop at the border to show their passports, how hijacked botnets in many countries can be combined to perform distributed denial of service attacks or infect computer systems with malicious code, and make tracing of the origins of attack almost impossible. Cyber threats often perforate sovereign borders, and thus make the classical distinction between the domestic and the international if not useless, then at least increasingly blurred.

Yet, despite or perhaps even because of the acknowledgment of the transnational and border-crossing nature of cyber threats, threat perceptions almost completely ignore the possibility of home-grown cyber culprits. The exception that proves the rule is the domestic campaign against child pornography, "grooming," trafficking, prostitution, and the like. When the government and its analysts explicitly talk about "national security threats," however, they are almost exclusively framing them in terms of "foreign" adversaries, whether or not some of them might operate from within Swedish territory.

Moreover, the Swedish government, particularly under the leadership of former foreign minister Carl Bildt, has also been a stalwart advocate for the US-led Internet Freedom Agenda (Bildt 2012). Indeed, even after his eight years in service as Sweden's foreign minister, Bildt continues his advocacy of Internet Freedom, chiefly though chairing the Global Commission of Internet Governance, a think-tank-based entity of his own creation, announced in 2014 at the World Economic Forum in Davos (MacAskill 2014). The Internet Freedom narrative portrays a clear distinction between democracy and autocracy, between the "free world" and those parts of the world in which liberal democracy, including free access to and use of the Internet, is either absent or strongly limited, censored and monitored. The Internet Freedom Agenda is also a continuation of the liberal idea of spreading democracy around the world, a way of democratizing the world with other means than military invasion followed by democratic state-building. Advocates believe, despite growing cyber censorship in the global East and South, that if people tweet, "they will tweet their way to freedom," and authoritarianism "becomes unstainable once the barriers to the free flow of information are removed" (Morozov 2012: xii).

At the same time as Sweden has framed cyber threats as being about how autocracies, hybrid-regimes and "foreign" terrorists around the world seek to control and limit access to cyber space, Sweden, like most Western governments, has maintained and developed its own cyber-surveillance systems. After an intense domestic debate, cutting across party lines, the Swedish Parliament in 2008 adopted a new law permitting the Swedish national signal intelligence agency, the FRA (the Swedish equivalent of the gigantic US National Security Agency), to tap telephone calls, Internet traffic and email that crosses the Swedish border. Thus, again, the potential threats were seen as originating from abroad rather than from within Sweden. Critics argued, however, that not only can savvy cyber culprits make international traffic go under the cyber border control radar, but also that the new law was a serious privacy infringement, and that a lot of communication between people located in Sweden goes through foreign routers, which is thus monitored. In a debate at an Internet conference in Stockholm, Bildt argued that surveillance is not itself a threat, on two conditions: if you are not aware of being tapped, and if only "good states" are doing it.[1] The Swedish debate on surveillance, which peaked when the new "FRA surveillance law" was taken in 2006, helped the new Pirate Party, which has "cyber freedom," private integrity and anti-surveillance as their main issues, getting voted into the European Parliament in 2011 (but then lost their seats in the 2014 elections).

According to British journalist and writer Duncan Campbell, the new law was a result of cooperation with the USA and the UK; Campbell described Sweden as an intelligence ally to the USA and the UK, of equal significance as Israel. A key reason for Sweden's usefulness to USA and UK cyber espionage is that Russian Internet traffic largely goes through cables passing through Swedish territorial waters, which Sweden has the capacity to tap.

Not surprisingly, then, when whistle-blower Edward Snowden revealed the global mass-surveillance system of the National Security Agency, Carl Bildt reacted with sympathy toward the USA and UK governments, and expressed concern for the alleged damage caused by Snowden's actions.[2]

Chinese threat perceptions

When looking at Chinese cyber-security strategy, one has to separate cyber-security strategy into two parts: the domestic and the international. Nation-states identify threats to their security both at home and abroad. In this section we focus mostly on the domestic cyber strategy of China, although China's much-debated capacity to perform transnational cyber attacks is worthy a deeper scrutiny. Counter-intuitive, as it may seem, on both sides of the existing digital divide there are mutual concerns over cyber security and how to handle state-market intermediary-citizen relations. The problem for Western governments is that authoritarian governments all too often view both the organizing of terrorist activities *and* dissenting political views as internal security threats. Especially after the Snowden revelations of mass surveillance of foreign and domestic US nationals, the line between necessary monitoring of terrorist cells and infringements of individual privacy have become even more blurred. As some observers point out, the clandestine activities of US intelligence agencies at home and abroad has made Washington's campaign against economic espionage "an uphill battle" (Segal 2014: 577) and in effect had led to a condition where the United States has lost "the high moral ground" (Bajaj 2014: 584). In China, private and state-owned commercial entities have over a decade become drawn into state efforts to police and monitor citizens' online expression (Lagerkvist 2010). This phenomenon is not altogether without precedents. In the Western world, the monarchy in eighteenth-century Britain sought to shift the burden of control of an emerging press system onto the new newspaper owners. All sorts of shunning responsibility to police and finally outright resistance followed. In a vastly different time-space-technological setting, 250 years later, China echoes some of the same problems that confronted English censorship hundreds of years ago.

And today we can identify the same kind of resistance (although different in scope) among media intermediaries in China, the United States and Sweden, whether the reasons relate to "homeland security" or "social and political stability."

Cyber-security methods

Swedish cyber-security methods: going offensive!

Swedish cyber-security methods are partly based on the surveillance of international communications mentioned above (made possible by the so-called FRA law from 2008). Of particular significance from a geostrategic point of view is the FRA's capacity to tap Internet traffic that goes to and from Russia, through cables in the Baltic Sea. The other part of Swedish cyber-security methods are measures taken to decrease vulnerability against cyber attacks on Swedish authorities. These measures include technical systems such as high-performance firewalls, 24/7 CERT functions (Computer Emergency Response Teams), continually updated security guidelines and training programs, and multi-agency coordination.

With the exception of child pornography, Sweden is not blocking access to Internet content. On at least one occasion, however, Sweden has blocked access not because of its criminal nature, but for political reasons. In February 2006, then foreign minister Laila Freivalds gave the order to shut down a website that belonged to the populist Sweden Democrats Party. The website contained anti-Islamic content, specifically a Mohammed cartoon, which the government believed could aggravate "dangerous" reactions.[3] The security police, together with foreign ministry personnel, made sure the web host (Levonline) took away the website.

Sweden's cyber security, much like its national security policy in general, has been defensively rather than offensively oriented. Yet in March 2015, a most significant shift occurred, as the Swedish Defence Minister Peter Hultqvist made the historic announcement that Sweden would no longer only defend itself from cyber attacks, but also conduct *offensive* cyber operations (Holmström 2015). In the words of the Defence Minister:

> The technical development takes its course and this is an area where, if you are serious in thinking about the future, you have to keep up and in some way develop our capabilities. And when you speak of capabilities, it means defensive as well as offensive ones.[4]

That Sweden has offensive cyber capacity is already known, since special IT units conducts "red team" exercises. The Swedish military has cyber-security units, whose main task is to defend military forces and the military command structure from cyber attacks. Also, one of the tasks of the signals agency FRA is to test Swedish authorities' resilience against cyber attacks. In addition, the Swedish Deference Research Agency (FOI) has capacity and expertise for testing cyber-security vulnerability, that is, they are known to conduct computer attacks (hacking, denial-of-service attacks, etc.), and commence tests on a regular basis.[5] That the FRA and the FOI conduct "penetration tests" and uses other methods of testing Swedish cyber defense, indicates that even if there is not yet an operative cyber-offensive system or cyber-warfare strategy, there is know-how. With the newly acknowledged cyber-offensive intentions, we should expect a continued build-up of offensive capabilities.

Chinese cyber-security methods: attacks no longer denied!

China runs one of the most successful and sophisticated systems of digital sur-veillance in the world. Yet, unlike Sweden and most countries in the Western world, the Chinese system routinely and widely blocks what the Chinese govern-ment calls "harmful information" on the global Internet from entering Chinese networks. Media giants such as Facebook, Twitter and Google are blocked from the Chinese market. Inside China, the state apparatus, communist party propa-ganda departments and commercial companies censor citizens' communication through key word filtering and manual deletion (Lagerkvist 2010; Klimburg 2011). Moreover, they seek to influence public opinion by skillful and modern packaging of state propaganda in all types of media. Just as for the international context, where China acts assertively to acquire sensitive information from its major rivals the United States and Japan, the Chinese strategy on cyber security in the domestic context entails both offensive and defensive dimensions.

While domestic cyber security in China is a joint project consisting of state agencies, commercial enterprises and vigilante teams of citizens who report inadvertent and "unhealthy" online behavior, work in the domain of international cyber security is harder to decipher. As the sources of cyber attacks are notori-ously difficult to affirm, Chinese officials alongside many of their foreign col-leagues have typically denied deny accusations that the People's Republic engages in cyber espionage.

Yet in March 2015, surprisingly simultaneous with the Swedish announce-ment of its cyber-offensive capabilities, also China admitted for the first time its cyber-offensive operations: a high-level research unit within the Chinese People's Liberation Army explicitly stated that "the country's military and its intelligence community have specialized units for waging war on computer net-works" (Harris 2015). Both the Swedish and the Chinese unexpected openness imply, if nothing else, a step away from hypocrisy. Usually, however, when asked about cyber attacks and in statements, Chinese institutions, companies and individuals are said to be one of the major victims of attacks on the Internet. A case in point is when Cao Mingzhu of the State Council Information Office opened a conference at Stanford University in 2013:

> China faces serious cyber threats. Between January and August this year, more than 20,000 websites based in China were modified by hackers and more than 8 million servers, 14 percent more than during the same period

last year, were compromised and controlled by overseas computers via zombie and Trojan programs. These activities have caused severe damage to our economy and the everyday life of the people. More than 80 percent of Chinese Internet users have fallen victim to cyberattacks at some time or other.

(Cao 2013)

Nonetheless, together with other major powers such as the United States and Russia, China is a major player in cyber espionage. The usual suspects engaging in overseas hacking are found within units of the People's Liberation Army (PLA) and nationalist hacker collectives and individuals who may or may not be affiliated with the PLA (Klimburg 2011: 45). However, despite the intent of China's government to promote innovation in the Chinese economy in general, and in the ICT sector in particular, there is evidence that censorship is blocking out not just communication, but also innovation and building of knowledge (Austin 2014).

Due to continued unwillingness to reform harsh media policies, resorting to cyber attacks of foreign companies and state agencies is one way to acquire new technologies to not fall further behind Western countries and stay both economically and strategically competitive. The attack on Google and other US companies in 2010 was a milestone that opened the eyes of the wider public to China's offensive capabilities in the area of cyber security (Nakashima and Wan 2014). That attack prompted former Secretary of State Hillary Clinton to publicly criticize China as an enemy of the Internet. However, that has not stopped Chinese attempts to acquire sophisticated and classified technologies in the United States and elsewhere. In February 2013, a report by the security firm Mandiant showed that a special unit of the People's Liberation Army was responsible for attacks on 141 companies (Mandiant 2013). Also in 2013, the *Washington Post* disclosed that Chinese hacker collectives had acquired top-secret information about advanced weapons systems such as the Patriot missile and the F-35 fighter jet.

Apart from other targets relating to economic and military security, such as ministries, embassies and news agencies, Chinese cyber attacks abroad also target exiled Chinese nationals. In particular, Tibetan and Uighur groups in exile, non-governmental organizations, and individuals that are judged to jeopardize domestic security are routinely targeted by Chinese hackers (Segal 2014: 577; Klimburg 2011).

Cyber-security organization

Swedish cyber-security organization

Swedish national cyber security is, despite a general trend toward outsourcing and public–private partnerships, mainly in the hands of governmental agencies. There is an inter-agency group called SAMFI, which coordinates cyber-security planning, strategy and information sharing. SAMFI consists of both military and civilian agencies, specifically the military signals intelligence agency (FRA), the military intelligence unit (MUST), the military central command and control unit, the military IT security and information warfare units (including the military CERT), the civil crisis management agency (MSB, including the civilian CERT), the national operative police command (RKP) and the postal and telecom authority (PTS) (cf. Eriksson 2004). There is also an MSB-led national IT security board, which gathers both public and private IT security actors in quarterly meetings with the purpose of increasing cyber-security awareness and preparedness (MSB 2012, 2014). While coordination and joint strategy development has been going on for almost twenty years in the realm of cyber security, voices are still heard that complain about turf battles and the lack of clear guidance and leadership. SAMFI, however, has developed a new strategy for "IT security" in 2010, followed up by a 2012 action plan (MSB 2012, 2014). Moreover, the signals agency FRA is developing a Technical Warning and Detection (TWD) system for cyber attacks (FRA 2010). Still, despite these organizational and technical efforts, there is recurrent critique that Swedish authorities are ignorant or weakly prepared with regard to cyber security. As observed in critical news coverage, these weaknesses have made governmental agencies vulnerable to digital break-ins, denial of service attacks, web defacing and leakage of classified or sensitive information.

Chinese cyber-security organization

The obedient posture of Chinese media entrepreneurs has been a long-standing theme, becoming more pronounced in 1999. Regulations to prohibit new media organizations were implemented to prevent media start-ups from running wild in the new territory of online journalism. By and large, a general climate of serving political masters permeates a business world and political scene of rampant corruption, have existed for decades despite recurring official rhetoric about the vice of embezzlement. Nonetheless, Chinese business leaders do not unconditionally accept the authoritarian information order. It is more probable that many pragmatically tolerate current arrangements because it brings more benefits than costs. Yet, as Dickson and Chen note, the "continuation of regime support is contingent on the government's policy performance" (2010: 17). Therefore, allegiance to the actually existing information order, and by extension, legitimacy for the party-state's authoritarian politics may be quite "thin."

It is extremely rare that business executives oppose government policies publicly. However, they do convey concerns about how state censorship and surveillance impact negatively on profits off-screen. Outsourcing surveillance and censorship features of the propaganda system to commercial media companies, and construction of a convincing narrative that views China's rise and domestic and foreign challenges that has the potential to curtail its rise through nationalistic glasses. Use of social media, like the digital communications practices that preceded it on the Chinese Internet, has challenged the Leninist political system and state-controlled mass media. Leaks of political scandals, social protests and other contested issues travel fast through the networked world of social media. China has the world's largest Internet population standing at 632 million.[6] Of these, 527 million are mobile Internet users, of whom a majority are active on social networking sites. Displaying how central media control had become for the party-state, the CCP decided at its third plenum in November 2013 that a new domestic security organization—the "National Security Commission" would be headed by General Secretary Xi Jinping. Under the commission's framework is another new task force: the Internet Security and Informatization Leading Group. Its creation shows that the leadership is cognizant of possible crises related to social protests enabled by social media. At the first meeting of the group Xi Jinping called for the Party to continue to mold online public opinion. He said that it was integral to the process of "making cyber space clean and bright."

The delegation of surveillance to private companies, however, could lead to potential foot-dragging, as it confers an extra cost for the industry. So far, however, the scheme to let companies do frontline spying on users of social media has been a cost-effective strategy of monitoring mobilizers of dissent in civil society. Regular leaks from Internet businesses of sensitive keywords to monitor on behalf of the state point to a principal-agent dilemma in the social media sector. News items in the immediate aftermath of the implementation of the real-name system for the Twitter-like social network Sina Weibo and its users in March 2012 indicated that Sina's design and operation was flawed, making possible the use of false identities. The system's failure was an example of foot-dragging between the agent (social media business) and the principal (party-state), which was also indicated by Sina's leader Zhao's signals about how negative the new regulations were for shareholders.

Concluding remarks: same–same, but different

Our analysis shows that although Sweden is a liberal democracy and China is an authoritarian one-party state, both states have advanced cyber-surveillance systems and recently for the first time acknowledged offensive cyber-warfare capabilities, which at least in the Swedish case breaks with its tradition of non-offensive defense. Yet, while cyber-offensive capabilities, cyber defence and cyber surveillance are similar in kind in Sweden and China, the main difference concerns access to cyber space, which is very liberal in Sweden, but greatly restricted in China through censorship, blocking and manual deletion of Internet content. Thus, the impact of political system—democracy or autocracy—is significant concerning censorship and filtering, but much less significant when it comes to other aspects of cyber security.

Finally, it is somewhat puzzling that Western strategies of cyber security have *not* become a major issue in public opinion and election campaigns in the Western world, despite legal and moral problems related to citizens' integrity and privacy, and the non-transparent nature of government surveillance. Thus, they become easy targets for authoritarian governments pointing to Western leaders who simultaneously vowed to fight for Internet freedom abroad *and* more Internet surveillance at home for security reasons (Andrejevic 2009). For example, in defending Chinese state monitoring of online activity, a diplomat at the Foreign Ministry in Beijing was quick to point to British Prime Minister David Cameron's promise to search and restrict social media to stabilize the situation in London after the suburban riots that took place in 2011 (Halliday 2011). The Chinese government and its officials have been quick to seize other such opportunities offered by Western governments and useful stories on their information management revealed by WikiLeaks—and especially the Snowden revelations of NSA's secret world of mass surveillance. There are certainly fundamental differences between democracies and autocracies concerning the many dimensions of cyber security, but obviously also many similarities, particularly regarding surveillance and its impact on trust and legitimacy. Further comparative research is required.

Notes

1 See transcript, at: www.dfri.se/wiki/users/linus/sif13-cb-transcript/ (accessed May 25, 2015). The talk is also available on YouTube, at: www.youtube.com/watch?v=stD l6ovmwrE (accessed May 25, 2015).
2 Indeed, when Edward Snowden in September 2014 was awarded the Right Livelihood prize (the so-called Alternative Nobel Prize), the foreign minister, breaking the previous tradition of having the ceremony at the foreign ministry, refused to allow Snowden to come—as revealed by Swedish television SVT: see www.expressen.se/nyheter/portas-fran-ud-efter-pris-till-snowden/ (accessed May 25, 2015).
3 This was reported widely in Swedish news media. See, for example: www.svd.se/nyheter/inrikes/kritik-mot-stangning-av-nattidning_275273.svd (accessed May 25, 2015).
4 This was reported widely in Swedish news media. See, for example, Swedish Radio website, at: http://sverigesradio.se/sida/artikel.aspx?programid=2054&artikel=5676813 (accessed May 25, 2015).
5 See the website of the Swedish Defence Research Agency (FOI), at: www.foi.se/en/Top-menu/Pressroom/News/2012/IT-sakerhetsforskning-i-fokus-vid-cyberattacker-/IT-security-research-in-focus-with-cyber-attacks-/ (accessed May 25, 2015).
6 See the announcement by the China Internet Network Information Center: "CNNIC Released its 34th Statistical Report on Internet Development in China," at: www1.cnnic.cn/AU/MediaC/rdxw/2014/201407/t20140723_47471.htm (accessed May 25, 2015).

References

Andreasson, Kim (ed.) 2012. *Cybersecurity: Public Sector Threats and Responses*. Boca Raton, FL: CRC Press/Taylor & Francis.
Andrejevic, Mark. 2009. *iSpy: Surveillance and Power in the Interactive Era*. Lawrence, KS: University Press of Kansas.
Austin, Greg. 2014. *China's Cyber Policy*. London: Polity Press.
Bajaj, Kamlesh. 2014. "Cyberspace: Post-Snowden." *Strategic Analysis* 38 (4): 582–87.
Bildt, Carl. 2012. "A Victory for the Internet." *New York Times*, July 5, at: http://mobile.nytimes.com/2012/07/06/opinion/carl-bildt-a-victory-for-the-internet.html?_r=0 (accessed May 25, 2015).

Cao, Mingzhu. 2013. "Making Joint Efforts to Maintain Cyber Security." Keynote speech presented at the Fourth World Cyberspace Cooperation Summit, November 5.

Clinton, Hillary. 2010. "Remarks on Internet Freedom," Statement by the State Secretary, Washington DC, January 21, at: www.state.gov/secretary/rm/2010/01/135519.htm (accessed May 25, 2015).

Dickson, Bruce J. and Jie Chen. 2010. *Allies of the State: China's Private Entrepreneurs and Democratic Change.* Cambridge, MA: Harvard University Press.

Dubai, L.S. 2012. "Internet Regulation: A digital Cold War?" *The Economist,* December 14, at: www.economist.com/blogs/babbage/2012/12/internet-regulation?fsrc=scn/tw_ec/a_digital_cold_war_ (accessed May 25, 2015).

Dunn Cavelty, Myriam. 2008. *Cyber-Security and Threat Politics: US Efforts to Secure the Information Age.* London: Routledge.

Eriksson, Johan. 2001a. "Cyberplagues, IT and Security: Threat Politics in the Information Age." *Journal of Contingencies and Crisis Management* 9 (4): 211–22.

Eriksson, Johan. 2001b. "Securitizing IT," in Johan Eriksson (ed.), *Threat Politics: New Perspectives on Security, Risk and Crisis Management.* Aldershot: Ashgate Publications, 145–163.

Eriksson, Johan. 2004. *Kampen om hotbilden. Rutin och drama i svensk säkerhetspolitik [The Politics of Threat Images: Routine and Drama in Swedish Security Policy].* Stockholm: Santérus förlag.

Farrell, Henry and Martha Finnemore. 2013. "End of hypocrisy: American Foreign Policy in the Age of Leaks." *Foreign Affairs,* November/December.

FRA. 2010. *Utformning av ett tekniskt detekterings- och varningssystem för samhälls- viktig verksamhet och kritisk infrastuktur [Developing a technical system for detection and warning for societal functions and critical infrastructure].* Report no. 2010–04–14 Fö nr. 14. Stockholm: National Defence Radio Establishment/Försvarets radioanstalt.

Halliday, Josh. 2011. "David Cameron Considers Banning Suspected Rioters from Social Media." *Guardian,* August 11, at: www.guardian.co.uk/media/2011/aug/11/david-cameron-rioters-social-media (accessed February 1, 2014).

Harris, Shane. 2015. "China Reveals its Cyberwar Secrets." *The Daily Beast,* March 18, at: www.thedailybeast.com/articles/2015/03/18/china-reveals-its-cyber-war-secrets.html (accessed March 25, 2015).

Holmström, Mikael. 2015. "Försvarsministern: Vi ska kunna genomföra cyberattacker." *Dagens Nyheter,* March 18, at: www.dn.se/nyheter/sverige/forsvarsministern-vi-ska-kunna-genomfora-cyberattacker/ (accessed March 25, 2015).

Klimburg, Alexander. 2011. "Mobilizing Cyber Power," *Survival,* 53 (1): 41–60.

Lagerkvist, Johan. 2010. *After the Internet, Before Democracy.* Bern: Peter Lang.

MacAskill, Ewen. 2014. "Independent Commission to Investigate Future of Internet after NSA Revelations." *Guardian,* January 22, at: www.theguardian.com/world/2014/jan/22/independent-commission-future-internet-nsa-revelations-davos (accessed May 25, 2015).

Mandiant. 2013. "APT1: Exposing One of China's Cyber Espionage Units." Report by Mandiant Intelligence Centre, February 18, at: http://intelreport.mandiant.com/Mandiant_APT1_Report.pdf (accessed May 25, 2015).

Morozov, Evgeny. 2012. *The Net Delusion: The Dark Side of Internet Freedom.* New York: PublicAffairs.

MSB. 2012. *Samhällets informationssäkerhet. Nationell handlingsplan 2012 [Societal Informatyion Security: National Action Plan 2014].* Stockholm: Swedish Civil Contingencies Agency (Myndigheten för samhällsskydd och beredskap).

MSB. 2014. *MSB:s informationssäkerhetsråd [MSB's Information Security Council].* Swedish Civil Contingencies Agency (Myndigheten för samhällskydd och beredskap), January, at: https://msb.se/Upload/Forebyggande/Informationssakerhet/Faktablad%20 Infos%c3%a4kr%c3%a5det2.pdf (accessed May 25, 2015).

Mueller, Milton and Andreas Kuehn. 2013. "Einsten on the Breach: Surveillance Technology, Cybersecurity and Organizational Change." Paper presented at the 12th Workshop on the Economics of Information Security (WEIS 2013), Georgetown University, Washington, DC, June 11–12.

Nakashima, Ellen and William Wan. 2014. "Report Ties Cyberattacks on U.S. Computers to Chinese Military." *Washington Post*, February 19, at: www.washingtonpost.com/world/ report-ties-100-plus-cyber-attacks-on-us-computers-to-chinese-military/2013/02/19/2700 228e-7a6a-11e2-9a75-dab0201670da_story.html (accessed May 25, 2015).

Norris, Pippa. 2001. *Digital Divide: Civic Engagement, Information Poverty, and the Internet Worldwide.* Cambridge: Cambridge University Press.

Segal, Adam. 2014. "Cyberspace: The New Strategic Realm in US-China Relations." *Strategic Analysis* 38 (4): 577–81.

Stalla-Bourdillon, Sofie Evangelia and Tim Chown. 2014. "From Porn to Cybersecurity Passing by Copyright: How Mass Surveillance Technologies are Gaining Legitimacy ... The Case of Deep Packet Inspection Technologies." *Computer Law & Security Review* 30 (6): 670–86.

6 Who pays for zero-days?

Balancing long-term stability in cyber space against short-term national security benefits

Michel Herzog and Jonas Schmid

Introduction

In their quest for coping with risks stemming from cyber space, some states have adopted contradictory approaches to managing them. Instead of working toward long-term international stability in cyber space, these states have been tempted by short-term benefits on national security grounds that have domestic and international negative externalities in the long run. This chapter aims to illustrate this two-sided state policy toward cyber security by focusing on these states' sustainment of and interaction with black markets for vulnerabilities and exploits (VEs).[1] It argues that if security in and through cyber space is one or even the key goal of cyber-security policies, then engaging in the market for VEs, as some state agencies do, creates unnecessary and counter-productive distrust for all actors involved. The current behavior, aimed at achieving more security, is actually leading to less virtual security and indirectly, less physical security (Dunn Cavelty 2012). This chapter argues for a shift in focus of national and international policy toward a defensive, long-term oriented approach to cyber security by reducing and responsibly disclosing vulnerabilities as well as ensuring cooperation between all relevant actors.

The primary task of the state is to protect the population against a variety of threats. However, responsibilities for the management of this new domain are distributed, as private technology companies and research centers, with the help of state agencies around the globe, have built up and are running the Internet as it is today. However, the problem with a multi-stakeholder governance approach is that goal-alignment becomes more difficult once many actors with diverging interests are involved—a fact that has become especially apparent through the narratives by some military agencies not in concert with the interests of civil society advocates (Nissenbaum 2005). In recent years, especially after the Snowden revelations, much of the cyber-space governance debate focused on the predominance of the United States. It has taken a turn for securitization, with the usual side effects of increased dominance of national governmental actors and national security-logic behaviors in such debates (Deibert and Rohozinski 2009; Mueller 2010; Dunn Cavelty 2012).

While states today are heavily promoting defensive cyber power, cyber resilience and preaching restraint, numerous reports show that the geopolitical heavyweight states are keen on ramping up their offensive capabilities to gain strategic, operational and tactical advantages over other states in the name of national security and to enable the formation of a deterrence posture (Lewis and Neuneck 2013; Sanger 2015; Lewis 2015).[2] In these developments, all national security tools are deemed legitimate in the current phase of doctrinal and institutional experimentation, as states are in the process of finding out how to deal with the international political dynamics of the domain. However, as cyber-arms arsenals are built up, the side-effects of these developments are a reduction of stability and less individual security in cyber space.[3]

Consequently, on a state level there is a misalignment between the narratives of different agencies of "public diplomacy" on the one hand, trying to keep cyber space a free and stable information domain for all, promoting cyber safety and good security practices for businesses, and measures in the name of national security on the other hand that include economic and military espionage, large-scale surveillance and intrusions leading to the malfunction of information systems (e.g., Stuxnet in 2010). Paradoxically, these intrusive efforts depend on the existence of underdeveloped security practices of the targeted actors. Thus, it can be argued that as the government still wants to be able to intrude for higher-level security reasons, it has no "real" interest in actually promoting good security practices either outside its own borders, or inside, as for example terrorism suspects are harder to control when they encrypt their data. All in all, the seemingly leviathan-like security agents' competence to breach into systems, perceived by many as counter-productive (e.g., Google, Facebook and co.), leaves stakeholders cynical and puzzled about the state's genuine intentions regarding cyber security.

This contradictory approach to cyber security of the state, resulting from the topic's subordination to physical national security and the short-term national focus on greater control leading to less cyber security in the long run internally and internationally, manifests itself in the markets for VEs. While detailed information on this topic is scarce due to the secretive nature of this trade, especially the journalists Nicole Perlroth and David Sanger from the *New York Times*, Ryan Gallagher from *Slate* magazine and Andy Greenberg from *Forbes*, as well as the Snowden revelations, in combination with work of the American Civil Liberties Union (ACLU) and an ever greater civil liberties community have allowed at least some amount of insight into the topic.

While the geopolitical heavyweight states have an impressive in-house capacity in terms of cyber operations, security actors also procure tools from black markets for defensive and offensive information tools, such as VEs (Perlroth and Sanger 2013). There is mounting evidence that state agencies sustain these black markets by buying knowledge on vulnerabilities[4] or full-scale weapons-grade exploits (Perlroth and Sanger 2013; Gallagher 2013). Thus, the important question for security policy becomes one of finding out how these markets affect the security prospects of the state and of Internet users in general over time. The reason is that unpatched vulnerabilities in software are not only a security issue for state agencies like the military or intelligence services, they equally threaten private businesses. By researching such vulnerabilities and keeping them deliberately unknown from the broader public, some states create security exploitation opportunities that they can either fix by publishing and patching—or exploit them themselves.[5] Caught in the present international strategic predicament of building up "cyber-arms" arsenals, the latter seems as viable as the former in the eyes of security personnel. However, such practices for national security gain severely undermine the long-term stability of cyber space, as: (1) the overall accident risks increase; (2) research goes into where the reward is: the financial incentive is currently heavily balanced toward writing exploits rather than detecting and reporting vulnerabilities; (3) software vendors are not encouraged to internalize their security costs and they routinely make the public pay; (4) crowd out other agencies' desirable stability efforts of good practices promotion; and (5) contribute to a cyber arms race.

In short, the effects of some state agencies' engagement in black markets in the name of security and other state agencies' contradictory approach of best practice promotion are what this chapter will focus on. The first section will outline the current stakeholders and their approaches to cyber security. It will also give an overview of the market for VEs and existing disclosure mechanisms. We will then process how states interact with these markets and what the implications are, arguing that states supporting these markets are actually reducing overall cyber and physical security. We will then discuss alternative solutions and finally conclude the chapter.

States, cyber security and the VE-markets: inherent contradictions

Having recognized the disruptive capacity of instable information systems, most countries have developed or are in the process of developing strategies to address threats from cyber space, including most Western countries and increasingly some developing countries.[6] For example, the US intelligence community lists cyber threats as the number one global risk to US security,[7] and the press reports "mega-hacks" on an almost daily basis putting hard pressure on policymakers. Even more so, developing countries are also energetically pushing for international governance reforms as a result of the Snowden disclosures of 2013 (Politorbis 2014: 33), further contributing to the processes of securitization that have been under way arguably since 9/11.[8] As a matter of fact, governmental security logics in cyber-space governance have started to dominate, which includes the extension of the subjugation of the domain to military and intelligence control reducing the influence of the more democratically organized, private and civil-society stakeholders.

Thus, states have elaborated doctrines designed to provide greater security. The means employed to this end have become more aligned with national security as well, meaning that covert operations to satisfy national interests in the short-term dominate, whereas a decade ago, national security implications were recognized (in the USA) but remained in the background compared to the ideal of keeping a free and open space for global exchange. Arguably, this shift has important negative implications for the long-term stability of the cross-national cyber space. One issue among many that reinforces this dilemma between long-term international stability versus short-term national stability is the market for vulnerabilities and exploits (VEs). This section illustrates this cyber-security policy tension by first explaining the markets' origins in a first subsection, presenting plausible reasons why the state engages in these markets in a second subsection and how it does this in a third subsection. It further discusses the implications of the state's involvement in the fourth and last subsection. All in all, this section mainly argues that for particularistic reasons, national security considerations trump international cyber-security stability and a more long-term security orientation of states.

The origins—establishing VE disclosure mechanisms

In the early days of software, it was common practice that the discoverer of a vulnerability would only notify the vendor and keep the knowledge a secret until a patch (neutralizing the vulnerability) had been distributed (Cavusoglu *et al.* 2007: 172). However, over the course of time, hackers, and increasingly also more security professionals, believed that "keeping bugs private only benefited two groups: the bad guys who were exploiting them, and the vendors like Microsoft that preferred to fix security holes without confessing the details of their screw-ups" (Poulsen in Maurushat 2013: 6). It is out of this motivation that disclosure mechanisms for a responsible handling of software security started to be put in practice. Subsequently, the question was raised which point in time was the most optimal for disclosure, meaning how much time is given to the software vendors to develop a patch. According to the literature, there is, unfortunately, no best practice minimizing total attack exposures (Cavusoglu *et al.* 2007; Arora *et al.* 2008).

Today, two main mechanisms associated with responsible disclosure[9] exist: self or third-party disclosure of vulnerabilities (Maurushat 2013: Ch. 2).[10] Self-disclosure refers to the rare event that companies voluntarily reveal a vulnerability (and patch) of their product. It can either be seen as being compliant with legal requirements, as ethically correct in the eyes of the customer, or both (Maurushat 2013: 17). Self-reporting is frequently associated with a previous data breach to which companies react by publishing the problem and notifying the customers (Maurushat 2013: 17–20). For example, when the Australian national telecommunications company, Telstra, was notified of a vulnerability exposing 734,000 user credentials of its customers in late 2011, it notified the people affected,[11] although there was no legal requirement to do so at the time (Maurushat 2013). There are numerous other examples where, after a data breach, companies were legally required to notify the public (e.g., the American company Choice Point in 2005 under Californian Law).

Third-party disclosure refers to the publication of vulnerability details by someone who is "not the author, owner or rights-holder of a piece of software, hardware, or of another aspect of a data system" (Maurushat 2013: 9). Proponents of this disclosure technique believe that it represents a good way of both putting pressure on vendors to quickly develop a patch and contribute to the quality of the software (Arora *et al.* 2008: 642). Whereas the discussion on the self-reported disclosure has been rather quiet due to its unchanging nature, it is the practice of third-party disclosure that has undergone rapid changes since the beginning of the new millennium. The earliest third-party disclosure mechanism, dating back to the late 1990s, is the "immediate disclosure" variant where security professionals would send their findings to interested parties via security mailing lists such as "Bug Traq" (Maurushat 2013: 7; Arora 2008: 642). This mechanism ensured that a wide audience of security professionals, hackers and vendors immediately received the information and could begin to work on it.

Other third-party disclosure methods have also emerged: the United States Computer Emergency Response Team (CERT), founded in 1988 as the first organization aiming to improve computer systems and increase their resilience, started to publish vulnerabilities in a "full disclosure" fashion in 2000 (Berinato 2007). The CERT (based at Carnegie-Mellon University) immediately notifies the software vendor of a vulnerability, only making this information public after a delay of forty-five days,[12] allowing the responsible company a reasonable time to develop a patch (Ransbotham *et al.* 2011: 4).

The last third-party disclosure avenue, which has recently received the greatest attention, is to sell the detected vulnerability/exploit via "institutionalized for-profit brokers." Several companies specialize in the pricing and trading of this merchandise, including the *"Zero-Day Initiative"* founded by the *"Tipping Point"* company in 2005, a subsidiary of the Hewlett-Packard Corporation. A second white market "transaction facilitator" is *"iDefense,"* which was purchased by the American Internet giant VeriSign in 2005 (Computerwoche.de 2005). *iDefense* functions by paying the discoverers of vulnerabilities as soon as they are submitted to an iDefence broker. The broker then immediately notifies the software vendor of the vulnerability details so the vendor can develop a patch. After a period of time the brokers also notify subscribers of special security measures before publishing the vulnerability. Security measures might include "[…] temporarily closing certain ports, disabling functionality in software, or further limiting access to the affected software" (Ransbotham *et al.* 2011: 6). Lastly, *iDefense* publicly announces vulnerability details after 133 days (Frei 2013a: 9). An important difference to the CERT-mechanism is that institutionalized brokers provide Intrusion Detection or Prevention Systems to the subscriber companies, where the encrypted vulnerability signature of the newly discovered weakness is included to provide at least some intermittent security (Ransbotham *et al.* 2011 : 4).

Searching a consensus on the extent of the "grace period," the head-start given to the software developer for working on a patch, is overall an argument about minimizing the social cost of vulnerabilities. Cavusoglu *et al.* (2007) as well as Arora *et al.* (2008) have conducted sophisticated empirical tests to determine this argument. Cavusoglu *et al.* have found that "none of the disclosure

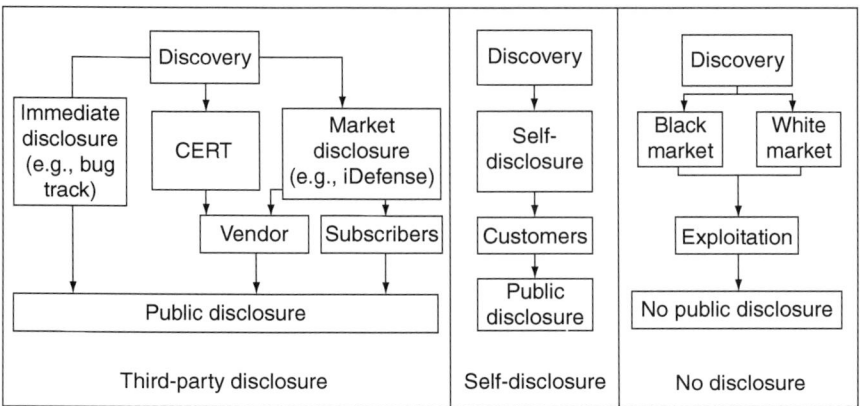

Figure 6.1 Summarizes the possible pathways to (non-) disclosure discussed above (source: adapted after Ransbotham *et al.* 2011: 4; Maurushat 2013: Chs 1 and 2 and extended).

policies, […] is always optimal. Characteristics of the vulnerability—risk, user population—and vendor's incentives determine the optimal vulnerability disclosure policy" (Cavusoglu *et al.* 2007: 184). Arora *et al.* conclude that "in general, both an instant disclosure and a secrecy policy are suboptimal" (Arora 2008: 655). Ransbotham *et al.* found that market-based mechanisms, as compared to immediate disclosure, can "delay the onset, reduce the penetration of the attack diffusion process, and decrease the volume of attacks corresponding to a vulnerability" (Ransbotham 2011: 17). In governmental risk assessments, the patching of vulnerabilities factors in positively, as it reduces both possible attack vectors and the amount of damage. However, as it reduces attack vectors, the state loses an exploitation possibility—and the provision of security based on current policies of supervision in case of suspicion is put in question.

To conclude, from the governmental perspective trying to increase overall cyber security, the challenge is to define appropriate disclosure mechanisms that minimize user security risks, taking all actors, including governments, into account. This difficult task though is further made more complex by diverging interests between different state security agencies, each having their own agenda.

Why states engage in the market—different needs and priorities

There are different risks stemming from cyber space that may be summarized under the umbrella term of insecurity: there are those associated with the user's involvement (mistaken clicks, malicious intentions, etc.) or the systemic risks stemming from the infrastructure independent of the user's involvement.

Because of that, the responsibility for cyber security is shared by and distributed amongst many different actors. The promotion of good practices is first and foremost concerned with user education rather than software or code improvements, where the latter is left to technical security specialists. Some state agencies thus target users for Internet literacy capacity building, whereas other agencies deal with coding mistakes or deliberate vulnerabilities. Different actors thus deal with different conceptions of security and consequently have different security needs. User education is not up for debate, as such activities align with the internationally shared aim of greater security and stability of cyber space. On the one hand, there are attempts to reduce the internal vulnerabilities and risks from cyber space. Because of the interdependencies and multidisciplinarity, most countries have opted for a voluntary public–private partnership (PPP) approach (e.g., USA, Germany, United Kingdom, Hungary, Canada, Japan, Switzerland, etc.).[13] The goal is to reduce the risks stemming from cyber space to the society and national economy and includes various initiatives like best-practices, reporting mechanisms, etc. In this sphere of matters of "everyday" cyber security, states are mostly restricted to support and cooperation, as the technical expertise of the systems mostly lies within the private industry and emphasizes the responsibility of the companies to keep their IT-systems secure. However, what is problematic is the secrecy of national security and the systemic, software architectural and stealthy security requirements that may run counter to international cyber-security efforts.

Caught in geopolitical tensions as well as institutional-, policy-, and strategy-experimentation (Lewis and Timlin 2011), intelligence, military or otherwise secretive approaches to national security provide incentives that may result in the amassment of arms to gain strategic advantage and develop a deterrence position. It is in this context of national rivalry that some states have resorted to procurement of information tools from outside—from black markets that are also home to criminals (Allodi *et al.* 2013: 165). Moreover, in national security strategies, cyber security is just one goal amongst many, meaning that in certain cases, physical security considerations take precedence and the breach of information security is willingly accepted. Information tools procurement thus meets physical security requirements. Nevertheless, the state (as a unitary agent) is left with contradictory goals: keep cyber space secure, but only if higher security considerations do not trump it. Higher-level, short-time considerations thus lead intelligence agencies and the military of some states to heavily invest (Pelroth and Sanger 2013; Gallagher 2013; Schneider 2013) in potentially offensive cyber capacities that draw on the very vulnerabilities that states are trying to diminish for the security of its own agents.

How states engage with and transform the market

Currently, no state openly highlights its involvement in the VEs market (Simonite 2013). Various reports though suggest that governments of the USA, Brazil, Russia, India, Malaysia, Singapore, Iran, North Korea, Israel and Britain are buyers of such vulnerabilities or their corresponding exploit-software (Perlroth and

Sanger 2013; Greenberg 2012; Gallagher 2013). That market is increasingly being viewed as a growing industry where states can buy arms customized to their targets and for their purposes (Simonite 2013). While there are also private companies active in this business, the VE vendor is frequently also a single person: a "hacker" or security researcher. The problem with these vendors is that many will sell to the highest bidder independent of its reputation or proposed use, resulting in uncontrolled selling activities of potentially extremely harmful information and code. Furthermore, there is evidence pointing to the fact that some of these "hackers" or "security researchers" have more or less loose ties to organized (cyber) crime, making the state's engagement with them indeed rather questionable (Radianti *et al.* 2009; Ablon *et al.* 2014).

Governmental agencies collaborate with many actors in a variety of marketplaces to procure VE-knowledge that is later used for both defensive and offensive purposes. It also has a growing and dedicated supply industry that, like in a gold rush, has quickly emerged and whose purpose is unequivocal: deliver exploits to governments. For example, VuPen openly stated[14] on its website that it "provides government-grade exploits specifically designed for the Intelligence community and national security agencies to help them achieve their offensive cyber security and lawful intercept missions" (Simonite 2013). The American NSA reportedly has (had) a contract with VuPen for the provision of exploits (Fidler 2014: 48). Even large defense contractors are becoming increasingly active in this area, as the following statement of Peter Singer from the Brookings Institution maintains: "It's a growing area of the defense business at the same time that the rest of the defense business is shrinking." Singer further claims that these defense contractors "[...] have identified two growth areas: drones and cyber." (Simonite 2013). On the one hand, the growing engagement of traditional military equipment providers is indicative of the fact that much money can be made. As a consequence, the market entry of more and more companies either means that black market procurement will be less necessary in the future, because the laws of supply and demand would dictate that prices of the commodity drop in case of greater supply. However, if governmental demand rises as more governments get involved in the trade, the direction of the price is unpredictable, but may well rise as demand rises more quickly than supply.

Moreover, even if fully institutionalized, the entry of many more security research companies is problematic for reasons of the market's incapacity of guaranteeing exclusive rights of information—and mostly, for the increasingly uncontrollable risk of disaster resulting from a worldwide build-up of a cyber-arms arsenal. Adrien Desautels, owner of the Netragard IT security company, states that he knows of "greedy and irresponsible" people who

> "will sell to anybody," to the extent that some exploits might be sold by the same hacker or broker to two separate governments not on friendly terms. This can feasibly lead to these countries unwittingly targeting each other's computer networks with the same exploit purchased from the same seller.
> (Gallagher 2013)

Netragard claims it only sells to American customers and the French company VuPen supposedly only sells to NATO partner countries, observing the voluntary (and rather shallow) Wassenaar Arrangement (WA) that governs the export of dual-use technologies.[15] But crucially, the more actors are involved, the higher the risk of such socially desirable statements being meaningless as competition gets harder.

For researchers or hackers wanting to sell their exploit, their information is "[...] only valuable, when it is not widely known" (Miller 2007: 3), meaning that the price of such information is subject to a large drop should it become public. Moreover, "there is usually no way to know when another researcher or the vendor will announce the same vulnerability" (Miller 2007: 3). This "exclusivity of rights" problem is fundamental "since, unlike physical commodities, the researcher cannot truly give up information. The researchers still possess knowledge about the vulnerability in question even if they destroy all traces of it from their computers" (Miller 2007: 5). In the case of non-consensual sharing, it may be very difficult to prove that the same researcher has sold the exploit to a third party, as the researcher may be selling under a different name. Possible is also that the vulnerability was legitimately discovered by someone else and this other researcher then sold it to this third party (Miller 2007: 5).

The value of a VE depends on a variety of factors, most of which are difficult to verify. Some pricing criteria for example are how widespread the affected application is, how critically an exploit could disturb the system, how reliable an exploit proves to be, if the VE affect an operating system application, whether standard firewalls block it, etc. (Miller 2007: 3). Moreover, as the VE derives its value from the exclusivity of information, it retains a price until the flaw or bug has been patched and is useless afterwards. Overall, in terms of pricing, very little is known in regard to the black markets, but experts suggest that prices for exploits vary widely, ranging from a few hundred dollars to $200,000–300,000 (Ablon *et al.* 2014: 26). Comparing them with available prices in the markets for responsible disclosure suggests that black market prices are 10–100 times higher on average (Frei 2013b; Ablon *et al.* 2014: 26), although this figure should be treated with the necessary caution. Most is known about the US involvement in the trade, thanks to the successful filing of an American "Freedom of Information" request (Fidler 2014: 48), which is why this country will serve as an example. For instance, NSS Labs estimated that in 2013 the NSA alone bought between 100 and 625 exploits[16] in addition to those developed by publicly employed security specialists (Frei 2013a: 15). For these exploits the US-American NSA has supposedly paid over $25 million to private firms in 2013 (Fnug 2013). In addition, the American Civil Liberties Union (ACLU) reports that government involvement has pushed up VE prices on the black markets. It also pointed out that "even civilian law-enforcement agencies pay for zero-days, in order to sneak spy software onto suspects' computers or mobile phones" (Simonite 2013). A very recent example became public in the course of the Italian company "Hacking Team," a provider of surveillance software, getting hacked themselves. Data stolen from their servers revealed that the police force of the Canton of Zurich, Switzerland, had bought a Trojan horse, going by the name of "Galileo," and paid almost €500,000 for this product.[17]

Policy implications of state engagement in these markets

The engagement of states in VE markets has many counter-productive effects, the most important of which shall be summarized in this subsection in nine arguments. *First* and most prominently, governmental participation generally drives up market prices for exploitative tools, thereby increasing the incentive of security researchers not to responsibly disclose their tools or knowledge, as the reward is much higher. For example, the earlier mentioned third-party disclosure path has not seriously undercut the development of black markets, as prices in these responsible disclosure schemes are still very low in comparison.[18] Motivation may also differ here between closed-source software and open-source software detection. Reporting in the open-source software is characterized by a gift-culture (Raymond 2001), where the social status of a developer is determined by "what you give away." Furthermore, the available funds in open-source software are very limited. Closed-source software products are based on market transactions, and it follows as a logical consequence that security researchers would want to be paid for their discoveries in closed-source software. In the current setting, incentives are skewed in favour of the black market: the loss of not selling the vulnerability or exploit on the black market is very high, as rewards on white markets are seen to be 10–100 times lower (Ablon *et al.* 2014: 26). By not engaging on the black market, states could lower black market prices by lowering demand, and also avoiding incentives that might encourage others to participate on the black market.

Second, by buying from those vendors, states actively support the market financially as well as morally. While information on this topic is scarce, there is increasing evidence that the borders between state-employed and controlled cyber-operation experts, freelance hackers and criminal hackers are increasingly diminishing (Stiennon 2015: 19; Shane and Lehren 2010). By increasing their reliance on these actors, states flood this industry with money, whereby the state sustains agents, many of who have no reservations about whom they sell to as long as the reward is high. Furthermore, many of these suppliers are also tied to criminal operations (Ablon *et al.* 2014). Large inflows of money also increase the know-how and specialization in these circles. This all leads to the increased growth in these markets in terms of knowledge, manpower and funds. In short, research goes into where the reward is high. But these resources are not only available for hire to one state, but also to potential enemy states, criminal organizations of terrorist organizations, increasing the risk of malicious cyber incidents reducing overall cyber security.

Third, information on vulnerabilities and exploits bought through these channels rarely seem to be disclosed in view of the high price paid for the exclusivity of information, but rather kept in secret to be used to expand the buyer's operational cyber capabilities. Of course, the legitimacy of buying such tools is only put in question in case of the state's offensive use, which is difficult to establish, as whether VEs are used offensively or defensively is not determined by the tool's characteristics (as the tool can be used for both). It only can be established after its use taking into account the user's intent. However, in view of the potential destructive power, the principle of precaution would call for responsible disclosure and in this regard, we argue that the chosen path of vulnerability (non-) disclosure might be drawn upon to provide the necessary cues to establish legitimacy of "weapon" possession. Following this argument, it is reasonable to assume a lack of legitimacy if the VE-knowledge is not inserted in a responsible disclosure process but is rather kept secret. Thus, keeping VEs deliberately from the public seems illegitimate and could potentially, by the incapacity of its offensive use, be labeled "offensive." It is reasonable to assume that government procurement which is committed in secret is not intended for responsible disclosure for two main reasons: First, a public agency would not spend so much money to let an opportunity to enforce its own interests pass away. Second, by disclosing them, governments may see its access window to black markets diminished, as sellers with criminal intentions and the public agency's actions are not aligned in terms of their goals.

Fourth, in the cyber domain, offensive operations like cyber espionage and cyber sabotage are usually kept clandestine, as numerous post-attack malware discoveries showed (Regin, Duqu and Duqu 2, Stuxnet, Snake, Flame, etc.). Even if the operation should be uncovered, technical issues and time make identifying the culprit very difficult. This issue (often referred to as the "attribution dilemma" within cyber security) (Tsagourias 2012) offers states the advantage of plausible deniability. A state can plausibly deny any connection to a cyber operation. States engaging in the purchase of VEs from the zero-day market make the attribution of cyber attacks more difficult. Because of the increasingly blurred lines between state-controlled actors and resources available on the black market, technically attributing an attack becomes even more difficult (Rowe 2015: 61ff.).[19] Furthermore, constructing a chain of evidence supporting the blaming of another country for example is extremely difficult, as all available proof (e.g., used software code, IP-addresses, etc.) point to a cyber-criminal organization that was hired to execute the cyber attack or at least provided the malware.

Fifth, knowledge and suspicion about states' activities on VE markets increase general mistrust toward the state as reliable actor and cooperation partner in cyber space. This effect is intensified by the increased vagueness of who works for whom on what agenda. Moreover, as the cyber-security stage is international and effectiveness of cooperation critically hinges upon trust (see e.g., Bryson *et al.* 2006), the establishment of confidence-building measures requires a clear commitment of the state toward non-offensive use of its cyber capacities. Non-transparent cyber-arms-procurement activities also cast a serious doubt on the positive, stability-enhancing user education initiatives of best practices promotion, confidence building measures (etc.) that arguably are hereby crowded out.

Sixth, and perhaps most disturbing in terms of potential damage, is the fear that by reducing trust in cyber space and by increasing the potential capabilities in terms of disruptive cyber operations, all states are increasingly encouraged to invest in the amassment of cyber weapons. Like in the nuclear weapons contest during the Cold War, armament amassment is the consequence of an increase in credibility of threats that other actors are thought to pose to national security (Lebow 2012: 394). Indeed, there is mounting evidence that states are arming themselves in a global "cyber-arms race" (Alexander 2012) with weapon-like information tools in accordance with model assumptions of a classical, game theoretic security dilemma, in which the actions taken by one actor (traditionally states) to enhance security decrease the security of (or increase the threats to) others unless cooperation can be achieved for a social optimum (Jervis 1978: 167–214). Actors arm themselves because they are worse off if their enemy is armed while they themselves are not, although the social optimum would be that both are unarmed (Mearsheimer 1990[20]). Consequently, states try to be ahead of the others in terms of cyber weapons' sophistication and number, and buying VEs on the black market is one of the methods to achieve this. Overall, the opaqueness of state engagement in such markets provides a boost to the cyber-arms race and leads to less security in cyber space due to the sheer risk of something going wrong.

Seventh, the use of zero-day exploits, being generally stealthy and difficult to detect, exacerbate the law enforcement problem of attribution of incidents to the perpetrator(s). For example, it is suspected that "heartbleed," the vulnerability published in April 2014 concerning OpenSSL, an encryption software for website traffic, had been known and used by the US-American secret services to intercept secure traffic from all over the world (Fidler 2014). But because the exploit left no traces, there is only mouth-to-mouth evidence supporting this claim. As a consequence, all servers and clients running OpenSSL had to be patched because the growing attention toward the vulnerability triggered an increase in exploitative attempts with resulting costs in the millions.[21]

Eight, by buying VEs, governments externalize costs to the public, which are presumably higher than the gain they receive from using them. The opaque procurement of VEs and the lack of public knowledge on how they are used does not mitigate the tendency of software developers to release a buggy product early due to reasons of competitive advantage. The issue is that the market has not priced the existence of vulnerabilities in software and hardware and software vendors externalize this cost to the public, which therefore needs to act to counter this "negative externality." Thus, by refraining from incentivizing software developers to internalize their costs, states allocate these costs to the public, only to have an opportunity to be strategically ahead of other actors.

Finally, rising incident numbers show that the current state approach to cyber security is not working. Indeed, cyber space does not seem to have become more secure, although there are potentially many reasons for that (Dunn Cavelty 2015: 83) besides the existence of illegitimate VE markets. The argument is simple: states invest in their own harm if they supply industries connected to cyber crime with their large sums of money. While numbers vary due to different reporting mechanisms, etc., the Ponemon Institute reports a 10.4 percent increase of cyberspace incidents in 2014 compared to the previous year (Ponemon Institute 2014). McAfee reports global estimates of the losses to be in the range of US$375–575 billion per annum. In terms of GDP, the annual loss of cyber crime incidents revolves around 0.5 to 1 percent in industrialized countries (McAfee and Intel Security 2014). Of course, incident numbers are not directly related to the market for VEs, but if the draining of cyber crime markets is a serious aim, then the state needs to credibly commit to it and disengage from procuring tools from these markets.

To conclude, proponents of current governmental cyber-security policies and practices argue that cyber espionage and cyber sabotage are needed for better national security.[22] Thus, the state's engagement in black markets for cyber-exploitation tools can be justified. Nevertheless, national security personnel do not seem to be interested in having "too much security," as overly difficult intrusion makes their mandate of control more difficult (as is visible in the data encryption debate) (Nakashima 2015). As a consequence, we argue that national security interests are met by building on the insecurity of the other actors. However, general user security and internal cyber security is not promoted through the acquisition of knowledge on exploitative tools—user security is furthered by its responsible disclosure of vulnerabilities as will be argued below (see Section 3 and Cavusoglu *et al.* 2007). Moreover, uncertainties regarding the geopolitically dominating states concerning their offensive and defensive capacities and their non-willingness to explicitly disclose all of them responsibly, has led to an arms race in cyber space that leaves all users less secure due to the risk of crisis escalation. Such intransparent security-relevant state engagement also impinges upon the credibility of other agencies' more positive contributions toward cyber security, leads to growth in these black markets, exacerbates law enforcement problems of attribution and does not mitigate the problem of software vendors externalizing their security costs.

Rethinking the approach

As discussed in Chapter 5, there is a mismatch in state behavior toward securing cyber space. It was also indicated that there are ways and means to increase overall security in cyber space without buying VEs from either brokers, security researchers or criminal online fora. In this section, the aim is to show that tackling the existing vulnerabilities and responsibly disclosing their existence, following the principle of precaution to counter armament escalation tendencies, is the right way forward. In this section we will thus discuss an alternative to the current approach.

Risk is usually defined by the damage multiplied with the probability of the incident. If we extend this model and apply it to the cyber sphere, the probability of an incident itself is a function of the threat assessment multiplied with the existing vulnerabilities. From this simple equation stems the reasoning that a reduction in vulnerabilities is beneficial to the overall risk level in cyber security.

Thus, states should focus their activity in cyber security toward reducing their risk from vulnerabilities, prioritizing their defense posture above in-transparent, offensively focused approaches. First, not only would such a policy generally reduce the potential for exploitation, and thus reduce risks and costs, but it would then also require a more highly sophisticated skill-set of the attackers to reach their intended goals (Gaycken and Lindner 2012). This again would impose higher costs on the malicious actors. Especially criminal groups, assuming that they think in terms of cost-benefit ratio, would be increasingly deterred. While opposed states would mostly still not be completely deterred and accept those increased hurdles as part of their national defense posture and operational capabilities, it seems safe to assume that also state-level operations would be increasingly reduced. The necessary surveillance would then be forced to go through hardened judicial procedures and the potential for an improvement in oversight is possible. This again would not only increase individual cyber security and the cyber security of companies, but would also benefit overall national security due to the diminished potential for physical damage through cyber attacks as well as reduced losses because of cyber crime and economic espionage. It would also enhance the necessary trust for international governance of cyber space. For states, such an approach would mean to mainly focus on setting incentives for reducing vulnerabilities as well as actively contributing toward diminishing VEs through information exchange, best practices and increasing trust in cyber space (through e.g., data breach notifications, confidence building measures, liability clarifications, etc.).

Trying another approach is advisable and is supported by the rising numbers of cyber incidents which show that the current take on cyber security is not working or existing efforts are insufficient. It is widely acknowledged that the United States, Russia, Israel, China and the UK have the most sophisticated cyber capabilities (*The Economist* 2012). Especially Western countries, but increasingly also the growing economies, are heavily dependent on IT-systems. While this increasing interconnectedness is a key aspect to their competitive advantages in economic and military terms, their high societal reliance on IT-systems makes these countries even more dependent on a well-functioning eradication of vulnerabilities. In the press, no week passes without the revelation of a significant new cyber-security incident resulting in identify theft, loss of money and intellectual property rights, reputation damage or endangering of national security through the loss of classified or restricted information.[23] Controversially, some of the above-mentioned states are allegedly also active purchasers of VEs on these black markets, despite the potential risk from knowledge and resources within those markets to their own economy and national security (Perlroth and Sanger 2013; Greenberg 2012; Gallagher 2013). Given the increasing sophistication of attacks, the rising monetary loss from cyber attacks and the potentially disastrous scenarios in case of an all-out attack on critical infrastructures or military infrastructure, the current approach to securing cyber space is not working.

For some authors, cyber war is inevitable unless security is built in (McGraw 2013: 109–19). While the authors of this chapter are not comfortable with using the concept of cyber war (due to lack of its occurrence), they do support the underlying arguments made by McGraw: first, offensive cyber-warfare operations, cyber espionage and cyber crime, the three major cyber-security concerns, all share the same root cause—the societies' dependency on insecure networked computer systems. Moreover, building systems properly from a security perspective will address cyber crime and espionage problems just as effectively as it deals with potential offensive cyber-warfare operations (McGraw 2013: 111). Reducing vulnerabilities not only reduces the risk of a successful cyber attack, but also reduces cyber espionage, risks for cyber crime and helps foster trust. In order to reach this goal, cooperation between states as well as between the private industry as primary technology developer and user is the key asset. Cooperation on a technical, operational and strategic level should be the central goal of all actors that take the long-term stability of cyber space seriously.

In order to achieve such long-term stability, states need to make a greater effort in various regards. *First*, a big effort could be made to promote a "safe by design"-approach in IT. This means setting incentives for developers to emphasize the security aspect of software and hardware much more than in the past to encourage them to internalize the security costs instead of externalizing them to the public. Otherwise, software developers will continue to release buggy products earlier for reasons of competitive advantage. A renewed contradiction-free state approach also includes the setting of incentives, or legal pressure, for private organizations to gain from responsible disclosure practices. Additionally, it would mean raising the financial rewards for rightfully found and reported vulnerabilities, making it more attractive for individual security experts to sell their knowledge in a legitimate setting.

Second, on an international level, existing cooperation on vulnerability information needs to be increased. At the moment, governments capitalize on threat assessments and have been less active in addressing vulnerabilities in software codes. This could be done through the establishment of high technology crime centers, or the addition of tasks to the CERT-portfolio, which facilitate responsible disclosure.

Third, cooperation and information exchange needs to be fostered, for example through increased establishment of collaborative arrangements that aim to internationally cooperate for greater information security. In this regard, the proliferation of national information sharing centers (ISACs) to the international stage would be desirable. Large international ISACs, such as for example, "ISACA," could take over greater responsibility in this regard.

Last but not least, some states need to seriously review their demeanor toward fostering cyber security. Even if they engage in all the above-mentioned activities, they also need to realize that they would profit more from a clearly communicated defensive posture focused on securing and hardening their own systems than exploiting other systems with all necessary means. Governments clearly have the potential to do much more to eliminate vulnerabilities, thereby not only contributing to security, but also advancing the state's credibility as a trustworthy actor in cyber space. By buying vulnerabilities on the black markets, states are subverting their own long-term economic health and security for short-term strategic gains over other states.

Conclusion

In this chapter, we highlighted the increasingly offensive stance some states are taking in the domain of cyber security. Amongst these capabilities are increasingly impressive means in the field of cyber espionage, cyber sabotage and cyber warfare. A lot of this activity can be explained with the ubiquity and novelty of the risks from cyber space as states are experimenting institutionally and from a point of view of policy, doctrine and strategy, trying to find ways and means to respond to these threats.

The state's dilemma between time horizons, international or national security and stability is well visible in some geopolitical heavyweight countries' engagement on the markets for vulnerabilities and exploits. Given the possible damage resulting from dubious participants' actions in these markets, we argue that even a state's national security interests would be best served by eliminating those markets. Perhaps the one positive aspect, from the perspective of overall cyber security, is the fact that these markets at least lead to some attention being paid to the VEs (by companies and states) being offered there. This does not defuse the main argument though: by actively buying VEs, states are not only supporting those markets but also giving growth incentives. In the light of an increasingly impressive list of cyber crime and cyber-espionage-related incidents originating from entities and individuals actively engaged in those markets, these states' behaviour seems contradictory at best.

From the authors' point of view, the only solution to foster cyber security in the long term is to focus on reducing vulnerabilities. States, in cooperation with software and hardware vendors, CERTs, technical communities, etc., need to reduce the amount of vulnerabilities. Only by taking this route will it be possible to align individual security with national security interests. While this would potentially mean a loss in exploit potential primarily on behalf of the intelligence services, it would also benefit the most developed countries, as they are the most highly networked and dependent in terms of critical infrastructures, their economies, etc. "Safe by design" should become the leading paradigm in the development of software and hardware, network solutions and so forth. While this process would be extremely challenging in technical and organizational terms and come with a high price tag in the short run, the benefits of such an inherently secure cyber space would be high pay-offs in the long term.

Notes

1 From now on referred to as "VEs."
2 www.atlanticcouncil.org/blogs/natosource/the-role-of-offensive-cyber-operations-in-nato-s-collective-defense (accessed June 12, 2015).
3 In this sense, this is classical securitization theory: the effect of an issue being securitized leads to extraordinary measures, outside the realm of public control.

4 Vulnerabilities are software defects that allow an attacker to violate an explicit (or implicit) security policy to achieve some impact (or consequence). Zero-day vulnerabilities are those that are unknown prior to exploitation and have no released patch at the time.

5 "Exploits" are software programs that can exploit the detected vulnerability. There is a variety of different sorts of exploits, the least common one of which is the "zero-day" version, in which the developers are not conscious of the vulnerability and the hacker(s) may exploit it to his/her/their advantage. For one vulnerability, there are a handful of possible exploits. One should be aware that exploits are always of a *dual-use nature*: professionals can use them to strengthen the software against intrusion or use them for intrusion into other computer systems as such.

6 Based on the up-to-date list compiled by the European Union Agency for Network and Information Security (ENISA), at: www.enisa.europa.eu/activities/Resilience-and-CIIP/national-cyber-security-strategies-ncsss/national-cyber-security-strategies-in-the-world (accessed June 8, 2015). Also see the overview of cyber-security strategy documents by the NATO Cooperative Cyber Defense Centre of Excellence, at: https://ccdcoe.org/strategies-policies.html (accessed June 1, 2015).

7 Worldwide Threat Assessment of the US Intelligence Community 2015.

8 See for example, Episode 7 of "do not track," at: https://donottrack-doc.com/en/ (accessed June 14, 2015).

9 The term "responsible disclosure" is used when talking about the publication of VEs with a delay to give the vendor or developer a head start to work on a patch.

10 Please note: non-publicized VE selling is not a disclosure method and the dynamics of non-public sales are therefore not analyzed in this line of research.

11 Allens, 2012, at: www.allens.com.au/pubs/priv/fopriv09jul12.htm (accessed June 5, 2015).

12 See: www.cert.org/vulnerability-analysis/vul-disclosure.cfm? (accessed June 6, 2015).

13 To name a few: Infragard (USA), Sicherheitskooperation Cybercrime (DE), Financial Services Information Exchange (UK), National Information Infrastructure Development Institute (HU), Dalhousie's Critical Infrastructure Protection Initiative (CA), Japan Vulnerability Notes (JP), MELANI (CH).

14 Not anymore—probably due to bad press.

15 See: www.vupen.com/english/services/lea-index.php (accessed June 1, 2015).

16 This information is based on the range of documented prices with the NSA as a buyer and the NSA's budget for the purchase of exploits of US$25 Million.

17 See: www.digitale-gesellschaft.ch/2015/07/11/einmal-trojaner-federal-fuer-die-zuercher-kantonspolizei/; and: www.inside-it.ch/articles/40773 (accessed June 4, 2015).

18 The impact of mandatory data breach notifications as they are discussed in the USA and in the EU on demand for VEs is not really foreseeable, as VEs are bought because of their stealth and an unrecognized breach cannot be reported. Nevertheless, as more breaches are notified, it might lead to a greater number of investigations, resulting in a greater supply of VEs that are responsibly disclosed of.

19 For a detailed discussion of the attribution dilemma, see: Rowe 2015: 61ff.

20 The realist argument that controlled proliferation of nuclear weapons actually stabilizes a domain (see e.g., Mearsheimer 1990) is hardly applicable for cyber space, because of the multiplicity of actors in a multi-polar world and incalculable risks that emerge.

21 See: www.theguardian.com/technology/2014/apr/18/heartbleed-bug-will-cost-millions, also www.eweek.com/security/heartbleed-ssl-flaws-true-cost-will-take-time-to-tally.html (accessed June 15, 2015).

22 See for example: the interview with Keith Alexander, former NSA Director, making a call for limited surveillance and intrusion at Aspen Security Forum, 2013, at: www.nsa.gov/public_info/_files/speeches_testimonies/GEN_A_Aspen_Security_Forum_Transcript_18_Jul_2013.pdf (accessed June 2, 2015).

23 Many overviews exist; for a comprehensive overview, see: http://hackmageddon.com/
    category/security/cyber-attacks-timeline/ (accessed June 15, 2015).

References

Ablon, Lillian, Martin C. Libicki and Andrea A. Golay. 2014. *Markets for Cybercrime Tools and Stolen Data*: *Hacker's Bazaar*. Rand Corporation.

Alexander, David. 2012. *Global Cyber Arms Race Engulfing Web—Defense Official*. Reuters, at: www.reuters.com/article/2012/04/11/net-us-usa-defense-cyber-idUSBRE83 A00520120411 (accessed June 5, 2015).

Alexander, Keith. 2013. *Clear and Present Danger: Cyber-Crime, Cyber-Espionage, Cyber-Terror and Cyber-War* at: www.nsa.gov/public_info/_files/speeches_testimonies/GEN_A_Aspen_Security_Forum_Transcript_18_Jul_2013.pdf (accessed June 18, 2015).

Allodi, Luca, Shim Woohyun and Fabio Massacci. 2013. *Quantitative Assessment of Risk Reduction with Cybercrime Black Market Monitoring*. 2013 IEEE Security and Privacy Workshops: 165–72.

Arora, Ashish, Rahul Telang and Hao Xu. 2008. "Optimal Policy for Software Vulnerability Disclosure." *Management Science* 54 (4): 642–56.

BAE Systems. 2014. *Snake Campaign and Cyber Espionage Toolkit*, at: http://info.bae-systemsdetica.com/rs/baesystems/images/snake_whitepaper.pdf (accessed June 18, 2015).

Berinato, Scott. 2007. "Software Vulnerability Disclosure: The Chilling Effect," at: www.csoonline.com/article/2121727/application-security/software-vulnerability-disclosure-the-chilling-effect.html (accessed June 6, 2015).

Boulanin, Vincent. 2013. *SIPRI yearbook 2013*: *Armaments, Disarmaments and International Security*. Oxford, New York: Oxford University Press.

Brito, Jerry and Tate Watkins. 2011. *Loving the Cyber Bomb? The Dangers of Threat Inflation in Cybersecurity Policy*, at: http://mercatus.org/sites/default/files/WP1124_Loving_cyber_bomb.pdf (accessed June 18, 2015).

Cavusoglu, Hasan, Huseyin Cavusoglu and Srinivasan Raghunathan. 2007. "Efficiency of Vulnerability Disclosure Mechanisms to Disseminate Vulnerability Knowledge." *IEEE Transactions on Software Engineering* 33 (3): 171–85.

Clapper, James. 2015. *Worldwide Threat Assessment of the US Intelligence Community*, at: www.dni.gov/files/documents/Unclassified_2015_ATA_SFR_-_SASC_FINAL.pdf (accessed June 19, 2015).

Computer Emergency Response Team (CERT). *Vulnerability Disclosure Policy*, at: www.cert.org/vulnerability-analysis/vul-disclosure.cfm? (accessed June 18, 2015).

Computerwoche.de. 2005. *Verisign übernimmt IT-Sicherheitsexperten iDefense*, at: www.computerwoche.de/a/verisign-uebernimmt-it-sicherheitsexperten-idefense,558438 (accessed June 14, 2015).

Dunn Cavelty, Myriam. 2012. "The Militarisation of Cyber Security as a Source of Global Tension," in Daniel Möckli (ed.), *Strategic Trends 2012*: *Key Developments in Global Affairs*. Zürich: Center for Security Studies, 103–24.

Dunn Cavelty, Myriam. 2014. "Breaking the Cybersecurity Dilemma: Aligning Security Needs and Removing Vulnerabilities." *Science and Engineering Ethics* 20 (3): 701–15.

Dunn Cavelty, Myriam. 2015. "The Normalization of Cyber-International Relations," in Oliver Thränert and Martin Zapfe (eds), *Strategic Trends 2015: Key Developments in Global Affairs*. Zürich: Center for Security Studies.

The Economist. 2012. "Hype and Fear." *The Economist*, December 8, at: www.economist.com/news/international/21567886-america-leading-way-developing-doctrines-cyber-warfare-other-countries-may (accessed June 19, 2015).

European Union Agency for Network and Information Security (ENISA*). National Cyber Security Strategies of the World*, at: www.enisa.europa.eu/activities/Resilience-and-CIIP/national-cyber-security-strategies-ncsss/national-cyber-security-strategies-in-the-world (accessed June 19, 2015).

Fidler, Maylin. 2014. *Anarchy or Regulation: Controlling the Global Trade in Zero-Day Vulnerabilities*. Stanford, CA: Stanford University Press.

Frei, Stefan. 2013. *The Known Unknowns*: *Empirical Analysis of Publicly Unknown Security Vulnerabilities*, at: www.nsslabs.com/reports/known-unknowns-0 (accessed June 10, 2015).

Frei, Stefan and Francisco Artes. 2013. *International Vulnerability Purchase Program*: *Why Buying All Vulnerabilities above Black Market Prices is Economically Sound*, at: www.nsslabs.com/reports/international-vulnerability-purchase-program (accessed June 14, 2015).

Fung, Brian. 2013. "The NSA Hacks other Countries by Buying Millions of Dollars' Worth of Computer Vulnerabilities." August 31, *Washington Post*.

Gallagher, Ryan. 2013. "Cyberwar's Gray Market." *Slate.com*.

Gaycken, Sandro and Felix Lindner. 2012. *Zero-Day Governance*: *An (Inexpensive) Solution to the Cyber Security Problem*. Toronto: Cyber Dialogue 2012, at: www.cyberdialogue.citizenlab.org/wp-content/uploads/2012/2012papers/CyberDialogue2012_gaycken-lindner.pdf (accessed June 13, 2015).

Greenberg, Andy. 2012a. "Meet The Hackers Who Sell Spies The Tools To Crack Your PC (And Get Paid Six-Figure Fees)." March 21, *Forbes*.

Greenberg, Andy. 2012b. "The Zero-Day Salesmen." March 28, *Forbes*.

Hern, Alex. 2014. "Heartbleed bug 'will cost millions'." *Guardian*, April 18.

Hewlett-Packard's Ponemon Institute. 2014. *2014 Global Report on the Cost of Cyber Crime*, at: www.ponemon.org/blog/2014-global-report-on-the-cost-of-cyber-crime (accessed June 6, 2015).

Jervis, Robert. 1978. "Cooperation under the Security Dilemma." *World Politics* 30 (2): 167–214.

Kerner, Sean Michael. 2014. "Heartbleed SSL Flaw's True Cost Will Take Time to Tally," at: www.eweek.com/security/heartbleed-ssl-flaws-true-cost-will-take-time-to-tally.html (accessed June 18, 2015).

Kurbalija, Jovan and Benno Laggner. 2014. *Switzerland and Internet Governance: Issues, Actors, and Challenges*, at: www.eda.admin.ch/content/dam/deza/de/documents/Themen/Politorbis57_en.pdf (accessed June 19, 2015).

Lebow, Richard Ned. 2010. "Deterrence," in Victor Mauer and Myriam Dunn Cavelty (eds), *The Routledge Handbook of Security Studies*. London: Routledge, 393–403.

Lewis, James. 2015. *The Role of Offensive Cyber Operations in NATO's Collective Defense*, at: www.atlanticcouncil.org/blogs/natosource/the-role-of-offensive-cyber-operations-in-nato-s-collective-defense (accessed June 18, 2015).

Lewis, James and Götz Neuneck. 2013. *The Cyber Index: International Security Trends and Realities*, at: www.unidir.org/files/publications/pdfs/cyber-index-2013-en-463.pdf (accessed June 18, 2015).

Lewis, James and Katrina Timlin. 2011. *Cybersecurity and Cyberwarfare*, at: www.unidir.org/files/publications/pdfs/cybersecurity-and-cyberwarfare-preliminary-assessment-of-national-doctrine-and-organization-380.pdf (accessed June 19, 2015).

Mauer, Victor and Myriam Dunn Cavelty (eds). 2010. *The Routledge Handbook of Security Studies*. London: Routledge.

Maurushat, Alana. 2013. *Disclosure of Security Vulnerabilities: Legal and Ethical Issues.* London, New York: Springer.

McAfee and Intel Security. 2014. *Net Losses: Estimating the Global Cost of Cybercrime,* at: www.mcafee.com/uk/resources/reports/rp-economic-impact-cybercrime2.pdf (accessed June 19, 2015).

McGraw, Gary. 2013. "Cyber War is Inevitable (Unless We Build Security In)." *The Journal of Strategic Studies* 36 (1): 109–19.

Mearsheimer, John. 1990. "Back to the Future: Instability in Europe after the Cold War." *International Security* 15 (1): 5–56.

Miller, Charlie. 2007. *The Legitimate Vulnerability Market: Inside the Secretive World of 0-Day Exploit Sales*. Independent Security Evaluators.

Mueller, Milton. 2010. *Networks and States*. Cambridge, MA: MIT Press.

Möckli, Daniel (ed.). 2012. *Strategic Trends 2012: Key Developments in Global Affairs.* Zürich: Center for Security Studies.

Nakashima, Ellen. 2015. "Tech giants don't want Obama to give police access to encrypted phone data." *Washington Post*, May 18, at: www.washingtonpost.com/world/national-security/tech-giants-urge-obama-to-resist-backdoors-into-encrypted-communications/2015/05/18/11781b4a-fd69-11e4-833c-a2de05b6b2a4_story.html?tid=hybrid_linearcol_1_na (accessed June 15, 2015).

NATO *Cooperative Cyber Defense Centre of Excellence (CCDCOE)*. Cyber Security Strategy Documents, at: https://ccdcoe.org/strategies-policies.html (accessed June 19, 2015).

Nissenbaum, Helen. 2005. "Where computer security meets national security." *Ethics and Information Technology* 7: 61–73.

Pattison, Michael and Margaret Walsh. 2012. *Focus: Privacy Commissioner Reports on Telstra Data Breaches*, at: www.allens.com.au/pubs/priv/fopriv09jul12.htm (accessed June 15, 2015).

Perlroth, Nicole. 2014. "Experts Find a Door Ajar in an Internet Security Method Thought Safe." *New York Times*, April 8.

Perlroth, Nicole and David E. Sanger. 2013. "Nations Buying as Hackers Sell Flaws in Computer Code." *New York Times*, July 13.

Poeter, Damon. 2011. "How Cybersecurity Has Changed Since 9/11." www.pcmag.com/article2/0,2817,2392642,00.asp (accessed June 4, 2015).

Politorbis. 2014. *Switzerland and Internet Governance: Issues, Actors, and Challenges.* 2: 33.

Ponemon Institute. 2014. 2014 Global Report on the Cost of Cyber Crime.

Radianti, Jaziar, Eliot Rich and Jose J. Gonzalez. 2009. "Vulnerability Black Markets: Empirical Evidence and Scenario Simulation," in Ralph H. Sprague (ed.), *Proceedings of the 42nd Annual Hawai'i International Conference on System Sciences*. Los Alamitos, CA: IEEE Computer Society Press, 1–10.

Ransbotham, Sam, Sabyaschi Mitra and Jon Ramsey. 2011. "Are Markets for Vulnerabilities Effective?" *MIS Quarterly* 35 (10): 1–22.

Raymond, Eric Steven. 2001. *The Cathedral and the Bazaar*, at: www.unterstein.net/su/docs/CathBaz.pdf (accessed June 2, 2015).

Rowe, Neil C. 2015. "The Attribution of Cyber Warfare," in James A. Green (ed.), *Cyber Warfare—A multidisciplinary analysis*. London: Routledge.

Sanger, David E. 2012. *Confront and Conceal: Obama's Secret Wars and Surprising Use of American Power.* New York: Crown Publishing.

Sanger, David E. 2015. "U.S. Must Step Up Capacity for Cyberattacks, Chief Argues." *New York Times*, March 19.

Schneier, Bruce. 2013. *Schneier on Security: US Offensive Cyberwar Policy*, at: www. schneier.com/blog/archives/2013/06/us_offensive_cy.html (accessed June 19, 2015).

Shane, Scott and Andrew W. Lehren, 2010. "Leaked Cables Offer Raw Look at U.S. Diplomacy." *New York Times*, November 28.

Silfversten, Erik. 2015. *The DoD Cyber Strategy*, at: www.linkedin.com/pulse/key-points-new-us-cyber-strategy-erik-silfversten (accessed June 19, 2015).

Simonite, Tom. 2013. *Welcome to the Malware-Industrial Complex*, at: www.technologyreview.com/news/507971/welcome-to-the-malware-industrial-complex/ (accessed June 19, 2015).

Sparrows, Paul. 2015. *Cyber Attacks Timeline*, at: http://hackmageddon.com/category/security/cyber-attacks-timeline/ (accessed June 18, 2015).

Sprague, Ralph H. (ed.). 2009. *Proceedings of the 42nd Annual Hawai'i International Conference on System Sciences*. Los Alamitos, CA: IEEE Computer Society Press.

Stiennon, Richard. 2015. "A Short History of Cyber Warfare," in James A. Green (ed.), *Cyber Warfare: A Multidisciplinary Analysis*. London: Routledge.

Thränert, Oliver and Martin Zapfe (eds). 2015. *Strategic Trends 2015: Key Developments in Global Affairs*. Zürich: Center for Security Studies.

Tsagourias, Nicholas. 2012. "Cyber Attacks, Self-Defence and the Problem of Attribution." *Journal of Conflict and Security Law* 17 (2): 229–44, at: http://jcsl.oxford journals.org/content/early/2012/07/23/jcsl.krs019.short (accessed June 4, 2015).

7   How to govern cyber security?

The limits of the multi-stakeholder approach and the need to rethink public–private cooperation

Lilly Pijnenburg Muller

Introduction

A secure cyber space is a necessity for the basic functioning of the economic, political and social structures of modern-day society. Because approximately 90 percent of what constitutes cyber space is owned by the private sector, the state has limited direct influence on cyber security. This makes cooperation mechanisms between the public and the private sector essential for the ongoing stability, growth and security of cyber space. However, such cooperation is poorly coordinated, on the international and national levels. Currently, cyber security is practiced in a neo-liberalist governance approach through *multi-stakeholder* initiatives (MSI) aimed at bringing state and non-state actors together to cooperate under indirect state rule. This approach is widely seen by the policy community as a panacea for securing cyber space, and has been implemented both nationally and internationally. In practice, however, the public–private cooperation dimension of cyber security has not been functioning adequately. The current approach, based on the idea of state facilitation of governance, has resulted in insufficient coordination of cooperation, in turn leading to unsatisfactory levels of cyber security today.

This chapter examines the suitability of the current form of governance for securing cyber space through MSI, taking as its point of departure the fact that cyber space has developed in the absence of the state and has not been privatized like other fields. It is decentralized by chance, not by choice. This chapter contributes to the debate on cyber-security governance by bringing the power dynamic between the public and private sectors into the discussion—a factor that has largely been ignored till now. It is argued that MSI are not functioning in governing cyber security, as the state has failed to fulfil its role as facilitator in a neo-liberal governance mode. The chapter is not intended not as an argument against public–private cooperation, but as a call for new assessments and approaches to cyber-security governance. Rather than viewing cyber security as a state-centric issue, the state should operate as a facilitator, bringing together those in the private sector who hold the crucial power in cyber space and securing coordinated cooperation.

Cyber-security governance and public–private interdependence

The emergence of a global computer network and our increasing reliance upon it has brought political challenges over the past two and a half decades. As secrecy surrounds the nature and extent of cyber operations conducted by governments and non-state actors alike, the complexity of intra- and intergovernmental relations complicates efforts to define and enforce cyber-security policy. Simultaneously most of what constitutes cyber space is owned by the private sector, making states heavily reliant on the private sector for the functioning of their everyday cyber-space operations. As Denardis and Raymond (2013) show, only a marginal part of cyber-security governance is the responsibility of the state. The main administrative task of cyber security concerns the private sector, as the primary institutional actor responsible for executing the responsibility for securing cyber space (ibid.). The securing of network infrastructure, designing encryption standards, correcting software security vulnerabilities, software patch management, securing routing, addressing, DNS, responding to security problems—all this is in the hands of the private sector. Most of the development, ownership, management and power in and of what constitutes cyber space thus lies with the private sector or individuals: little of what is cyber space can function on a daily basis without the private sector.

There are many obstacles to a clear understanding of cyber security[1] and to create effective private sector–state cooperation to secure cyber space has proven challenging. States themselves and the academic community are not able to reach agreement as to what cyber security entails which makes it difficult to create cooperation between states and non-state actors. The result is an inconsistent focus on cyber security on the part of governments, with an inadequate legal framework to facilitate security coordination and protect user-rights, imperfect alignment between fast-changing technology and slow-moving policy, and insufficient public awareness of the risks involved (Yuxiao and Lu 2015). In other words: an insecure cyber space. Today the number of cyber attacks on states and non-state actors are increasing at an accelerating pace, with new and progressively complex instances detected every day (Lindsay, Cheung and Revron 2015). The attacks on the German Bundestag and on the United States Office of Personal Management (OPM) are only two recent examples. In Germany up to 20,000 PCs were communicating with the hackers, sending back sensitive data. Computers had to be replaced at a cost of several million euros (BBC 2015). In the US case, millions of people were affected by a colossal breach of government computer systems, involving the theft of vast amounts of personal information, including social security numbers and some fingerprints (opm.gov 2015). As our society becomes increasingly more connected and dependent on cyber space, such incidents are likely to continue to occur. This calls into question the current public–private sector cooperation mechanisms and forms of governance for securing cyber space.

State of the art in the literature on cyber-security governance

It is commonly agreed upon that cooperation is needed to secure cyber space, yet the academic literature on cyber-security governance is underdeveloped. There is a large and expanding technical literature on computer network security, as well as an emerging discussion of the economic incentives and market failures that shape the problem. Further, there exists a relatively coherent and hierarchical regime on the technical function of connectivity, such as the domain name system (DNS) and technical standards (Nye 2014). Equally, whereas it was once widely assumed that cyber space was immune to government regulation because of its dynamic nature and distributed architecture, a growing body of scholarship is now assessing how governments can shape and constrain access to information, freedom of speech and other elements of cyber space within their jurisdiction (Deibert and Crete-Nishihata 2012). With this the debate has moved from whether the state is losing or gaining sovereignty and power, to recent studies calling for a renewed assessment of the role of the state (Christou and Simpson 2009; Drezner 2007; Goldsmith and Wu 2006). Disputing earlier claims about the marginalization of the state, they see the shadow of state power extending across the governance of Internet resources. Drezner (2004: 479) argues that non-state actors "often ... act as the agents of state interests." Christou and Simpson (2009) conclude that "state-shadowed private interest governance is the order of the day" (Christou and Simpson 2009: 600).

Thus, the state remains highly relevant to the governance of cyber space. And so, a focus on the nation-state has re-emerged in the debate as the primary unit of analysis, and the deepening and widening of state controls within domestic context are recognized. Moreover, organizations like IGF and the Internet Corporation for Assigned Names and Numbers (ICANN) are becoming increasingly important, creating a need for wider discussions outside of state control.

Numerous studies have focused on civil society participation, on how state and non-state actors share power and the MSI structure and processes (Froomkin 2003; Klein 2004; Kleinwachter 2004b; Koppell 2005; Palfrey 2004; Pavane and Diani 2008). Part of this debate centers on a UN multi-stakeholder approach versus an approach to cyber governance and security with the focus on direct partnerships (Dunn Cavelty and Suter 2009; Denardis and Raymond 2013). That MSI are not suitable for all areas that are governed in cyber space has been recognized in the academic literature (Denardis and Raymond 2013; Carr 2014)—but *why* this is the case has not been discussed sufficiently. The academic discussion tends to assume that power rests with the states that govern these institutions; their power to govern cyber space itself is not questioned. As Eeten and Mueller (2013) point out, the literature *assumes* that governance of cyber space takes place at these institutions, and then proceeds to ask questions about the institutions, rather than questioning cyber-security governance in itself and studying where and how it is actually conducted. This leads the academic discussion to stagnate at whether MSI is suitable for cyber-space governance. But why it is not suitable is largely overlooked. In order to explain why the current MSI do not work in practice we need to analyze who holds the power and expertise to secure cyber space and how cyber security is practiced today.

From liberal governance to a multi-stakeholder approach

In the academic literature of governance, two interrelated modes of governing, broadly classifiable as *liberal* and *neo-liberal*, are seen as pervasive in global politics (Neumann and Sending 2010). These two modes affect state conduct, internally and externally (Dean 1999: 10). In the liberal governance mode, the focus is on security and control. Aspiring to govern more areas, the state aims to increase its detailed knowledge and direct form of governing by means of regulation, control and policing.

In recent decades, states in the Western world have sought to govern through a less resource-demanding logic where they have has less direct control. To this end they have applied a neo-liberal mode of governing where the content of governing practices develops from being direct to being indirect, and from being "political" and hierarchical in the sense of deciding authoritatively on the ends and means of governing, to being far more horizontal, voluntary and thereby less "political" (Neumann and Sending 2010). The state becomes less centralized and more network-based; instead of ruling through a centralized top-down approach, it takes on a new role as facilitator for cooperation and collaboration between state and non-state actors. The state's delegation of power to non-state actors in this mode is thus a conscious decision. To govern less, the state gives away control through legislation and regulation. To perform such indirect rule, states often employ a multi-stakeholder framework. There is no clear agreement on a definition of MSI, but all descriptions define it as an open form of cooperation based on an idea of equal parties that come together under conditions of transparency and equality (Huijstee 2012; Carr 2014). Further it is implemented with the goal of increasing the effectiveness of an area of crucial importance to all involved. By effectively recognizing and accommodating the multitude of interests around an issue, MSI promise optimal utilization of expertise (ibid.).

Cyber space is viewed broadly as yet another domain to facilitate the horizontal rule of state governance through the lowest common denominator, and MSI are thus largely seen in the (Western) policy community as a panacea for cyber-space governance. When discussing MSI, Markus Kummer, executive coordinator for the Internet Governance Forum (IGF) secretariat, described multi-stakeholder governance as a vehicle "for policy dialogue where all stakeholders took part on an equal footing" via a process that is open, inclusive and transparent (Kummer 2013). Further:

> while multi-stakeholder participants in the World Group on internet governance (WGIG) and IGF meant and means that all stakeholders participate on an equal footing, it is also clear that in most organizations, whether intergovernmental or not, some structures are in place to facilitate decision-making processes.
>
> (Krummer 2013)

Employing MSI in cyber-security governance is a seemingly logical step from the state, as MSI are implemented for cyber security with the aim of including, as Carr (2014) puts it, "those closest to the bleeding edge of the technology (...) to offer insights and perspectives not accessible to policy makers or international bureaucrats" (Carr 2014: 649). Indeed, over the past decade, multi-stakeholderism has become almost synonymous with the governance of cyber space. Multi-stakeholder cyber-security governance is not only regarded by many as the best way to organize around this particular issue, it is also held up as a possible template for managing of other "post-state" issues (ibid.).

In cyber space, however, the state has never governed through direct control. Unlike other fields where the state acts as facilitator, there have been no clear instances of privatization: cyber space has basically always been private. As such, the governance of cyber space cannot be thought of purely as a changing logic or rationality of governance, as the state never has had the governance thereof. As the case studies below will show, the state struggles to understand its own role, and that of the private sector. When states attempt to implement MSIs in cyber space, the central question of power is overlooked. The considerable influence of the private sector, its impact and responsibility, are not reflected in the implementation of MSI. An adequate understanding of the technical and political picture that allows MSI to work is simply lacking—an inadequacy that has profound effects on cyber-space security.

Because of the nature of cyber space, the public and private sector are not on an "equal footing" in cyber space, as the above quotes might indicate. Neither are all private actors equal—some provide software, others hardware, some control networks, others do not. Similarly, the various public agencies differ in competencies and roles. Based on a neo-liberal mode, MSI require that power is spread equally between the parties. However, when the power has always been with private-sector actors, more is needed to bring them over to MSI than the promise of more effective governance (Dunn Cavelty and Sutter 2009). In other areas where the state in a neo-liberal mode implements MSI to govern, considerations of effectiveness and economic benefits from cooperation bring the stakeholders to cooperate (ibid.). However, in cyber space what is needed is not efficiency and economic benefit—but security. As improved security of cyber space is the main goal of all parties, coordinated cooperation and dialogue are essential factors that must be in place for MSI to function. These factors can help the private sector to improve security, but as the next section will show they are not in place in today's MSI.

National cyber-security governance: the case of Norway

The level of public–private sector cooperation in securing cyber space in Norway is widely regarded internationally as advanced, and Norway's national cyber strategy clearly shows that the state wants close cooperation with the private sector through MSI (Norwegian Ministries 2012: 17–22). Norway offers an interesting case study because of the high levels of operational cooperation and trust, exemplified with the implementation of a voluntary "Alert System for Digital Infrastructure" (VDI) sensor.[2] The VDI is a sensor box placed out on consumers' and partners' networks to detect whether someone is attempting to carry out hostile activities against critical digital infrastructure in Norway.[3] No other country has been able to create a similar system based solely on trust. Implemented in the 1980s, Norwegian Computer Emergency Response Team (NorCERT) and the VDI have been the main drivers and creators of a public–private cooperation system in Norway. These digital sensors are located in various companies that pay US$200,000 to be members of NORCERT Warning System and US$500,000 to be partners (Hommedal 2015[4] [interview]; Kirknes 2010). The VDI allows for information exchange between the public and private sectors and helps to overcome issues of transparency concerning threats and attacks, a problem that the private sector experiences and is rarely interested in sharing (Dunn Cavelty and Sutter 2009; Campbell *et al.* 2013; Dunn and Mauer eds 2006).[5] The VDI makes it possible for NorCERT to read anything that comes out and in of the member companies and businesses, so member companies have to trust the state that this information will not be misused (Sveinbjørnsson 2012). In theory, the VDI means that the state facilitates both protection and warning for private-sector cyber security by gaining better insight into the threat level in Norway and can warn the private sector about likely future dangers.

The high levels of cooperation are taken by the state to mean that there is success in bringing multiple stakeholders together to cooperate to secure cyber space. In practice, however the essential part of MSI—dialogue, transparency *between* the parties, and that cooperation is coordinated—does not take place, for two main reasons. First, the VDI tends to become a one-way communication mechanism for the public sector to gain information from the private sector. In practice, then, not all parties are sharing equally, and the power-holders in cyber space—the private sector—cannot communicate in a coordinated manner. Although NorCERT sees the information collected of singular actors to help the others, actors in the private sector do not communicate amongst themselves. This is not unwillingness on behalf of the private sector to cooperate with the public sector.[6] In Norway, actors in the private sector have largely recognized the need for cooperation amongst themselves and with the state, for their own security (as demonstrated by the sizeable VDI membership). It is rather that their ability to do so is hindered by lack of a platform or coordinated communication where information can be shared, building trust and cooperation mechanisms. The VDI in a sense acts to prevent essential communication, opportunities and the development of trust-sharing mechanisms. Instead of facilitating cooperation, the Norwegian state's approach to securing cyber space through VDI is found to limit communication between the parties, as well as their security.

Second, insufficient regulation and legislation hinders the development of coordinated cooperation. One of the main roles of the state in a neo-liberal mode of governance is to regulate and enforce through legislation (Denardis and Raymond 2013). For MSI to be successful, clear legislation and regulation need to be in place. In Norway this is not the case, which in turn affects the ability and possibilities for public–private cooperation through MSI, in three main areas. First, current legislation stands in contradiction to the state's encouragement and effort to create security through the VDI. For the private sector to cooperate with the state and receive security, it must join the VDI. However, for companies like Telenor and NRK (the national broadcasting cooperation), this contravenes Norway's Personal Data Act of 2000, as the VDI in theory gives the state the means for surveillance of anything that goes over the private sector Internet. The private sector is caught between the state's wish for it to use the VDI to cooperate with the state, and legislation that requires it to protect its customers from surveillance. The second area that creates problems for coordinated cooperation through legislation concerns the unclear division of responsibility between the public and private sector on what is to be secured, and by whom (Hommedal 2015 [interview]). This forces the private sector itself to interpret the existing legal framework in shaping and defining its own role. Instead of the state facilitating cooperation through legislation, private-sector actors thus take on this role themselves, to the extent they wish to do so. The third area affected by the lack of legislation is the internal division and understanding of who and which governmental department has responsibility for securing cyber space. Without clarity here, the state's decision-making ability, and also the capacity of the private sector to cooperate with the public sector, becomes restricted. It becomes difficult for the private sector to communicate and work together with the public sector, obstructing dialogue and cooperation across sectors.

Arguably, the challenge in achieving neo-liberal governance of cyber space security lies in the state's ability to take responsibility for a field that is fragmented, while simultaneously building on the existing collaboration to boost cooperation. With the lack of situational awareness, responsibility and with legislation that is hard to interpret, comes weak cyber security. The state might believe that it is facilitating cooperation through MSI, as it is cooperating with the private sector through the VDI and ad hoc meetings. However, in a facilitator mode, the state is expected to bring the different stakeholders together to cooperate and coordinate through legislation. A question of power is arguably the main problem: how it is utilized and who is involved. This directly affects trust, cooperation and reliance between the two sectors—resulting in weakened cooperation and lower cyber security.

Two predominant characteristics can be noted as regards the current level of cyber-security governance in Norway: first, the Norwegian state is either generally uninvolved, or is involved only as a participant without superordinate decision-making authority. This means that the technical and private communities can take the lead in developing and securing cyber space, with the public sector functioning mainly as a bystander. Second, decision-making has typically been driven by technical and market considerations. Throughout most of the world, the focus has been on letting cyber space flourish and develop freely, leaving the state with marginal involvement on technical or strategic levels. In Norway, the result has been that the public sector only has a limited say in the securing of cyber space. This, again, has two main consequences.

First, in the improvement of cyber space and the Internet, economic benefit and profits are the main priority, leaving security sidelined. The focus on advancement and growth of cyber space, combined with minimal state involvement, results in less than optimal security. Second, there is no clear division of competencies and responsibilities between governmental departments as regards responsibility for securing cyber space. The state and the private sector work together to secure cyber space, but largely in an uncoordinated manner. The factors for the proclaimed MSI are thus not in place. Cooperation is ad hoc and bilateral between government and individual private actors, with little overarching strategic planning or facilitation of coordination. This, we shall see, is also an important reason for the negative progress in cyber-security governance on the international level.

International cyber-security governance

Since the mid-1990s, efforts have been underway to construct international regimes for global cyber-security governance. Based on an understanding that international cross-sector cooperation is necessary to secure cyber space, states and the private sector have created initiatives for cooperation. While the institutions, actors and processes of governance vary greatly, they all indicate a collective, policy-motivated shaping of a socio-technical system (Bauer 2005; Eeten and Mueller 2013).

The term "multi-stakeholder" was first used in an international cyber context to describe the encounter with the problems that culminated in the creation of the Internet Corporation of Assigned Names and Numbers (ICANN)[7] in 1998 as a private, not-for-profit organization. Registered in California and linked by a zero-dollar contract to the US Department of Commerce,[8] it is a unilateral construction of a global regime under US law. After the creation of ICANN, the term "multi-stakeholder" was consolidated at the Working Group on Internet Governance (WGIG) in the establishment of a UN World Summit on the Information Society (WSIS).[9] In this state-centric series of diplomatic conferences held between 2002 and 2005, WSIS provided a platform for developing countries and the European Union to challenge the pre-eminence of the United States.[10] However, few of the international political conflicts that led to the WSIS were resolved. Although WSIS involved potentially influential and powerful state actors, they could not agree on how to alter or institutionalize any governance practices or rules for cyber space, other than to create another MSI initiative—the United Nation's Internet Governance Forum (IGF). The community of discourse through multi-stakeholder initiatives that had formed around ICANN and WSIS was extended to the IGF, designed to provide a relatively nonthreatening, non-binding venue for "multi-stakeholder dialogue" (Eeten and Mueller 2013).

As one multi-stakeholder initiative replaces another with the promise of more effective recognition and accommodation of cyber security and Internet governance, the multitude of interests around cyber security has continued to grow.

However, the initiatives do not solve the problems they have been created to deal with. The IGF, for example, is assumed to be relevant for governance of the Internet because that is where the state leaders come together to talk about cyber-security governance (Eeten and Mueller 2013). However, most of the actors with operational control over cyber-security resources are *not* involved in IGF. Not surprisingly, these state-initiated MSI have produced no collective resolutions, let alone binding agreements or decisions; and even if they did, they would have had little leverage over the actors who actually operate the Internet, as they are absent from the discussions. The open character of these organizations could be well suited as a platform for dialogue, but not as a body that needs to make decisions.

Governments generally fail to acknowledge that most cyber-security governance takes place elsewhere than within the state. As a result, there is remarkably little multi-stakeholderism in the multi-stakeholder initiatives of the formalized institutions that are officially designated for creating cyber-security governance on the international level. To counter this, private-sector actors have initiated several MSI efforts aimed at improving cyber security. One example can be found in the Forums for Incident Response and Security Teams (FIRST) that attempt to coordinate the activities of government and private Computer Emergency Response Teams (CERTS) to create cyber-security standards, although the focus is on the technical level. Members work together on securing cyber space by developing and sharing technical information, tools, methodologies, processes and best practices; and they use their combined knowledge, skills and experience to promote a safer, more secure Internet environment. Similarly, the annual meeting of National Computer Security Incident Response Teams (NatC-SIRT) hosts technical gatherings for CSIRTs with national responsibility. Here the organizations responsible for protecting the security of nations, economies and critical infrastructures can discuss the challenges they face. However, although such initiatives exist, they have had limited effect on how states view cyber security—the public sector has shown little interest in participating in these private-sector-initiated initiatives.

With the public and private sector creating different MSIs, systems are developing on two separate tracks: one for the public sector, and one for the private. In the MSI-initiated work of either sector, the other part (to the extent that it is involved at all) seems to treat it as part of its own public relations efforts to signal that something is indeed being done—and not as a collaborative/bargaining process where the management of their resources is modified and coordinated with others to achieve effective forms of collective action (Eeten and Mueller 2013). Without the involvement of the other parties that hold power—as creators and owners of what constitutes cyber space, or as legislators—such initiatives risk becoming mere talk-shops and information exchange hubs within sectors. To take decisions that have impact, both the public and private sector must be involved. Those with power to act and enforce need to be consolidated and lead the discussion, instead of remaining as bystanders. With state-led incentives, this means that the private sector, which holds the expertise and technology, must be included in the decisions made regarding delivery. Similarly, with initiatives led by the private sector, the public sector needs to be involved, in order to create legislation that can be followed up in practice.

None of today's international MSI have proven able to create greater security. This is firstly because the "wrong" people are at the table: not all the power-holders are included. Second, the unclear division of responsibility from the national level is transmitted to the international level, with the question of power structures largely overlooked. This means that internationally who is to be included in securing cyber space is unclear in the various initiatives that aim to govern cyber security—in turn, resulting in inadequate cyber security.

Conclusions: toward an expanded governance model for cyber security?

The current approach to cyber-security governance has been profoundly shaped, if not defined, by the idea of multi-stakeholder initiatives, rather than by an in-depth assessment of the power dynamics inherent in cyber space. This has led to inadequate coordination of cooperation, which affects all levels of cyber security. Instead of aiming at facilitation, MSI become the state's entry-point to cyber security. As Carr points out, "contrary to one of the key claims about it, multi-stakeholder Internet governance serves largely to reinforce existing power relations rather than disrupt them" (Carr 2014: 642). Examining the role of power, we find that the state may think it is facilitating cooperation, but it is doing this on the wrong premises. The state focus on MSI to secure cyber space means that the importance of legislation, regulation and to coordinate cooperation is overlooked. With the lack of situational awareness and responsibility, plus legislation that is hard to interpret, comes weak cyber security.

By means of governmentality theory, an understanding of the technical and political picture that is needed for MSI to work can be established. States think, and declare, that they are implementing MSI to govern cyber-security governance in cyber space, without the necessary conditions for such governance being in place. To secure cyber space, those who hold the "real power" must be included, both nationally and internationally—otherwise, cyber space is only partially secured. Further, rather than trying to secure cyber space by "governing less," the state must act as a facilitator for those who hold the power in cyber space, and it must clarify through legislation what is required to secure cyber space. This entails not a limitation of state power, nor controlling the private sector, but rather a clarification of roles and responsibilities. To act as a facilitator in cyber space, the state will need to work to ensure coordinated cooperation between the public and private sector, by creating an adequate legal framework. What the state does nationally spreads to the international level: the unclear division of responsibility from the national level gets transmitted to the international level, and the question of power structures remains largely overlooked. With the "wrong" people are at the table, the actual power-holders in cyber space are not included. Just who is to be included in securing cyber space is unclear in the various initiatives that aim to govern cyber security—leading to poor results. Rather than approaching cyber security as a state-centric issue, the "state as a facilitator" under neo-liberal state governance needs to help those who hold the power in cyber space to come together.

While some aspects of cyber-security governance are a matter of technical coordination, the political, commercial, legal and cultural implications also need to be included. Acknowledging the political side of cyber-security governance is imperative, as governments will continue to promote their own national interests in this context. Governments, NGOs and other stakeholders are often misled by the assumption that cyber-security governance is what happens at international forums like the IGF. The range of issues stakeholders try to put on the agenda keeps expanding, despite the limited actual mandates of those institutions. This has important implications for our understanding of the role of the state in cyber-security governance. Coordinated cooperation is needed between the public and private sector both nationally and internationally—but an MSI is no silver bullet, and should not be valued in and of itself. What is needed is another form of coordinated cooperation other than MSIs, one that can include a broader range of stakeholders with the power to secure cyber space.

Examining how power is understood within these systems, how interests are articulated and pursued, the kinds of ideas and discourses from which power and interests draw substance, as well as those that help to establish, maintain and perpetuate the system—this has brought us one step closer to understanding why MSIs have failed to secure cyber space today. The more we understand about the opportunities and weaknesses of MSI for cyber security, the better equipped will we be for refining and amending the practices, functions and roles involved.

Notes

1 Cyber security is defined in the Introduction.
2 Virtual desktop infrastructure (VDI) is the practice of hosting a desktop operating system within a virtual machine (VM) running on a centralized server. VDI is a variation on the client/server computing model, sometimes referred to as "server-based computing."
3 Concretely this means that companies and agencies that participate in the scheme have received physical boxes that monitor network traffic. This includes "deep-packet inspection": NorCERT can check the file-level of what is being submitted to a corporate network and what is being sent out.
4 F. Hommedal, 2015. Interview with the author. Oslo, June 13, 2015.
5 Private companies fear that sensitive information on previous security incidents that is passed on to the state might not be treated with the necessary degree of confidentiality, causing damage to their reputation and thus future profits. Studies have shown a negative correlation between the publication of security values and the market value of the companies concerned.
6 One of the points often brought up when explaining why public–private cooperation does not work is that the private sector does not wish to share information about attacks under transparent conditions, as they are worried about the economic consequences (Dunn Cavelty and Sutter 2009).

7 As Eeten and Mueller (2013) point out, this has produced a misunderstanding that haunts many academic and policy debates to this date: that the Internet is somehow "governed" by the ICANN. As recently as September 2009, *The Economist* referred to the negotiations over a new contract between the ICANN and the US government as being about "control over cyber space."

8 At the time of writing, ICANN operates under a zero-dollar contract with the US Department of Commerce, although this is up for review in 2015.

9 The WGIG Report itself uses the term eleven times and, among other things, identifies the need for a "global multi-stakeholder forum to address Internet-related public policy issues." Also the WGIG Background Report uses the term eleven times. Finally, it was via WGIG that the term found its way into the Tunis Agenda. The Tunis Agenda has eighteen references to "multi-stakeholder," four of them related to the Internet Governance Forum (IGF).

10 WGIG invites to MSI by asking non-governmental actors like private industry and civil society to become directly involved into the political process, but reality is a different matter. In any case, the vague "invitation" for non-state actors has led to disagreements between governments themselves and between governmental and non-governmental participants. The invitation challenges non-governmental stakeholders to counter the governmental argument that "observers" are not representative and unable to speak with a coordinated voice by organizing themselves and demonstrating legitimacy, expertise and constructive engagement.

References

AbeleWigert, Isabelle. 2006. "Challenges Governments Face in the Field of Critical Information Infrastructure Protection: Shareholders and Perspectives," in Myriam Dunn and Victor Mauer (eds), *International CIIP Handbook 2006, Vol. II: Analyzing Issues, Challenges, and Prospects*. Zurich: Center for Security Studies, 69–99.

Bauer, Johannes M. 2005. "Internet Governance: Theory and First Principles." Paper presented at the 33rd annual telecommunication policy research conference, Arlington, VA, September 23–25.

BBC News. 2015. "German Parliament Cyber-Attack Still 'Live.'" *BBC News*. June 11, at: www.bbc.com/news/technology-33093895 (accessed August 20, 2015).

Campbell, Katherine, Lawrence A. Gordon, Martin P. Loeb and Lei Zhou. 2003. "The Economic Cost of Publicly Announced Information Security Breaches: Empirical Evidence from the Stock Market." *Journal of Computer Security* 11: 431–48.

Carr, Madeline. 2015. "Power Plays in Global Internet Governance" Millennium: *Journal of International Studies* 43 (2): 640–59.

CERT. n.d. *CSIRT Frequently Asked Questions (FAQ)*, at: www.cert.org/incident-management/csirt-development/csirt-faq.cfm (accessed July 3, 2015).

Chehadé, Fadi. 2014. *Largest Ever ICANN Meeting Convenes in London Affirmation of Multistakeholder Model for Internet Governance by World Leaders*. ICANN, June 2, at: www.icann.org/news/announcement-2014-06-23-en (accessed July 2, 2015).

Christou, George and Seamus Simpson. 2009. "New Governance, the Internet, and Country Code Top-Level Domains in Europe." *Governance: An International Journal of Policy Administration and Institutions* 22: 599–624.

Dean, Mitchell. 1999. *Governmentality: Power and Rule in Modern Society*. London: Sage.

Deibert, Ronald J. and Masashi Crete-Nishihata. 2012. "Global Governance and the Spread of Cyber Controls." *Global Governance* 18: 339–61.

Deibert, Ronald J. and Rafal Rhozomski. 2011. "The New Cyber Military–Industrial Complex." *Globe and Mail.* March 28.

DeNardis, Laura and Mark Raymond. 2013. "Thinking Clearly about Multistakeholder Internet Governance." Paper presented at eighth annual GigaNet Symposium, Bali, Indonesia, October 21.

Drezner, Daniel W. 2004. "The Global Governance of the Internet: Bringing the State Back In." *Political Science Quarterly* 119: 447–98.

Drezner, Daniel W. 2007. *All Politics Is Global: Explaining International Regulatory Regimes.* Princeton, NJ: Princeton University Press.

Dunn, Myriam and Victor Mauer (eds). 2006. "Analyzing Issues, Challenges, and Pro-spects." *International CIIP Handbook 2006 Vol. II.* Center for Security Studies, Zurich, 69–88.

Dunn Cavelty, Myriam. 2012. "The Militarisation of Cyber Security as a Source of Global Tension," in Daniel Möckli and Andreas Wenger (eds), *Strategic Trends Study.* Zurich: Center for Security Studies.

Dunn Cavelty, Myriam. 2012. *Public–Private Partnerships are No Silver Bullet: An Expanded Governance Model for Critical Infrastructure Protection.* Zurich: Center for Security Studies.

Dunn Cavelty, Myriam and Manuel Suter. 2009. "Public–Private Partnerships are No Silver Bullet: An Expanded Governance Model for Critical Infrastructure Protection." *International Journal of Critical InfraStructure Protection* 2 (4): 179–87.

The Economist. 2009. *Regulating the Internet: ICANN be Independent.* ICANN September 24, at: www.economist.com/node/14517430 (accessed July 2, 2015).

Eeten, Michel J.G. and Milton Mueller. 2013. "Where is the Governance in Internet Governance?" *New Media & Society* 15 (5): 720–36.

Farrell, Henry. 2003. "Constructing the International Foundations of E-Commerce. The EU–US Safe Harbour Agreement." *International Organization* 57: 277–306.

Froomkin, A. Michael. 2003. "ICANN 2.0: Meet the New Boss." *Loyola of Los Angeles Law Review* 36 (3): 1087–1102.

Goldsmith, Jack and Tim Wu. 2006. *Who Controls the Internet? Illusions of a Borderless World.* New York: Oxford University Press.

Hansen, Lene and Helen Nissenbaum. 2009. "Digital Disaster, Cyber Security, and the Copenhagen School." *International Studies Quarterly* 53: 1155–75.

Hindess, Barry. 2005. "Politics as Government: Michel Foucault's Analysis of Political Reason." *Alternatives* 30: 389–413.

Huijstee, Mariette. V. 2012. *Multistakeholder Initatives: A Strategic Guide for Civil Society Organizations.* Stichting Onderzoek Multinationale Ondernemingen. Amster-dam: The Netherlands.

Kirknes, Leif M. 2010. "Flere kritiske til NSM-samarbeid." *Computer World*, December 1, at: www.cw.no/artikkel/offentlig-sektor/flere-kritiske-til-nsm-samarbeid (accessed June 13, 2015).

Klein, Hans. 2004. "Understanding WSIS: An Institutional Analysis of the UN World Summit on the Information Society." *Information Technology & International Development* 1 (3–4): 3–14.

Kleinwächter, Wolfgang. 2004. "WSIS: A New Diplomacy? Multistakeholder Approach and Bottom Up Policy in Global ICT Governance." *Information Technology & International Development* 1 (3–4): 3–13.

Koppell, Jonathan G.S. 2005. "Pathologies of Accountability: ICANN and the Challenge of "Multiple Accountabilities Disorder." *Public Administration Review* 65 (1): 94–108.

Kummer, Markus. 2013. "Multistakeholder Cooperation: Reflections on the Emergence of a New Phraseology in International Cooperation, Internet Society." *Internet Society* May 14, at: www.internetsociety.org/blog/2013/05/multistakeholder-cooperation-reflections-emergence-new-phraseology-international (accessed June 29, 2015).

Lindsay, Jon R., Tai Min Cheung and Derek S. Reveron. 2015. *China and Cybersecurity*. New York: Oxford University Press.

Neumann, Iver B. and Ole Jacob Sending. 2010. *Governing the Global Polity*. Ann Arbor, MI: University of Michigan Press.

Norwegian ministries (Justice and Public Security, Defence, Transport and Communications, Government Administration, Reform and Church Affairs). 2012. *Cyber Security Strategy for Norway*, at: www.regjeringen.no/globalassets/upload/FAD/Vedlegg/IKT-politikk/Cyber_Security_Strategy_Norway.pdf (accessed August 1, 2015).

Nye, Joseph S. 2014. *The Regime Complex for Managing Global Cyber Activities*. Global Commission on Internet Governance, paper series, No. 1, May.

Opm.gov. 2015. *Information about OPM Cybersecurity Incidents*. OPM.gov., at: www.opm.gov/cybersecurity (accessed August 10, 2015).

Palfrey, John. 2004. "The End of the Experiment: How ICANN'S Foray into Global Internet Democracy Failed." *Harvard Journal of Law and Technology* 17 (2): 409–73.

Pavan, Elena and Mario Diani. 2008. "Structuring Online and Offline Discursive Spaces of Internet Governance: Insights from a Network Approach to Map an Emerging Field." Paper presented at the annual GigaNet symposium, Hyderabad, India, December 2.

Personal Data Act. 2000. *Relating to the Processing of Personal Data (Personal Data Act)*. Datatilsynet, April 14, No. 31, at: www.datatilsynet.no/English/Regulations/Personal-Data-Act-/ (accessed August 5, 2015).

Sveinbjørnsson, S. 2012. "NRK kastet ut statens 'spionboks'." *Digi.no*, November 5, at: www.digi.no/sikkerhet/2012/11/05/nrk-kastet-ut-statens-spionboks (accessed August 1, 2015).

Yuxiao, Li and Xu Lu. 2015. "China's Cybersecurity Situation and the Potential for International Cooperation," in John R. Lindsay, Tai Ming Cheung and Derek S. Reveron (eds), *China and Cybersecurity*. New York: Oxford University Press, 225–41.

8 Cyber warfare by social network media

Thomas Elkjer Nissen

Introduction

Cyber warfare, what it is and what it entails, has been widely debated in recent years including the political, ethical and not least legal aspects of it. Most of this debate has though been centered around cyber attack on, protection of so-called "critical infrastructure," and state-sponsored cyber espionage. Social network media has also been mentioned a lot in connection with recent conflicts. Most recently, as we will discuss later, in connection with The Islamic State in Iraq and Syria's use of social network media to create effects regionally and internationally. But also in connection with the civil war in Syria where social network media has been used extensively throughout by all actors to create effects in the international system and within the conflict area in a very strategic way. A tendency that also has been clearly visible in the ongoing conflict in Ukraine and in connection with Russian Information Warfare. The majority of the debate concerning social network media have, however, been focused on the use of these for propaganda purposes. The two debates, however, have not for real been merged and social network media have therefore not been seen as a distinct subset to cyber warfare in the debate.

To this end, it is this chapter's main argument that cyber warfare is too narrowly interpreted in the current debate and that social network media has to be viewed as specific subset of "cyber warfare," which only occurs in and through social network media. Furthermore, that social network media as a specific subset of cyber warfare has been subject to an intensified strategic use within recent years. That has resulted in a coordinated use of social network media for intelligence collection, targeting, propaganda, offensive and defensive "cyber operations" and for command and control purposes.

To provide a context for this argument the chapter will first discuss some characteristics of the contemporary conflict environment, which is facilitating the effectiveness of social network media as a "war-fighting platform" to include what is meant with the term "global information environment." Furthermore the chapter will discuss how social network media fit into cyber warfare through the "military" activities which they can be used for. Finally will the chapter present two short case studies on how social network media has been strategically employed in the Syrian civil war and by the terror organization "Islamic State" in order to draw some general deductions on how social network media are used for warfare purposes within the cyber-warfare context.

Character of the contemporary conflict environment

First and foremost, contemporary conflicts are characterized as being so-called "wars of choice" for Western liberal democracies, although less so for a series authoritarian regimes, and by being "low intensity conflicts" or LIC. This means that they take the form of uprisings, insurgencies, intra-state wars and civil wars, rather than inter-state conflicts fought with conventional forces. When conventional forces are used, they are often employed against non-state actors, or as leverage supporting other instruments of power (diplomatic, economic or informational). These characteristics also result in an increased number of possible actors, both state and non-state, who are empowered by information and communication technology. The objectives of these actors also tend to be more focused on affecting public perception, political decision-making and media agendas rather than territorial control in many instances, in order to achieve their objectives. Although there is still fought over terrain, in order to achieve the desired behavioral or contextual change, terrain seems to be secondary. The disputed "terrain" also tends to be more centred on urban areas, which often are more developed in respect to information and communication technology, giving even more lavage to technologically savvy actors. The methods to achieve the desired objectives are as a result changing. Contemporary conflicts are fought with integrated overt and covert military, paramilitary and civilian means, including cyber activities, often with conventional military forces in a supporting role, as it has been seen in Ukraine. It is therefore also increasingly difficult to identify exactly when a conflict start and end. One could perhaps say that they have a running start and no real end, as a lot of what they entail (the methods) is "under the threshold" activity in respect to what can be codified as war or conflict (Sloan 2012; Kaldor 2013).[1] As with the actors, the methods and objectives are multiple, and to a high degree targeted at perception and decision-making behavior, which is why the global information environment, particularly "cyber space" for lack of a better term, increasingly becomes the main battle-space.

The global information environment, where the developments within information and communication technology (reach of the internet, number of mobile phones and other devices and social network media) has been exponential, is creating an unprecedented connectivity and democratisation of the technology further empowering the many actors in contemporary conflicts.

Events in the world are now transmitted as information through digital networks in near real-time. This has created an increased reliance on information technology for waging warfare introducing new opportunities that can be exploited, but also new vulnerabilities. Information technology now provides almost universal direct access to information via the Internet especially through social network media (Nissen 2015) and thereby also possibilities for affecting international developments. In turn, this also means affecting social network media, systems and networks, individual profiles and accounts, and the information (text, images, video, etc.) or content they are used to share, and not to forget the humans behind the networks and accounts (or some of them, as others may be fake), can pay enormous dividends. Through Computer Network Operation activities, in and through social network media, actors can create or shift agendas and discourses, aid or hamper access to information use of decision-making, project and counter narratives, in turn, effectively redistributing power in the global information environment and potentially also in the physical domain. Alone due to the effect(s) possible to create in and through social network media, and these association with the cyber domain, firmly puts them within the cyberwarfare arena.

Cyber warfare

Many definitions of what cyber warfare is exist in current literature. One has been developed by Adam Liff, who defines cyber warfare as:

> the deliberate hostile and cost-inducing use of CNA [Computer Network Attack] against an adversary's critical civilian or military infrastructure with coercive intent or to extract political concessions, as a brute force measure against military or civilian networks in order to reduce the adversary's ability to defend itself or retaliate in kind or with conventional force, or against civilian and/or military targets in order to frame another actor for strategic purposes.
>
> (Liff 2012: 408)

This definition firmly puts cyber warfare within a more conventional warfighting paradigm and does not separate cyber activities from conventional use of military power by portraying them as something completely different things. It also points to that cyber warfare is not something that only goes on in "cyber space," but as something that will be conducted in concert with "real-life" physical activities. It will therefore be a question of combining "armed attacks" with "cyber attacks" in order to simultaneously create effects in both domains. Cyber attack will in this understanding therefore be conducted in the framework of conventional kinetic attack or other "military" activities, perhaps covert actions, used as an opening salvo to disable defenses in immediate advance of a conventional attack, giving an offensive advantage (Liff 2012). This offensive advantage can, however, also be a question of paralyzing, deceiving or confusing decision makers, media and publics.

A "cyber attack" can on the other hand be defined as: "activities that are carried out over information networks ranging from hacking and defacing of webpages to large-scale destruction of the military or civilian computer based systems, networks or infrastructure" (Waxmann 2011: 422). The targets of a cyber attack can therefore range from critical infrastructure to open information networks as social network media. The use of social network media for creating military effects, either alone or in concert with other (physical) military activities can subsequently also be framed or explained within these two definitions.

First, looking at the definition of cyber warfare then, social network media is used deliberately hostile and can be cost-inducing through the use of CNA-like activities or hacking. Although these activities mostly are targeted against adversary's, sometimes private, civilian or military communication and information infrastructure it is still with coercive intent or to extract political concessions through manipulation and excreting influence on decision-making processes. Social network media is not on the other hand particularly adapt as a brute force measure against military or civilian networks in order to reduce the adversary's ability to defend itself (unless it is a question of so-called "psychological defense," e.g., the achievement and maintenance of information resilience against propaganda within own population or armed forces).[2] Social network media is not likely to be used to retaliate in kind either, but social network media can be used against civilian and/or military targets in order to frame another actor for strategic purposes. This was for example seen very clearly in connection with the downing of MH17 over Ukraine, where multiple stories about what in reality happen was disseminated in order to confuse audiences.[3] The cyber-warfare definition, however, only provide clarity over some of the effects that can be created in and through social network media. As it is, it only encompasses the effects resulting from direct action in either the cognitive or physical network domains, for example, what Thomas Rid besides espionage labels, subversion and sabotage (Rid 2012: 5–23). It does not encompass other "warfare activities," or effects, as actual intelligence collection, support to targeting and the facilitating/supporting warfare activities associated with command and control.

For further depth we secondly have to look at the cyber-attack definition. Stating that it is activities that are carried out over information networks clearly implies that this also can be a question of social network alone. Further pointing out that it is ranging from hacking, as discussed above, and defacing of web-pages to large-scale destruction of the military or civilian computer based systems, networks or infrastructure. The latter though not being of particular relevance when talking about social network media in terms of "destruction." It is on the other hand interesting in term of affecting systems, networks and infrastructure. Particularly in respect to the distribution of malware in order to facilitate tracking and monitoring (intelligence collection) and mapping networks and content flow for targeting purposes (of both networks and individual user profiles). In respect to targeting this can be a question of identifying "personas" (virtual actors) as well as "persons" (humans behind one or more personas). Affecting networks can furthermore be a question of actual attacks on the social network media profiles/accounts themselves or the network or servers on which they reside. The predominant and most mentioned utilization of social network media in warfare is, however, to extract political concessions through manipulation and excreting influence on decision-making processes (leading to actual behavior) and to frame or deceive other actors in and through social network media, for example, their use for propaganda purposes. Surely as social network media first and foremost are for communication and dialogue they can also be used to communicate, coordinate and synchronize actions and messages making them useful for "command and control" activities as well.

In order to see this demonstrated in contemporary conflicts we can look on the ongoing conflicts in respectively Syria and Iraq. First, the civil war in Syria, from 2010 to present day, between the Syrian regime and multiple opposition groups where social network media increasingly have been used as an integral part of the war-fighting efforts. Second, on the terror organization Islamic State's strategic use of social network media to achieve both offensive and defensive objectives.

The social network media battle-space of Syria

In 2010 it caught the attention of the world media when the news about a Syrian lesbian blogger in Damascus spread globally very quickly. "She" was blogging about life in Syria in the context of the ongoing unrest in the rest of the Arab world. Just as quickly, however, the world discovered that "she" was a "he," more precisely a middle-aged American man named Tom MacMaster living in Scotland.[4] This case illustrates just how difficult the attribution of the information disseminated on social network media really is. The Syrian conflict, however, offers many other examples of how social network media has been used by the regime, the opposition and a variety of external third parties. These examples also illustrate how actors continuously develop their capabilities based on experiences from earlier and other conflicts on how to use social network media in order to create "political" or "military" effects.

"The Syrian conflict is the world's first cyber civil war. Cyber communications are central to strategy and tactics employed by both Assad and the rebels" (Farwell and Arakelian 2013). This statement was put forward by Rafal Rohozinski who is leading the Canadian based firm SecDev Group's efforts on monitoring internet activities in amongst other places Syria. He goes on pointing out "that it is hard to overstate how heavily both sides depend on cyber tools to articulate their narrative, stories, themes and messages. The war has integrated kinetic and information warfare tactics in an unprecedented ways" (Farwell and Arakelian 2013). The internet and especially social network media are used for Command and Control purposes, providing lines of communication between dispersed groups for coordination and synchronizing of tactics on the ground. Social network media are also used for intelligence purposes, including surveillance and reconnaissance, obtaining and maintaining situational awareness through for example gathering of information from people living within denied areas, and to receive training and advice on military matters from actors outside Syria. Last, but definitely not least, the cyber domain and social network media are used by all actors for propaganda purposes in order to influence and shape perceptions, attitudes and behaviors of audiences both inside Syria and internationally. Basically striving to make their voice heard and silence the voices of the opposition. The Syrian civil war is thereby the first to happen in the full throes of the global information environment saturated by cyber, where mobile technology, social network media and tech-savvy digital natives[5] have created a potent mix influencing the character of the conflict (Frizpatrick 2013).

Looking at the conflict in Syria, and particularly the cyber warfare elements of it, you find that social network media has been used to collect intelligence, target opponents, conduct propaganda and cyber operations and facilitate command and control in support of the war-fighting efforts by nearly all actors.

Intelligence collection and targeting in and through social network media

From a targeting point of view, information from social network media has been used by various actors in Syria to identify and target individuals posting information and updates to single out accounts and profiles for computer network attack or hacking. But also to identify opinion-leaders to counter their messaging and narrative, and for identifying the individuals behind the accounts for "real-life" targeting (Clayton 2012).

This process of cause requires knowledge about the "targets." A pre-condition for this targeting is therefore intelligence collection. This intelligence collection has been done through the application of monitoring and tracking software, often provided by outside actors, to identify networks and individual accounts and profiles within these networks belonging to the opponents or their supporters. Also techniques as crowdsourcing are being used for collecting simple information on opponent's social network media presence from their followers. In Syria amongst others the Syrian Electronic Army (SEA) (Zambelis 2013; Note Syria 2013 and Flash Note Syria 2013)[6] have had detailed instructions on their Facebook page dealing with how to report opposition Facebook pages.[7] For example, collecting information through crowdsourcing upon which targeting can be done. Internet (live streamed news reports on web-television) and social network media (example journalists tweeting from within Syria) is also being used by non-state actors without sophisticated Intelligence, Surveillance and Recognisance (ISR) assets to conduct Bomb Damage Assessment (BDA) on the effect of their rocket attacks and other so-called indirect fires. In Syria it has been used as a way to verify, at least partially, other social network media reports of collateral damage, where no other sources are available, by actors inside Syria to include both opposition and regime entities as well as human rights organizations.

The predominant use of social network media in Syria by all actors has though been for propaganda purposes. In particularly to distribute emotional imagery or video and associated stories (sometimes fake or taken out of context) in order to influence audience's perception of the situation, ultimately their behavior. One thing is, however, the extensive messaging in social network media, another is more sophisticated methods like the use of "botnets."[8] These have been seen multiple times in Syria. In one instance the regime allegedly produced more than four million tweets and retweets over a four-month time-frame in 2012, before the botnet was brought to twitters attention and subsequently shut down.[9] The content was predominantly tweets of pro-regime news outlets in order to draw attention to them while at the same time provide plausible deniability for the regime; hence the problem of attribution of online activity. The same methodology has also been seen applied on Facebook, where accounts have appeared to belong to human rights organizations offering news about the humanitarian situation in Syria. However, when logging onto the site using a Facebook account, as required, the username and password has been "pinched." This information can potentially thereafter be used for either intelligence or targeting purposes or for distributing propaganda to your social network using your Facebook account (Clayton 2013). The utilization of social network media in Syria therefore also provides insight into the convergence between the informational or content aspects and the more technical, or traditional, aspects of cyber warfare.

Offensive utilization of social network media in Syria

Besides collecting intelligence, single out "targets" and disseminating propaganda several actors in Syria also conduct actual cyber operations, or computer network attack (e.g., hacking), against opponents and outside third party social network media accounts and profiles. The use of computer network attack on example news organization's social network media platforms and accounts have been widespread in Syria. One example of this is SEA's computer network attack on the news company AP's Twitter account releasing a false tweet claiming the White House had been bombed and that the US president Obama was injured. This one tweet resulted in a US$135 billion dip on the Dow Jones S&P 500 index within minutes (Fischer 2013). The effect was though not sustainable and the marked was quickly restored when it became apparent that it was not correct. But as examples of this accumulates it does have a secondary effect; lack of trust in news disseminated by major news agencies and also drawing these news agencies closer into the war-fighting than previously seen. Other examples include posting fake news stories about opposition commanders prompting internal repercussions against them (Tomlinson 2015). Another purpose of cyber operations in and through social network media is to hamper other actor's ability to use social network media for their "war-fighting" purposes by conducting operations against an opponent's capabilities. This can be done through denying them access to their accounts and profiles through DDOS (distributed denial of service) attacks, or by defacing their accounts on Twitter or Facebook, replacing the original content with other content. The latter is not necessarily a question of completely changing the content, it can also be more covert—just changing language slightly so that the content gives a different impression, without the owner of the account knowing it. One example of DDOS from Syria is the Syrian Electronic Army attacking, or hacking, opposition group's area-specific Facebook accounts in an attempt to deny the opposition the possibility of reporting news about on-going events on ground to outside observers (Clayton and SecDev Group 2013a: 2).

Several times during the Syrian civil war the internet has also been disabled. The Syrian regime has claimed either that it is the opposition (or in their terminology; the terrorists) that have done it, or that is has been caused by technical problems. Conversely, the opposition have continually claimed that it is the regime that deliberately shut down access to the Internet. Why the regime has done this, however, is debated. That the opposition should have been able to do it is highly unlikely taken into account the much centralized way the internet is configured in Syria. The regime itself is also to a degree dependent on the internet for command and control purposes and for intelligence gathering. This suggests that the regime either needed time to install detection and tracking software or it has been an attempt to prompt the opposition to use other communication means for specific periods of time which have been easier for the regime to monitor. In other instances it have been seen that the regime has disable the internet in areas where attacks on opposition units have been imminent in order to prevent communication, in particularly through social network media, to the outside world and to coordinate actions between the opposition groups (Goldman 2012; SecDey Group 2013; Flash Note Syria 2013). Allegedly Al-Assad was supported by Iranian specialists, when creating the Syrian Electronic Army (SEA) in order to collect intelligence but also to harass activists, hack opposition websites and social network media accounts and spread propaganda and misinformation (Kilcullen 2013: 220–21). The SEA's actions also include trying to counter the dissemination of censorship circumvention tools, blocking Virtual Private Networks (PVNs), and the sites from where they can be downloaded, in order to prevent the opposition to use this technique to bypass censorship and avoid monitoring. This shows that the use of social network media represents an, at the very least perceived, threat to the regime (SecDev Group 2012: 1). Syrian regime awareness of this aspect of the conflict has led to an increase in their "cyber warfare" efforts particularly directed at social network media (SecDev Group 2013; Flash Note Syria 2013).

Finally has social network media been used for command and control purposes in Syria. This is in itself not new knowledge. Social network media have for long been used by terror organizations for communicating and coordinating efforts, also real-time, and thereby for command and control purposes. An example of this utilization of social network media is the Mumbai terrorists that had a "control room" in Karachi where social network media, among other media, such as mobile devices, was used to coordinate the actions of the terrorists, partly based on feed-back gained through the monitoring of mainstream news coverage of the terror attack, and partly based on conversations about the event in social network media. Similarly, in the conflict in Libya, Twitter was used to coordinate information, medical requirements, radio frequencies and telephone numbers along with new satellite frequencies for television stations that were being jammed. These are all examples of social network media being used for command and control purposes (Kilcullen 2013: 202). Social network media has, however, much more systematically emerged in Syria as remote command and control nodes playing a large practical coordination and logistical role. Most notably in connection with opposition group's attempts of synchronizing and coordinating the "combat power" of geographically dispersed groups in order to conduct unified attacks on regime security forces, and for general internal communication. This is probably also why the regime is so heavily focused on the cyber operations against the oppositions use of social technology and why external actors, such as the United States, in what is called "non-lethal support" to the moderate Syrian opposition has focused on delivering social technology and training in order to provide the opposition with secure Command and Control.[10]

The bottom line is that all parties and other actors in the Syrian civil war exploit cyber space and in particularly social network media to advance their strategic objectives (SecDev Group 2013d: 1). But not only internally in Syria, they are also used to achieve effects on outside audiences predominantly through propaganda. The other way around has virtual networks of international support for Syria represented a complete logistical, informational and command-and-control hinterland for the uprisings, providing instant strategic depth as the movements gathered momentum (Kilcullen, 2013: 204). As a consequence each opposition "battalion" in Syria for example now has its own online presence on social network media (SecDev Group 2013; Flash Note 2013: 1). A methodology the Islamic State has taken to another level in their online strategy, as we will now discuss.

Islamic State's social media warfare

For a while now, like other non-state actors, the terror organization Islamic State (IS) in Iraq and Syria has employed a social network media strategy in order to advance their strategic objectives. At the moment, however, IS seems to be more successful in their online activities than other similar organizations. For example, IS uses social media strategically as an integral, and sometimes leading, part of its armed activities in Syria and Iraq and worldwide.

Strategy

From a strategic point of view, IS has employed social media to gain the attention of mass media and strategic audiences, amplify and control its messaging in support of its narrative in order to radicalize and recruit followers, deter their opponents and raise funds. Amongst other things, this strategy displays an understanding of the importance of having a single goal (the Caliphate) and a common purpose (articulated in a strategic narrative). It also shows an understanding of how to exploit user experience and visual media (infotainment) in order to gain attention and engage their followers and other strategic audiences in an emotional way—for good (cats) and bad (beheadings) (Powell 2014). At the same time they manage to construct their "self-image" in a way that supports their narrative. Simultaneously, they display an understanding of how to disrupt the opponent's narrative and on-line activities by exploiting their opponent's messages, in order to position IS and their "brand" amongst other jihadist factions in the Middle East (Borkowski 2014).

The strategy also builds on the notion of "Force Multiplication" through the use of social media in order to make IS seem more powerful than it may actually be. Part of this is done to create large volume of on-line output to assure visibility among strategic audiences, as well as gaining mass media attention and thereby further exposure of their message. This also serves the added purpose of creating the impression of a large mass of followers, in turn creating social proof or fake peer endorsement, potentially leading to even more "real" followers. Amongst other things this is achieved through the use of "disseminators"; individuals who although not officially affiliated with IS spread their tweets and other postings to their thousands of followers (Townsend 2014; Bartlett 2014; Kingsley 2014; Reilly 2014; Matthews 2014).

Another dimension of this strategy is to rely on these "disseminators" using hashtags crafted to look like grass-root initiatives exploiting "astro-turfing" techniques,[11] in some cases also hijacking existing hashtags, and thereby lending third-party credibility to the narrative. Not least "hashtag hijacking" where IS uses # of trending topics to get attention from audiences how would normally not search for IS content or # (Bloom 2014). IS also utilizes techniques normally associated with political campaigning, for example, by sounding out possible support through feedback on potential ideas, terms and graphics. This can also be viewed as a form of both target-audience analysis and pre-testing of products (both messages and images) in support of the campaign.

Multi-layered approach to social-network media

The use of social-network media also indicates that they are relying on both a top-down approach as well as being comfortable with bottom-up initiatives (disseminators, or "fan boys," acting in IS interest). According to Rose Powell you can identify four levels of online activities. All four levels use the centralized strategic narrative as the framework (or direction and guidance) for their use of images and messages in the different social-media platforms supporting their propaganda activities (Powell 2014). The content is therefore initially very coordinated, but as it makes its way either vertically downwards or is retweeted, re-posted or adapted to local circumstances and networks, the content changes. This results in some loss of control of the message, and hence the narrative.

The top-level element consists of IS's own Twitter account and other social-media platform accounts where most video is uploaded centrally. These video clips appear very professional and in many cases resemble Hollywood-style productions. They make use of a number of techniques, including slow-motion sequences and first-person-shooter like graphics. IS does, however, also use other and much simpler yet still violent videos, like it was seen with the video shoving the burning of a Jordanian pilot.[12]

The second level consists of regional or provincial accounts posting both live reports from strikes (words and images) and localized messaging, in some cases including live feeds and live streaming.

The third level consists of individual fighters that post updates about their experiences on what is to appear as personal accounts. These are more personal, emotional and therefore appealing to for example young potential recruits.

The fourth level is more or less outside the control of IS media "management" and consists of sympathisers and supporters (the disseminators) either retweeting or re-posting IS content or their user-generated content (UGC) based on the authorized IS messaging. Sometimes this is translated into the local language, including Western languages.

The platforms used are most notably Twitter, including an (Android and Apple) app called "The Dawn of Glad Tidings" (this has apparently been closed now) to promote IS messages and images and the use of hashtags and links (Berger 2014), Facebook profiles, Instagram and YouTube accounts and the Skype-like platform Viber. These platforms originate at the top-level, and at lower levels links are used to connect to content. IS is also using links to selected outside articles and images from respected news outlets that support their message or overall narrative in order to gain further credibility.

Some message and content production is also crowd-sourced/crowd-distributed (and translated). This indicates IS has access to highly skilled multimedia designers and state-of-the-art software (such as Adobe applications like InDesign, Photoshop, etc.) The bottom line is that when it comes to the strategic utilization of social network media, IS seems to be in the lead at the moment although they are increasingly challenged at their own game.

Cyber warfare by social network media—the "military" utilization

Based on the two case studies on the use of social network media in the Syrian civil war, and the terror organization Islamic State's strategic use of them, we can draw some general deductions on how social network media can be utilized for a series of "military" activities, whether by state or non-state actors (even down to the individual level), for example, for Intelligence, Targeting, Propaganda, Cyber Operations and Command and Control. Common denominator is though that all these activities, regardless that they can have both online and offline effects, can be conducted in and through social network media in support of warfare, or as a particular type of warfare itself, within the framework of cyber warfare, effectively broadening the scope of it.

Intelligence

Intelligence can be seen as the product resulting from the collection, processing, integration, analysis, evaluation and interpretation of available information concerning countries or areas of interest, to include specific domains that are not geographical in nature, such as the global information environment, including social network media. But Intelligence is also an activity in itself. In respect to social network media, intelligence is about monitoring online activity and behavior in order to collect and aggregate information and data on and from networks, sites and platforms considered as social network media. Furthermore to analyze this information and data in order to generate knowledge and understanding in general and in particular in order to support the targeting process. Taken the open access to social network media into consideration, the utilization for intelligence purposes is no longer exclusive to nation-states or international organizations. Non-state actors or private individuals for that matter can today collect and analyze information and data from social network media and turn this into intelligence. One example of this is the site bellingcat.com where data from social network media from several contemporary conflicts are aggregated and analyzed.[13]

Some of what differentiates intelligence collection in social network media from other intelligence activities is the possibility for overt or covert "crowdsourcing" and things as mapping of existing narratives. Firstly looking at crowdsourcing it is a neologism between the terms "crowd" and "outsourcing." According to journalist Jeff Howe, who invented the term in 2006, crowdsourcing represents the act of a company or institution taking a function once performed by employees and outsourcing it to an undefined (and generally large) network of people in the form of an open call. This can take the form of peer-production (when the job is performed collaboratively), but is also often undertaken by sole individuals. The fact that social network media platforms (e.g., YouTube, Wikipedia, iStockphoto or InnoCentive) are successful, prove that normal people are willing to create content or to solve problems on the internet (Howe 2006a, 2006b). Something that can also be exploited in connection with conflicts for intelligence purposes either overt or covert. Second looking at narratives in social network media it is to be understood as the identification and mapping of existing narratives (of multiple actors) related to the conflict at hand in social network media and amongst key audiences and stakeholders, whether they are in the crisis-area or not. For example IS's narrative as it is projected through multiple social network media platforms, how it is received at further projected in other networks. In terms of intelligence analysis of social network media content it can include but are not limited to Trend-, Network-, Sentiment-, Geo-, Content-, Behavioral-, Systemic, Information and Target Audience Analysis, all contributing to understanding of the information environment as a component of cyber space.

Social network media analysis is therefore a strategic tool for uncovering insights into posted content, trends, networks and online behavior of audiences and other stakeholders. In the context of systemic intelligence collection and analysis, it offers a detailed picture of networks, actors, and related communication (interaction), with the help of monitoring tools, all of which has to be tailored to gain a comprehensive understanding of the social network media information environment. It also provides possibilities for mapping who the disseminators, influencers or key opinion-makers are and how they drive the conversation around topics of interest, and people's conversations and actions on-line that can be mined for insights and understanding. What also makes social media particularly interesting within an intelligence context is the possibility for collection of real-time data—depending on the speed of monitoring and analysis software. In addition to that, social network media allows for intelligence collection and analysis without boots on the ground, or even physical presence in the area of interest (theatre of operations). This feature of social network media (intelligence) makes it particularly interesting from an "remote warfare" point of view, which is when access to an operational area is initially contested or even impossible for several reasons (political mandate, Rules of Engagement (RoE), for security reasons or lack of capability), or when mostly non-state actors desire to create effects within a conflict area. Basically it provides options for leveraging online sharing and conversations in a "theatre of operation," which ultimately can lead to engagement with, or targeting of, current and future audiences and influencers.

Targeting

Targeting is not per say an activity in itself. It can be described as the guidance concerning the coordination of target nominations (targets and target audiences) in support of the creation of desired effects. It is a process to coordinate and synchronize the desired effects with the other activities, conducted in or through social network media, which should create the effects in time and space. Targeting as a process is therefore directly linked to Intelligence, Cyber Operations and Propaganda. The use of social network media for intelligence allows for more accurate monitoring, tracking and targeting of potential persons/personas, groups, nodes or networks, platforms and content of interest (for example, mapping of existing narratives and actual messaging). Intelligence collected thereby supports the nomination of targets—be that social media profiles, sites, accounts, computers behind these (system level), where to place information (words and images) and other content, influence conversations, how to link things and or directly address target audiences in order to influence their perception, attitude and ultimately behavior (online and offline). Finally intelligence collected from social network media can be used for identifying and nominating targets in the physical domain based on geo-tacked pictures, updates/postings and more. Conversely can information from social network media conversations also be used for "Battle Damage Assessment" (BDA) in order to verify the effect of traditional employment of weapon systems (e.g., air delivered munitions, artillery or car bombs, etc.).

Cyber operations

Cyber operations can generally be divided into three separate but complementary activities; Computer Network Attack (CAN), Computer Network Exploitation

(CNE) and Computer Network Defence (CND).[14] The first two can furthermore be categorized as "offensive" and the third as "defensive." The offensive operations referees in this contest primarily to activities associated with "computer network attack" (CNA), as described in the in the cyber-warfare definition discussed earlier. This can include Distributed Denial of Service (DDoS) attacks on websites (example Blog), breaching (hacking) of password protected chat sites, emails or cell-phones with the purpose of later exposure of the content, intrusion on news agencies cable news and altering news stories, or altering content and imagery on example a Facebook profile, etc. It can also be a question of "pinching" the identity information like usernames and passwords from people unsuspecting trying to gain access to specific sites. It can, however, also be a question of intrusion into example databases in order to undetected extract information for intelligence purposes, also known as "computer network exploitation" (CNE).[15] All of these "offensive" activities can be conducted in and through social network media by all types of actors, state as well as non-state, and is typically aimed at technically preventing other actors from using specific social network media platforms, at least temporarily. This can be to prevent other actors from communicating with each other, coordinating and synchronizing actions in time and space, accessing information or distribution of messages and propaganda. In the case of the latter it can be an act of propaganda in itself to deface a social network media account.

Cyber operations can, however, also be of a defensive character. Defensive cyber operations are in this context about the protection of own social network media platforms, sties, profiles and accounts in the form of "computer network defense" (CND). At the technical or systemic level this can include "Information Assurance" (IA), meaning the continuous efforts to ensure the integrity of information on own networks (e.g., social network media in this context). At the human level defence refers to "Operational Security" (OPSEC) and "Counter Intelligence" (CI) to detect and prevent the revilement of sensitive or classified information on social network media accounts and attempts to conduct espionage in or through own networks and against individuals. The latter is widespread as it is often seen that the fake LinkedIn and Facebook accounts are used for sending invitations to connect to military or civil servants.[16] Defensive activities can include the use of example encryption-, anti-tracking- and IP-concealing-software in connection with social network media (example the TOR project).[17]

Propaganda

The largest utility for using social network media for "military" activities exists within propaganda, which is closely related to cross-media communication and strategic narratives. Propaganda refers in this context to activities associated with the use of media in order to influence a target audience's value and belief system, perceptions, emotions, motives, reasoning, or behavior. It is used to induce or reinforce perceptions, attitudes and behaviors favorable to the originator's objectives, either directly or indirectly. This can be done both overtly and covertly in and through social network media. In connection with the latter it is sometimes combined with "black operations" or "false flag tactics," which can involve untruthful attribution of information or the source behind specific information (content) or outlets (social network media platforms or accounts).[18] The Target audiences can be governments, organizations, groups, and individuals.[19] Either directly or through networks they belong to or are a part of. Propaganda can also include activities like deception and subversion (Pomerantsev 2014). Utilizing cross-media communication methods propaganda conducted in and through social network media can be exponentially more effective, in combination with traditional means of communication and media, than more classical on-way communication means.

Command and control

Lastly social network media can be used for Command and Control (C2)[20] purposes. In respect to social network media, C2 is about internal communication, information sharing, coordination and synchronisation of actions and facilitates more agile decision making. Command and Control generally applies to endeavors undertaken by collections of individuals and organizations of vastly different characteristics and sizes for many different purposes. The most interesting and challenging endeavors are those that involve a collection of military and civilian sovereign entities with overlapping interests that can best be met by sharing information and collaboration that cuts across the boundaries of the individual entities (Alberts and Hayes 2011). This is often the case when looking at, for example, non-state actors, who like opposition groups in Syria, have a need for distributing information, internally and externally, and for coordinating and synchronising actions, and in some cases giving commands or direction and guidance (D&G) to other groups or entities. Particularly when these groups or entities have no formal structure or are dispersed over large geographical areas, social network media can afford them with means and capabilities to conduct C2 activities. They have, though, to be very cognisant of operational security (OPSEC) issues.

Command and Control is scalable. At an organizational level, C2 is about shaping the organization and determining its purpose and priorities. Information and output from this process can, of course, be distributed through social network media to the rest of the organization. The more interesting elements are, however, at the "mission" level. At the mission level, C2 is about employing the organization's assets and capabilities (people, systems, material and the relationships between them) toward a specific objective or task.[21]

Conclusion

Over the course of the last more than fifteen years from NATO air-campaign over Serbian and Kosovo over Iraq, Afghanistan, Libya to present-day Syria and

Ukraine, social network media has become ever more pervasive in conflicts—arguably affecting the character of contemporary conflicts. One observable tendency is that the emergence of social network media has given all actors and stakeholders, as well as apparent irrelevant third parties, a much more direct access to the target audiences, whose perception and behavior they for some reason desire to influence. Actors are thereby no longer solely dependent on traditional media outlets to reach the target audiences. Social network media are, however, not just another media platform that can be used to disseminate information or propaganda, in the form of messages and images. They are also interactive, can facilitate dialogue, and content can be redistributed as well as altered by the users and new contexts can emerge through so-called User Generated Content (UCG), which again can inform how a conflict is perceived by various actors and stakeholders leading to behavior change. There is also a tendency for the traditional news media to lose access to conflict areas leaving social network media even more important. Mechanisms actors' using social network media in contemporary conflicts seem to be very aware of and exploit strategically.

Changed conditions under which contemporary wars and conflicts are conducted; enhanced digital connectivity, democratisation of technology, urbanization and more tech-savvy populations has also led to the emergence of "virtual theatres." Non-state actors that can conduct "remote warfare" and "social net-war" having effect both inside and outside of a conflict area not possible before.

Social network media is, however, not only a potent tool for creating informational effects on audience's perception and ultimately their behavior. Social network media are also used for achieving direct "cyber-operations" effects through hacking and attacking opponent's and other stakeholder's accounts and profiles.

Regardless, however, of ones interpretation of cyber warfare and view on to which degree the use of social network media in contemporary conflicts at all is "warfare," it remains a challenge for all actors; but also a reality that must be dealt with. Especially within contemporary conflicts, where the threshold for where war can be said to a reality is not reached, and where the lines between peace and war is blurred and the activity, whatever it is, have no easily identifiable start and end. The use of social network media in contemporary conflicts is therefore not just a question of petty disinformation, forgeries, lies, leaks, and cyber sabotage normally associated with "information warfare." It is, as the case studies also indicated, a question of a strategic use of social network media for creating a series of "military" effects. Furthermore as all of the activities ranging from targeting, over intelligence and propaganda to cyber operations and command and control are conducted in concert with "real-life" military activities, but in a parallel domain, it makes it a subset of cyber warfare, which now is an integral part of contemporary conflicts.

The developments have empowered multiple state and non-state, leading to a redistribution of power in the international system and in the operational environment. This operational environment is as a result changing as well. The traditional notion of "battle space" is challenged to a point where you no longer are able to only talk about a "theatre of operation" or a "joint operational area" in their traditional geographical sense, even though it still exists, but you also have to talk about a "virtual theatre" which in principle is worldwide. With the strategic use of social network media in contemporary conflicts for "military" purposes to create effects both online and offline on information itself (content), systemically on software and potentially also on hardware, as well as on actors perceptions and behavior, today we see cyber warfare also effectively being waged in and through social network media.

Notes

1 Social network media can in this context be defined as:

> Social network media refers to internet connected platforms and software used to collect, store, aggregate, share, process, discuss or deliver user-generated and general media content, that can influence knowledge, perception and thereby directly or indirectly prompt behaviour as a result of interaction.

2 See ex. National Defence Strategy of Estonia for an explanation of "psychological defense," p. 23, at: www.kaitseministeerium.ee/files/kmin/img/files/KM_riigikaitse_strateegia_eng(2).pdf (accessed April 2, 2015).

3 See NATO CoE for StratCom "Analysis of Russia's Information Campaign," at: www.stratcomcoe.org/~/media/SCCE/Ukraine_report_StratComCOE_Public_Fin2.ashx (accessed February 9, 2015), and Pomerantsev (OpCit).

4 www.guardian.co.uk/world/2011/jun/13/syrian-lesbian-blogger-tom-macmaster (accessed February 6, 2013).

5 "Digital Native" refers to the generation born into the digital era that therefore has a greater understanding of its concepts.

6 Syrian Electronic Army (SEA) is just one of many groupings conducting "cyber activities" on behalf of or in support of the regime or the different opposition groupings. SEA was created in early 2011 to fight a cyber war on behalf of the regime. It does, however, claim to independent. The SEA targets both websites and social network media accounts of opposition groups and interests and of Western and Arab news sources. The SEA has also engaged in Computer Network Attack (CNA) to include defacing and DDOS attacks and replacing content with centralized pro-regime messaging. The SEAs stated mission is to "counter the media and information war against Syria." Another regime grouping is the "Electronic National Defence Force" (ENDF) associated with the regime loyal paramilitant group National Defence Force (NDF). ENDF's declared mission is "dedicated to crushing the pages of the revolution and their NATO agents/clients."

7 SecDev Group (2013a): Flash Note Syria—Syrian electronic Army Goes on the Offensive, Intensifies Targeting of Opposition Facebook Pages. Page 1. Published online 4 June 2013, at: www.secdev.com (accessed April 4, 2014).

8

> A botnet is a collection of computers, connected to the Internet, that interact to accomplish some distributed task. Although such a collection of computers can be used for useful and constructive applications, the term botnet typically refers to such a system designed and used for illegal purposes. Such systems are composed of compromised machines that are assimilated without their owner's knowledge. The compromised machines are referred to as drones or zombies, the malicious software running on them as "bot."
> (source: www.shadowserver.org/wiki/pmwiki.php/Information/Botnets)

9 SecDev Group: Syria Cyber Watch. Published online 25 November 2012, at: www.secdev.com (accessed April 4, 2014).

10 See US Department of State, at: www.state.gov/r/pa/prs/ps/2014/09/232266.htm (accessed February 13, 2015).

11 Astroturfing is in this context to be understood as:

> the act of creating a small interest organization or a grouping many seemingly individual people, that never existed, and making it appear to represent something popular for the purpose of promoting a particular entity or cause in order to boost its image online with fake comments, paid-for reviews, made-up claims and testimonials.
> [A play on grassroots in the sense of a popular movement originating among the common people, ultimately from AstroTurf, a brand of artificial grass].
> (Source: Description is derived from proposed definitions on http://da.urbandictionary.com/define.php?term=astroturfing. Accessed May 13, 2015)

12 See:www.dailymail.co.uk/news/article-2946587/Jordanian-pilot-burned-death-sickening-ISIS-video-heavily-sedated-unaware-happen-him.html (accessed December 2, 2015).

13 See: www.bellingcat.com/ (accessed February 12, 2015).

14 According to NATO doctrine on Information Operations CAN, CNE and CND can be described as follows:

> **Computer Network Attack.** Software and hardware vulnerabilities allow computers, storage devices and networking equipment to be attacked through insertion of malicious code, such as viruses, or through more subtle manipulation of data, changing the characteristics and performance of the devices or the expression and display of the information contained therein. This capability is enhanced by the increasing use of commercial off-the-shelf software in military systems (including social network media technology).
>
> **"Computer Network Exploitation.** (…) the ability to get information about computers and computer networks, by gaining access to information hosted on those and the ability to make use of the information and the computers/computer networks" [without being detected].
>
> **Computer Network Defence.** The purpose of CND is to protect against CNA and CNE. CND is action taken to protect against disruption, denial, degradation or destruction of information resident in computers and computer networks or the computers and networks themselves. CND is essential to maintain decision-making capability; as well as maintaining a defensive posture, it will use monitoring and penetration protection techniques to detect, characterise, and respond to an attack, instigating containment and recovery action as required.
> (Source: NATO Allied Joint Publication—AJP 3.10 Information Operations, NATO 2009, 1–11. https://info.publicintelligence.net/NATO-IO.pdf (accessed February 9, 2015)

15 For more on computer network attack and social media, see ex. Jaitner, Margarita: "Exercising Power in Social Media," in Jari Rantapelkonen and Mirva Salminen (eds), *The Fog of Cyber Defence*. National Defence University Department of Leadership and Military Pedagogy. Publication Series 2. Article Collection no. 10. Helsinki, Finland, 2013.

16 See Simon Tomlinson, 2013a. "Hackers Posing as Beautiful Women Sent 'Selfies' to Syrian Rebels on Skype … and Stole Battle Plans with Hidden Viruses." *Daily Mail*, at: www.dailymail.co.uk/news/article-2937644/Hackers-posing-beautiful-women-sent-selfies-Syrian-rebels-using-online-dating-sites-stole-battle-plans-hidden-viruses.html (accessed April 2, 2015).

17 See: http://en.wikipedia.org/wiki/Tor_(anonymity_network) (accessed December 2, 2015).

18 For more on attribution of messaging, see: Thomas Elkjer Nissen (2012): Black and White and 256 Shades of Grey in Between—Reflections on the question of Attribution of Psychological Operations. RDDC Brief, March 2012, at: http://forsvaret.dk/FAK/ENG/PUBLICATIONS/Pages/default.aspx (accessed March 26, 2014).
19 See: http://en.wikipedia.org/wiki/Psychological_warfare (accessed March 25, 2014).
20 Command and Control in NATO is defined as: "Command and control (C2) encompasses the exercise of authority and direction by a commander over assigned and attached forces in the accomplishment of the mission." The doctrine goes on to state that:

> Command includes both the authority and responsibility for effectively using available resources to achieve desired outcomes. Command at all levels is the art of motivating and directing people and organizations into action. The art of command lies in conscious and skilful exercise of command authority through decision-making, and leadership. Using judgment and intuition acquired from experience, training, study, and creative thinking; commanders visualise the situation and make sound and timely decisions. Effective decision-making combines judgment with information; it requires knowing if to decide, when to decide, and what to decide. Timeliness is the speed required to maintain the initiative over the adversary.
>
> (Source: NATO Allied Joint Doctrine (AJP) 03 (B)—Operations, paragraph 0147 + 0148)

21 NATO System Analysis and Studies (SAS) research project 050: Exploring New Command and Control Capabilities. Final Report, January 2006, 5–7.

References

Alberts, David S. and Richard E. Hayes. *Understanding Command and Control*. The Command and Control Research Program (CCRP), at: www.dodccrp.org (accessed December 2, 2015).
Bartlett, Jamie. 2014. "ISIS and their so-called social media genius." *The Telegraph*, at: http://blogs.telegraph.co.uk/technology/jamiebartlett/100013899/isis-and-their-so-called-social-media-genius/ (accessed June 30, 2014).
Berger, J.M. 2014. "How ISIS Games Twitter." *The Atlantic*, at: www.theatlantic.com/international/archive/2014/06/isis-iraq-twitter-social-media-strategy/372856/ (accessed June 16, 2014).
Bloom, Dan. 2015. "ISIS Use US Journalist Hostage as Focus of Latest Terror Campaign on Social Media by Hijacking Discussions Using #StenensHeadInObamas Hands hsahtag." *Daily Mail*, at: www.dailymail.co.uk/news/article-2734534/ISIS-use-US-journalist-hostage-focus-latest-terror-campaign-social-media-hijacking-discussions-using-StevensHeadInObamasHands-hashtag.html (accessed February 13, 2015).
Borkowski, Mark. 2014. "ISIS and the Propaganda War: How the Social-Savvy Extremists are Dominating the Headlines." *The Drum*, at: www.thedrum.com/opinion/2014/06/25/isis-and-propaganda-war-how-social-savvy-extremists-are-dominating-headlines (accessed June 27, 2014).
Clayton, Mark. 2012. "Syrian's Cyberwars: Using Social Media Against Dissent." *The CS Monitor*, at: www.csmonitor.com/USA/2012/0725/Syria-s-cyberwars-using-social-media-against-dissent (accessed July 25, 2012).
Farwell, James and Darby Arakelian. 2013. *A Better Syria Option: Cyber War. The National Interest*, at: http://nationalinterest.org/commentary/better-syria-option-cyber-war-9003 (accessed December 18, 2013).

Fischer, Max. 2013. "Syrian Hackers Claim AP Hack that Tipped Stock Market by $136 Billion. Is it Terrorism?" *Washington Post*, April 23, at: www.washingtonpost.com/blogs/worldviews/wp/2013/04/23/syrian-hackers-claim-ap-hack-that-tipped-stock-market-by-136-billion-is-it-terrorism/ (accessed February 11, 2015).

Frizpatrick, Alex. 2012. *Social Media Becoming Online Battlefield in Syria*, at: http://mashable.com/2012/08/09/social-media-syria/ (accessed December 2, 2015).

Goldman, Lisa. 2012. *In Syria's Civil War, Cyber Attacks are the "New Modern Warfare"*, at: www.techpresident.com (accessed December 2, 2015).

Howe, Jeff. 2006a. "The Rise of Crowdsourcing." *The Wired Magazine*, at: www.wired.com/wired/archive/14.06/crowds.html (accessed March 26, 2014).

Howe, Jeff. 2006b. "Crowdsourcing: A Definition." *The Wired Magazine*, at: http://crowdsourcing.typepad.com/cs/2006/06/crowdsourcing_a.html (accessed March 26, 2014).

Kaldor, Mary. 2013. "In Defence of New Wars." *Stability* 2 (1): 4. DOI: http://dx.doi.org/10.5334/sta.at.

Kilcullen, David. 2013. *Out of the Mountains—The Coming Age of the Urban Guerrilla*. New York: Oxford University Press.

Kingsley, Patrick. 2014. "Who is Behind ISIS's Terrifying Online Propaganda Operation?" *Guardian*, June 23, at: www.theguardian.com/world/2014/jun/23/who-behind-isis-propaganda-operation-iraq (accessed June 26, 2014).

Liff, Adam P. 2012. "Cyberwar: A New 'Absolute Weapon'? The Proliferation of Cyberwarfare Capabilities and Interstate War." *The Journal of Strategic Studies* 35 (3).

Matthews, Dylan. 2014. "The Surreal Infographics ISIS is Producing, Translated." *VOX*, at: www.vox.com/2014/6/24/5834068/the-iraqi-rebels-make-annual-reports-with-infographics-we-translated (accessed June 27, 2014).

National Defence Strategy of Estonia for an explanation of "Psychological Defence": 23, at: www.kaitseministeerium.ee/files/kmin/img/files/KM_riigikaitse_strateegia_eng(2).pdf (accessed April 2, 2015).

NATO CoE for StratCom "Analysis of Russia's Information Campaign", at: www.stratcomcoc.org/~/media/SCCE/Ukraine_report_StratComCOE_Public_Fin2.ashx (accessed February 9, 2015).

NATO System Analysis and Studies (SAS) research project 050: *Exploring New Command and Control Capabilities*. Final Report, January 2006: 5–7.

Nissen, Thomas Elkjer. 2012. *Black and White and 256 Shades of Grey in Between—Reflections on the question of Attribution of Psychological Operations*. RDDC Brief, at: http://forsvaret.dk/FAK/ENG/PUBLICATIONS/Pages/default.aspx (accessed March 26, 2014).

Nissen, Thomas Elkjer. 2015. *#TheWeaponizationOfSocialMedia*. Royal Danish Defence College.

Reilly, Richard Byrne. 2014. *Iraq Cracks Down Further on Social Media—But Leaves ISIS-Affiliated Web Sites Alone*, at: http://venturebeat.com/2014/06/23/iraq-cracks-down-further-on-social-media-but-leaves-isis-affiliated-web-sites-alone/ (accessed December 2, 2015).

Rid, Thomas. 2012. "Cyber War Will Not Take Place." *Journal of Strategic Studies* 35 (1).

Pomerantsev, Peter. 2014. "Russia and the Menace of Unreality." *The Atlantic*, at: www.theatlantic.com/international/archive/2014/09/russia-putin-revolutionizing-information-warfare/379880/ (accessed February 9, 2015).

Powell, Rose. 2014. "Cats and Kalashnikovs: Behind the ISIL Social Media Strategy." *The Sydney Morning Herald*, at: www.smh.com.au/world/cats-and-kalashnikovs-behind-the-isil-social-media-strategy-20140625-zsk50.html (accessed June 26, 2014).

SecDev Group. November 25, 2012. *Syria Cyber Watch*, at: www.secdev.com (accessed April 4, 2014).

SecDev Group April 23, 2013. *Flash Note Syria—Syrian Regime Tightens Access to Secure Online Communications*, at: www.secdev.com (accessed April 4, 2014).

SecDev Group. May 8, 2013. *Flash Note Syria—The Internet in Syria—Down, But Not Out*, at: www.secdec.com (accessed April 4, 2014).

SecDev Group. June 4, 2013. *Flash Note Syria—Syrian Electronic Army Goes on the Offensive, Intensifies Targeting of Opposition Facebook Pages*, at: www.secdev.com (accessed April 4, 2014).

SecDev Group September 30, 2013. *Flash Note Syria—Syria's National Defence Forces take the Battle to Cyberspace*, at: www.secdev.com (accessed April 4, 2014).

SecDev Group. October 8, 2013. *Flash Note Syria—Syria's Hacker Wars*, at: www.secdev.com (accessed April 4, 2014).

Sloan, Elinor C. 2012. *Modern Military Strategy: An Introduction*. New York: Routledge.

Tomlinson, Simon. 2013a. "Hackers Posing as Beautiful Women Sent 'Selfies' to Syrian Rebels on Skype ... and Stole Battle Plans with Hidden Viruses." *Daily Mail*, at: www.dailymail.co.uk/news/article-2937644/Hackers-posing-beautiful-women-sent-selfies-Syrian-rebels-using-online-dating-sites-stole-battle-plans-hidden-viruses.html(accessed April 2, 2015).

Townsend, Mark. 2014. "Jihad in a Social Media Age: How Can the West Win an Online War?" *Guardian*. August 23, at: www.theguardian.com/world/2014/aug/23/jihad-social-media-age-west-win-online-war (accessed August 24, 2014).

US Department of State. 2014, at: www.state.gov/r/pa/prs/ps/2014/09/232266.htm (accessed February 13, 2015).

Waxmann, Matthew C. 2011. "Cyber-Attacks and the Use of Force: Back to the Future of Article 2(4)." *Yale Journal of International Law* 36.

Zambelis, Chris. 2012. *Information Wars—Assessing the Social Media Battlefield in Syria*. The International Relations and Security Network, at: www.isn.ethz.ch/ (accessed August 22, 2012).

9 Politics and the development of legal norms in cyber space

Anders Henriksen

Introduction

In late 2014, a group calling itself "Guardians of Peace" orchestrated a campaign of cyber attacks against Sony Pictures Entertainment that destroyed systems and stole large quantities of personal and commercial data, such as unreleased movies. In addition, the group threatened anyone who were to attend the opening of a movie—*The Interview*—about North Korea that included an assassination of its ruler Kim Jong-Un (Carr 2013). The United States blamed North Korea for the attack (Federal Bureau of Investigations 2014) and responded by ordering a new round of sanctions against North Korean government officials and its defense industry (Associated Press 2015). The American response was the first ever response to a concrete cyber attack. North Korea, however, denied any involvement in the hacking of Sony and for their part accused the United States of being responsible for cutting of the nation's already very limited connections to the Internet (Fackler 2014).

The Sony hack and the American responses thereto illustrate the extent to the threat from cyber attacks and other forms of harmful cyber incidents (Schreier 2015; Arquilla and Ronfeldt 1993; Kello 2013).[1] It is becoming one of the most pressing national security concerns and why a multitude of national governmental agencies are currently engaged in developing strategies and guidelines for both the offensive and defensive use of computer network operations.[2] One of the more pressing issues with regard to the ongoing efforts to develop cyber strategies relates to the identification of the legal landscape that governs both the offensive and defensive use of computer network operations that may have an effect on the territory of another state, including on the latter's electronic infrastructure. In short, to formulate a proper strategy in cyber space states need to know what offensive activities are lawful and how a targeted state is allowed to respond defensively.

Interestingly, among its users, in its early years, cyber space was perceived of as a *sui generis* domain outside the reach of individual states. In contrast to the physical domains (land, sea, air and space), cyber space was supposed to be governed by the users themselves. In its 1996 "Declaration of Independence of Cyberspace," for example, the *Electronic Frontier Foundation* had this to say to all the states of the world:

You are not welcome among us. You have no sovereignty where we gather.... We did not invite you. You do not know us, nor do you know our world. Cyberspace does not lie within your borders.... You claim there are problems among us that you need to solve. You use this claim as an excuse to invade our precincts. Many of these problems don't exist. Where there are real conflicts, where there are wrongs, we will identify them and address them by our means. We are forming our own Social Contract. This governance will arise according to the conditions of our world, not yours. Our world is different.

(Barlow 1996)

Today, however, in an age of Trojan horses, Distributed Denial of Service Attacks and Botnets, no one would any more seriously make such an argument. Indeed, the virtual domain never became self-regulated, it never became borderless and states never became absent. If anything, states have become ever more present in cyber space and everyone agrees that the fundamental principles of international law also apply in the virtual domain (Goldsmith 2006).[3]

The overall agreement that international law (also) applies in cyber space is not, however, yet matched by universal consensus on how, exact, that law must be applied. To legal historians, of course, this is not surprising. New technologies and new modes of coercion have a tendency to challenge existing frameworks and led to confusion about the proper application of the law. When the airplane was invented and introduced into the military arsenal of states in the 1920s, questions were raised about the compatibility of aerial warfare with the existing laws of war. Similar questions were raised following the invention and early use of nuclear weapons in the 1940s and 1950s and in recent years, the emergence of remotely operated vehicles, such as armed drones, has yet again made lawyers and policymakers debate the application of existing rules and principles to new technologies.

The purpose of this chapter is to provide an overview of some of the existing uncertainties regarding the application of international law to cyber operations conducted in peacetime and to link those uncertainties to the ongoing domestic efforts to develop national strategies for cyber space. Hence, the object of this piece is not to offer a "black-letter law" analysis of the exact contours of the legal landscape that governs computer network operations but instead to bring attention to some of the implications of the difficulties of doing so. To be more precise, the article will make two interrelated arguments. First of all, it will argue that it is still fairly uncertain how computer network operations fit the existing legal framework for lawful and unlawful interferences in times of peace. Second, building on work done by, among others, Professor Matthew Waxmann (Waxman 2011), the article will argue that these uncertainties can be as much about politics as they can be about law. For that reason, the ongoing efforts in the Nordic countries to identify the proper legal norms for conducting computer network operations should be part of a much larger and more principled political and strategic debate about cyber security in the twenty-first century. Hence, rather than simply asking their governmental lawyers how international law governs cyber space, policymakers should start by asking themselves what kind of cyber space and therefore also what sort of legal interpretations they prefer.

The article proceeds as follows. Section II introduces the international legal framework that assists in separating lawful from unlawful international interferences and in determining the character of the response that is available to a state that is the target of a particular unlawful activity. On the basis of that overview, Article III will discuss why it is not only difficult to apply the legal framework to computer network operations but also unlikely that international agreement on the application of at least some of the principles will be obtained anytime soon. Lastly, Section IV will offer some thoughts on the implications of the latter conclusion for the ongoing efforts to formulate national strategies for cyber space.

The international law of interferences

In practical terms, the international legal regime that regulates the measures states may resort to against each other outside times of armed conflict can be conceived of as a hierarchy consisting of various thresholds. The first and clearly most important of those is the threshold that differentiates between *those measures and activities that are lawful and those that are not*. Concretely, the line is drawn between, on the one hand, activities that constitute a *violation of sovereignty* of another state and those that do not. Mutual state respect for territorial sovereignty is: "an essential foundation of international relations" according to the *Corfu Canal Case* (UK vs Albania 1949), and with a few exceptions[4] (Parks 1990; Silver 2005), *any* state activity in another state constitutes *prima facie* violations of the latter's sovereignty. Hence, if a state sends it agents into another state in order to secure the arrest of a suspected criminal in the absence of consent from the territorial state, it will violate that state's sovereignty. Just like the sending of an airplane into the airspace of another state without permission will violate the territorial state's airspace and constitute a violation of sovereignty.

If an activity that violates the sovereignty of another state attempts to coerce the state—that is, to make it change its policy—in a matter in which it is permitted to decide freely, the violation of sovereignty will also constitute an *unlawful intervention*[5] (Jamnejad and M. Wood 2009: 348) Under international law, states are entitled to freely determine their own political, economic, cultural and social systems, to develop their own foreign policies and to exercise permanent sovereignty over its natural resources.[6] States also have the right to: "free access to information and to develop fully, without interference, their system of information and mass media and to use their information media in order to promote their political, social, economic and cultural interests and aspirations."[7] Furthermore, no state must resort to subversive activities against other states that promote, encourage or support, direct or indirect, "rebellious or secessionist activities," or seeks to "disrupt the unity or to undermine or subvert the political order" according to UNGA "Declaration on the Inadmissibility of Intervention and Interference in the Internal Affairs of States."[8]

To the extent a state's efforts to coerce another state involves the use of force, the former will not only be guilty of an unlawful intervention but also violate the *prohibition on the use of force* in Article 2(4) of the 1945 UN Charter. According to that article: "All Members shall refrain in their international relations from the threat or use of force against the territorial integrity or political independence of any state, or in any other manner inconsistent with the Purposes of the United Nations."

Lastly, if an instance of the use of force is particularly serious it may constitute an armed attack under Article 51 of the UN Charter.[9] However, according to case-law from the International Court of Justice, only the gravest forms of the use of force" will qualify[10] and so-called "frontier incidents" falls outside the concept of an armed attack.[11]

The hierarchy of lawful and unlawful international interferences not only assists in determining when certain measures violate international law, but also when and how a state that is targeted by a particular unlawful interference may respond in order to bring the latter to a halt. Not surprisingly, the higher one moves up the hierarchy of unlawful interferences, the more serious the breach of international law and the more authority for the targeted state to respond. In practical terms, the law operates with a clear distinction between, on the one hand, those interferences that are so intense and serious as to qualify as an armed attack under Article 51 and, on the other, all those interferences that, while still constituting a violation of international law, are less serious. While the former triggers a right to employ necessary and proportionate armed means in self-defense, the latter form merely triggers the application of other, less drastic, responses, the primary of which are proportionate counter-measures (Henriksen 2015: 323–51).

The difficulties of applying the law to operations in cyber space

On the basis of the overview provided above, it would appear to be a simple task for those states that are in the process of formulating national cyber strategies to determine how cyber operations are governed by international law. For all manner and purposes, the analysis boils down to the lawyers' art of drawing analogies and determining how cyber operations fit the hierarchy of lawful and unlawful interferences and the principles for responding thereto. So when does computer network operations cross the threshold that separates lawful from unlawful activities and become a violation of sovereignty? When does an operation in cyber space constitute an unlawful intervention or an instance of a prohibited use of force or even an armed attack that may trigger the resort to self-defense? And how should one translate the principles for the lawful exercise of self-defense or countermeasures to incidents in cyber space?

Unfortunately, despite the existence of an rapidly expanding literature on the "international law of cyber space"[12] and a number of recent international initiatives within the area, such as reports by a United Nations Group of Governmental

Experts on Developments in the Field of Information and Telecommunications in the Context of International Security[13] and the publication in 2013 by a group of international legal experts of a manual on the international law applicable to cyber warfare—the so-called Tallinn Manual" (Schmitt 2013),[14] the analogies remain anything but easy to draw. Obviously, this is primarily due to the fundamental difference between operations in cyber space and operations in the "real" world. Unlike the physical domains, cyber space is primarily a virtual and electronic domain in which humans and machines communicate. Hence, operations in cyber space are inherently non-kinetic in the sense that one cannot (at least for now) create a direct physical effect by pressing a button on a dashboard. In contrast to the firing of a missile or the detonation of a bomb, cyber operations can only create physical destruction in an *indirect* manner and it is that non-violent/non-kinetic character that makes cyber operations a hard fit for at least some of the traditional categories of either lawful or unlawful interferences mentioned above.

As a result of the difficulties in drawing the required analogies, a number of highly important issues remain unresolved. For example, it is not yet resolved when a computer network operation constitutes a violation of sovereignty of another state.[15] As indicated earlier, while as a point of departure at least, under a traditional understanding of the law, all state activities on the territory of another state violates the latter state's sovereignty, it is not entirely clear if *all* cyber activities on the "networks" of other states also constitute violations of sovereignty. Is there not, after all, a substantial difference between a state's physical presence, that is, in the form of agents or airplanes, and a "virtual" presence with electronic signals? (Ziolkowski 2013b: 459–89). The authors of the Tallinn Manual seem to think so when they conclude that a computer network operation only constitutes a violation of sovereignty if it causes a certain minimum of damage (Schmitt 2013: supra note 10, rule 1[6). The uncertainty about what constitutes a violation of sovereignty in cyber space is particularly relevant with regard to the issue of cyber espionage, a topic that has been receiving increasing attention lately.[16] While the act of collecting intelligence is usually proscribed under domestic law, its status is less clear in international law.[17] Although, the most prevalent view holds that intelligence gathering does not *in itself* violate international law unless it is aimed at certain individuals, documents or locations/facilities that are explicitly protected from such activities (Ziolkowski 2013b: 425–64),[18] it is worth noting that the traditional means whereby the actual spying is done, such as the unauthorized presence of foreign agents or airplanes on the territory of another state, would appear to constitute a violation of sovereignty (Ziolkowski 2013b: 457–59). However, if a mere unauthorized "virtual trespass" (Ziolkowski 2013b: 458) does not suffice, the whole "enterprise" of cyber espionage would not seem to be proscribed by international law.[19]

Another grey area of great importance relates to the determination of whether or not cyber attacks may constitute "force" as that concept is understood in *Article 2 (4) of the UN Charter* (Henriksen 2015: 344–45). The concept of "force" has been debated ever since the adoption of the Charter in 1945 and the prevailing view has always been that it only covers *armed* measures (Randelzhofer 2002: 112–17). It seems, in other words, that the Charter was intended to outlawing the use of certain *means*—armed force—and not coercion as such (Schmitt 2011: 573). So while non-armed means of coercion, such as economic and political measures, may violate the principle of non-intervention they cannot constitute "force" for the purposes of Article 2(4).[20] For instance, when the Charter was drafted, a Brazilian proposal to extend the reach of the prohibition on the use of force to economic sanctions did not find support,[21] and in *Nicaragua* the International Court of Justice did not find that fairly extensive economic pressure exerted by the United States against Nicaragua violated Article 2(4).[22] But to conclude that computer network attacks cannot constitute "force" for the purposes of the UN Charter will have fairly wide-ranging consequences for global stability and the maintenance of international peace and security. It would mean, for example, that a wide range of potentially very coercive and damaging activities like the widespread Destributed Denial of Service (DDOS) attacks that hit Estonia in 2007 would not be proscribed by the Charter.[23] And neither would very sophisticated and targeted cyber operations, such as the 2010 Stuxnet attack on the alleged Iranian nuclear enrichment program (Stark 2011; Borad *et al.* 2011).

The existing uncertainties about the application of at least some of the areas of international law to computer network operations is obviously a cause of much frustration to those states and governmental lawyers who are in the process of drafting national strategies for cyber space. But since we are probably still in the early stages in the evolution of "cyber coercion," it is likely that the years to come will bring more legal clarity to the field. As the states become more vocal—and certain—about how they themselves interpret the relevant parts of international law and international and national courts will decide concrete cases involving computer network operations, a least some of the interpretations and analogies will be easier to make.

Fundamental obstacles to achieving legal clarity are likely to remain, however. For one thing, the area is likely to remain shrouded in secrecy and in the absence of concrete and reliable information about the character of attacks that occur and the type of responses targeted states employ, it will always be difficult for lawyers to identify concrete cases upon which legal interpretations can be made.[24] A second and more important obstacle to achieving legal clarity has to do with the fact that at least some of the legal uncertainties are as much about distribution of power and differences in ideology as they are about law and legal interpretation. International law and international politics are inherently intertwined and whenever there is uncertainty about the proper interpretation of an international legal norm, politics will enter the fray. Since, for all manner and purposes, the answers to some of the existing legal questions about the extent to which computer network operations are regulated will decide how states are allowed to rely on computer network operations to pursue their foreign policy goals, we should not be surprised that the *legal* debate about these issues will also be perceived of as a vital *political* debate about the exertion of power and influence in cyber space as such. Clearly, the current uncertainties about the proper interpretation of important parts of international law within the cyber realm reflects a lack of political agreement among states on the extent to which cyber space can be used as a tool for the realization of foreign policy objectives. And on such questions, states are bound to disagree.

The link between legal interpretations and politics is, of course, not unique to the cyber context. States have historically interpreted their obligations under international law in furtherance of their national interests, and the strategic and political reliance on international law has always been particularly visible within the area of the regulation of the use of force. Here, states frequently rely on interpretations that reflect their strategic strengths and weaknesses. Hence, militarily weak and/or vulnerable states have usually relied on a very strict interpretation of the prohibition on the use of force in the Charter while stronger and/or less vulnerable states have done the opposite. As Matthew Waxman persuasively argues, the current debate about the proper application of the legal framework that governs computer network operations is simply the latest example of this recurring dynamic (Waxman 2011; Tiirmaa-Klaar 2013: 509–31). Within the cyber context, therefore, we should expect that states with different capabilities and vulnerabilities will disagree on the right interpretation of the legal framework. A state with a strong offensive cyber capability and a correspondingly low vulnerability to cyber attacks is likely to stress a legal interpretation that is different from a state that is highly vulnerable to attacks and at the same time has limited capability (ibid.: 456). For example, to the extent that a strong cyber capability will help alleviate an existing weakness in conventional military capability, it is unrealistic to expect militarily vulnerable states to agree to a wide-ranging prohibition on the employment of cyber-related capabilities, in particular if the states in question are not themselves very vulnerable to computer network operations.

But it is not only differences in capabilities and domestic vulnerability that will make it difficult to reach universal agreement on the application of important parts of international law to computer network operations. Of potentially equal importance are national differences with respect to more general notions of internet freedom and universal norms and values (Waxman 2011: 456). It is no secret that states differ on the extent to which openness and the free flow of information in cyber space is an inherent "good" worth protecting or a potential threat that must be curbed. While the West generally considers cyber space as a fundamentally positive contribution to the world that serves as an important tool for the spread of freedom and fundamental freedoms, other states are less positive. In some quarters of the world, most notably in places like China and in states around the Middle East, a free cyber space poses a threat to existing authoritarian governmental structures (Healey 2012: 7). The existing differences in attitude to openness and dissemination of ideas and expressions are bound to be expressed in different interpretations of the existing international legal framework and make it hard for states to find common ground (Waxman 2011: 456–57; Healey 2012). For instance, states that consider the free flow of information and ideas to be detrimental to the efforts to sustain an existing authoritarian political order will be more prone to interpret the law in a more government-friendly manner than a well-functioning liberal democracy.

Not surprisingly, the major players in the world are keenly aware of the link between legal interpretation and the distribution of power and politics and that the strategic and therefore also legal battle for the future of cyber space has begun. The United States, for example, have for a long time been trying to influence the interpretation of international law in accordance with its strategic goals and domestic vulnerabilities. As Matthew Waxman demonstrates, the fact that the United States is militarily very strong but at the same time very vulnerable to hostile computer network operations against its critical infrastructure is reflected in the American interpretations of what constitutes a use of "force" in cyber space (Waxman 2011: 448). American strength and weakness within the realm of cyber espionage is also likely to manifest itself in the manner in which the USA will interpret the relevant parts of international law. The American vulnerability to industrial espionage and the theft of intellectual property is likely to influence the extent to which the USA will be ready to conclude that such forms of espionage should be considered a national security concern and lawful under international law (Ziolkowski 2013: 459–62). Just like the advanced cyber capabilities of its intelligence services, most notably the National Security Agency, is likely to have an impact on the way the Americans interpret other parts of international law. The Americans are not the only ones engaged in the legal/strategic battle for the future of cyber space, however. Through, among other things, the Shanghai Cooperation Organization (SCO), states like Russia and China are working to advance *their* preferred interpretation of the international norms that apply or ought to apply in cyber space (Upadhyay 2013). Not surprisingly, SCO stresses the importance of ensuring national control over cyber systems and content, including speech which may be considered politically destabilizing. In a September 2014 summit declaration on cyber-related security issues, the organization stated that the member states will continue to exercise oversight of the Internet on their territories without foreign interference, which can be linked with the aim to have better control over the flow and content of information. The declaration reaffirms that governing "the Internet in their respective national segments" is regarded as a sovereign right of states.[25] In recent years, the strategic/legal battle for the future of cyber space has also found its way into the United Nations where a Group of Governmental Experts on Developments in the Field of Information and Telecommunications in the Context of International Security has met and issued a number of reports on the issue.[26]

Conclusion

The existing uncertainties about the application of parts of international law to computer network operations is bound to be a cause of frustration to those states and governmental lawyers who are in the process of drafting national strategies for cyber space. The uncertainties should also, however, be considered a welcomed opportunity for states to further their strategic and political interests in cyber space. Hence, for domestic policymakers the question about how computer network operations are currently regulated in international law evolves into a question about how international law *should* regulate such operations. In practical terms, then, before instructing their lawyers to tell them what the legal landscape looks like and what is lawful and unlawful behavior in cyber space, policymakers should begin the important discussion about what kind of cyber space they would prefer in the long run. What is, in other words, the strategic importance of cyber space? What are the weaknesses in cyber space and what should those weaknesses tell the policymakers about the preferred legal framework? What are the advantages and disadvantages of an open and free cyber space? How much freedom is worth sacrificing in order to enhance protection from harmful acts in cyber space? It is only be asking—and answering—such questions that the government lawyers will be able to draw the preferred legal analogies. In conclusion, then, all states must think carefully about the approaches and legal interpretations they apply to instances of harmful cyber incidents. The ongoing efforts to identify the proper legal framework for computer network operations should be considered as a vital part of the much larger and more principled debate about cyber security in the twenty-first century.

Notes

1 Traditionally, hostile cyber activities are classified according to three basic categories, see F. Schreier, Geneva Centre for the Democratic Control of Armed Forces, *On Cyberwarfare*, at: www.dcaf.ch/Publications/On-Cyberwarfare (accessed April 3, 2014): 10–14. See also J. Arquilla and D. Ronfeldt. 1993. "Cyberwar is Coming!" *Comparative Strategy* 12: 141–65; L. Kello. 2013. "The Meaning of the Cyber Revolution: Perils to Theory and Statecraft." *International Security* 38: 7–50. Cyber crime covers all those acts that, whether consisting of internet credit card fraud, bank account manipulation, identity theft, traditional forms of industrial espionage, cyber vandalism or the exchange of child pornography, are not politically motivated. Cyber espionage, on the other hand, refers to politically motivated intrusions into other state's (or private actor's) computer networks with the intent of gaining access to information. Unlike traditional cyber attacks (see below), successful acts of cyber espionage does not require manipulation of information or data. To the contrary, it usually requires an invisible digital presence. Lastly, cyber attacks are politically or strategically motivated hostile cyber activities that "disrupt, deny, degrade, or destroy information resident in computers and computer networks, or the computers or networks themselves," see US Department of Defense, *United States National Military Strategy for Cyberspace Operations*, November 2006, at: www.dod.mil/pubs/foi/joint_staff/jointStaff_jointOperations/07-F-2105doc1.pdf (accessed March 16, 2014). Terms such as "cyber exploitation" and "computer network exploitation" are also used instead of "cyber espionage," as is the term "computer network attacks" instead of "cyber attack."

2 For an overview of national cyber strategies, see: www.ccdcoe.org/strategies-policies. html (accessed December 3, 2015). The threat from disruptive cyber incidents is also visible within the United Nations, see, for example, the latest report by the Group of Governmental Experts on Developments in the Field of Information and Telecommunications in the Context of International Security, GA.Res. A/68/98, June 24, 2013,

§6: "Threats to individuals, businesses, national infrastructure and Governments have grown more acute and incidents more damaging."

3 See also the 2013 report by the Group of Governmental Experts on Developments in the Field of Information and Telecommunications in the Context of International Security, GA.Res. A/68/98, June 24, 2013, §20.

4 Charter of the United Nations (adopted June 26, 1945, entered into for October 24, 1945) 1 UNTS XVI, Arts. 42 and 51. In addition, espionage only violates international law if it targets individuals, documents or locations/facilities explicitly protected from such activities, see, *inter alia*, Vienna Convention on Diplomatic Relations (adopted April 14, 1961, entered into force April 24, 1964) 500 UNTS 95, Art. 27, and the overview in W.H. Parks. 1990. "The International Law of Intelligence Collection," in J.N. Moore and R.F. Turner (eds), *National Security Law*. Durham, NC: Carolina Academic Press, 433–34, and D.B. Silver. 2005. "Intelligence and Counterintelligence," in J.N. Moore and R.F. Turner (eds), *National Security Law*. Durham, NC: Carolina Academic Press, 935.

5 *Case Concerning Military and Paramilitary Activities in and against Nicaragua (Nicaragua vs USA)* (Merits) [1986] ICJ Rep 14, para. 205. M. Jamnejad and M. Wood. 2009. "The Principle of Non-intervention." *Leiden Journal of International Law* 22: 348. See also UNGA UNGA 'Declaration on Principles of International Law concerning Friendly Relations and Co-operation among States in accordance with the Charter of the United Nations' (October 24, 1970) UN Doc A/RES/25/2625(XXV).

6 UNGA, "Declaration on the Inadmissibility of Intervention and Interference in the Internal Affairs of States," *supra* note 41, section 2(b). *See also Nicaragua, supra* note 56, para. 205.

7 UNGA, "Declaration on the Inadmissibility of Intervention and Interference in the Internal Affairs of States," *supra* note 41, section 2(c).

8 Ibid., section 2(f).

9 Article 51:

> Nothing in the present Charter shall impair the inherent right of individual or collective self-defence if an armed attack occurs against a Member of the United Nations, until the Security Council has taken measures necessary to maintain international peace and security.

10 Nicaragua, para. 191. See also Oil Platforms (*Islamic Republic of Iran* v. *United States of America*) (Judgement) [2003] ICJ Rep 161, para. 191.

11 *Nicaragua*, para. 195; *Oil Platforms*, para. 51. *See also* UNGA "Definition on Aggression" (December 14, 1974) UN Doc A/RES/3314 (XXIX). For an attempt at a definition, see Y. Dinstein. 2012. *War, Aggression and Self-Defence*. Cambridge: Cambridge University Press: 193.

12 For the rapidly increasing literature on such issues, see, among others, Y. Dinstein. 2002. "Computer Network Attacks and Self-Defense." *International Law Studies* 76: 99–119; M.N. Schmitt. 1999. "Computer Network Attack and the Use of Force in International Law—Thoughts on a Normative Framework." *Columbia Journal of Transnational Law* 37: 885–937; M.N. Schmitt. 2011. "Cyber Operations and the *Jus ad Bellum* Revisited." *Villanova Law Review* 56: 569–605; C.C. Joyner and C. Lotrionte. 2001. "Information Warfare as International Coercion: Elements of a Legal Framework." *European Journal of International Law* 12: 849; H. Lin. 2010. "Offensive Cyber Operations and the Use of Force." *Journal of National Security Law and Policy* 4: 63–86; M. Roscini. 2010. "World Wide Warfare—Jus ad bellum and the Use of Cyber Force." *Max Planck Yearbook of United Nations Law* 14: 85–130; E. Talbot. 2002. "Computer Attacks on Critical National Infrastructure: A Use of Force Invoking the Right of Self-Defense." *Stanford Journal of International Law* 38: 207–40; D.B. Silver. 2002. "Computer Network Attack as a Use of Force under Article 2(4) of the United Nations Charter." *International Law Studies* 76: 73–97; J.

Barkham. 2001–2002. "Information Warfare and International Law on the Use of Force." *New York University Journal of International Law and Politics* 34: 57–113; M. Hoisington. 2009. "Cyberwarfare and the Use of Force Giving Rise to the Right to Self-Defense." *Boston College International & Comparative Law Review* 32: 439–54; H.B. Robertson, Jr. 2002. "Self-Defense against Computer Network Attack under International Law." *International Law Studies* 76: 121–45; P. Cornish *et al.* 2010. *On Cyber Warfare*. November. Chatham House, at: www.chathamhouse.org/sites/default/files/public/Research/International%20Security/r1110_cyberwarfare.pdf (accessed March 16, 2014); S.J. Shackelford. 2009. "From Nuclear War to Net War: Analogizing Cyber Attacks in International Law." *Berkeley Journal of International Law* 25: 192–251; T.D. Gill and P.A.L. Ducheine. 2013. "Anticipatory Self-Defense in the Cyber Context." *International Law Studies* 89: 438–71. Among others, see H.H. Dinniss. 2012. *Cyber Warfare and the Laws of War*. New York: Cambridge University Press; H. Lin. 2012. "Cyber conflict and international humanitarian law." *International Review of the Red Cross* 94: 515–31; C. Droege. 2012. "Get Off My Cloud: Cyber Warfare, International Humanitarian Law, and the Protection of Civilians." *International Review of the Red Cross* 94: 533–78; N. Lubell. 2013. "Lawful Targets in Cyber Operations: Does the Principle of Distinction Apply?" *International Law Studies* 89: 252–75; E.T. Jensen. 2013. "Cyber Attacks: Proportionality and Precautions in Attack." *International Law Studies* 89: 198–217; M.N. Schmitt. 2011. "Cyber Operations and the Jus in Bello: Key Issues." *International Law Studies* 87: 90–110; T. Huntley. 2010. "Controlling the Use of Force in Cyber Space: The Application of the Law of Armed Conflict During a Time of Fundamental Change in the Nature of Warfare." *Naval Law Review* 60: 1–40; R. Geiss. 2013. "Cyber Warfare: Implications for Non-international Armed Conflicts." *International Law Studies* 89: 627–45; D. Wallace and S.R. Reeves. 2013. "The Law of Armed Conflict's "Wicked" Problem: *Levée in Masse* in Cyber Warfare." *International Law Studies* 89: 646–68.

13 See the Groups reports of July 30, 2010 (A/65/201) and June 24, 2013 (A/68/98), at: www.un.org/disarmament/topics/informationsecurity/ (accessed December 3, 2015).
14 United Nations General Assembly, "The Promotion and Enjoyment of Human Rights on the Internet," UN Doc. A/HRC/20/L.13.
15 See also Benedikt Pirker. 2013. "Territorial Sovereignty and Integrity and the Challenges of Cyberspace," in Katharina Ziolkowski (ed.), *Peacetime Regime for State Activities in Cyberspace; International Law, International Relations and Diplomacy*. CCDCOE: 216; Anders Henriksen. 2015. "Lawful State Responses to Low Level Cyber Attacks." *Nordic Journal of International Law* 84: 331–36.
16 For a thorough overview of surveillance issues and international law, see Ashley Deeks. 2015. Forthcoming. "An International Legal Framework for Surveillance." *Virginia Journal of International Law* 55.
17 Ibid.
18 *See also* W.H. Parks. 1990. "The International Law of Intelligence Collection," in J.N. Moore and R.F. Turner (eds), *National Security Law*. Durham, NC: Carolina Academic Press, 433–34; and D.B. Silver. 2005. "Intelligence and Counterintelligence," in J.N. Moore and R.F. Turner (eds), *National Security Law*. Durham, NC: Carolina Academic Press, 935. A specific prohibition against espionage is found in the Vienna Convention on Diplomatic Relations (adopted April 14, 1961, entered into force April 24, 1964) 500 UNTS 95, Art. 27.
19 See also Benedikt Pirker. 2013. "Territorial Sovereignty and Integrity and the Challenges of Cyberspace," in Katharina Ziolkowski (ed.), *Peacetime Regime for State Activities in Cyberspace; International Law, International Relations and Diplomacy*. CCDCOE: 201–03.
20 Waxman, *supra* note 8, 427; Lin, *supra* note 8, 71–72 and 80; Silver, *supra* note 8, 81.
21 United Nations. 1945. *Documents of the United Nations Conference on International Organization*, Vol. VI, 559, 720–21.

22 Both the 1970 Declaration on Principles of International Law concerning Friendly Relations' and the 1987 Declaration on the Enhancement of the Effectiveness of the Principles of Refraining from the Threat or Use of Force in International Relations' (November 18, 1987) UN Doc A/RES/42/22. strongly indicate that article 2(4) only covers the use of armed force.
23 For background on the attacks on Estonia, see Tikk *et al.* (2010), 15–22.
24 See also Benedikt Pirker. 2013. "Territorial Sovereignty and Integrity and the Challenges of Cyberspace," in Katharina Ziolkowski (ed.), *Peacetime Regime for State Activities in Cyberspace; International Law, International Relations and Diplomacy.* CCDCOE: 216.
25 For more on the Dushanbe Summit Declaration, see www.ccdcoe.org/information-security-discussed-dushanbe-summit-shanghai-cooperation-organisation.html (accessed December 3, 2015).
26 See the Groups reports of July 30, 2010 (A/65/201) and June 24, 2013 (A/68/98), at: www.un.org/disarmament/topics/informationsecurity/ (accessed December 3, 2015).

References

Associated Press. 2015. "US Slaps Sanctions on North Korea After Sony Hack." *New York Times*, January 2, at: www.nytimes.com/aponline/2015/01/02/us/ap-us-united-states-nkorea-.html (accessed January 5, 2015).

Barlow, J. P. 1996. "Declaration of Independence of Cyberspace." *Electronic Frontier Foundation*, February, at: projects.eff.org/~barlow/Declaration-Final.html (accessed March 16, 2014).

Barkham, J. 2001–2002. "Information Warfare and International Law on the Use of Force." *New York University Journal of International Law and Politics* 34.

Borad, William J. *et al.* 2011. "Israeli Test on Worm Called Crucial in Iran Nuclear Delay." *New York Times*, January 15.

Carr, David, ed. 2013. "How the Hacking at Sony Over 'The Interview' Became a Horror Movie." *New York Times*, December 21, at: www.nytimes.com/2014/12/22/business/media/hacking-at-sony-over-the-interview-reveals-hollywoods-failings-too.html (accessed January 5, 2015).

Case Concerning Military and Paramilitary Activities in and against Nicaragua (Nicaragua vs USA) (Merits). 1986. ICJ Rep 14, para. 205.

Corfu Channel Case (UK vs Albania) (Merits).1949. ICJ Rep 4: 35.

Cornish, P. *et al.* 2010. *On Cyber Warfare.* Chatham House, November, at: www.chathamhouse.org/sites/default/files/public/Research/International%20Security/r1110_cyberwarfare.pdf (accessed March 16, 2014).

Deeks, Ashley. 2015. Forthcoming. "An International Legal Framework for Surveillance." *Virginia Journal of International Law* 55.

Dinniss, H.H. 2012. *Cyber Warfare and the Laws of War.* New York: Cambridge University Press.

Dinstein, Y. 2002. "Computer Network Attacks and Self-Defense." *International Law Studies* 76.

Droege, C. 2012. "Get Off My Cloud: Cyber Warfare, International Humanitarian Law, and the Protection of Civilians." *International Review of the Red Cross* 94.

Fackler, Martin. 2014. "North Korea Accuses U.S. of Staging Internet Failure." *New York Times*, December 27, at: www.nytimes.com/2014/12/28/world/asia/north-korea-sony-hacking-the-interview.html (accessed January 5, 2015).

Federal Bureau of Investigations. 2014. *Update on Sony Investigation.* December 19.

Geiss, R. 2013. "Cyber Warfare: Implications for Non-international Armed Conflicts." *International Law Studies* 89.

Gill T.D. and P.A.L. Ducheine. 2013. "Anticipatory Self-Defense in the Cyber Context." *International Law Studies* 89.

Goldsmith, J. 2006. *Who Controls the Internet? Illusions of a Borderless World*. New York: Oxford University Press.

Healey, J. 2012. "Beyond Attribution: Seeking National Responsibility for Cyber Attacks." *Atlantic Council*, January 7, at: www.atlanticcouncil.org/publications/issue-briefs/beyond-attribution-seeking-national-responsibility-in-cyberspace (accessed March 17, 2014).

Henriksen, Anders. 2015. "Lawful State Responses to Low Level Cyber Attacks." *Nordic Journal of International Law* 84.

Hoisington, M. 2009. "Cyberwarfare and the Use of Force Giving Rise to the Right to Self-Defense." *Boston College International & Comparative Law Review* 32.

Huntley, T. 2010. "Controlling the Use of Force in Cyber Space: The Application of the Law of Armed Conflict During a Time of Fundamental Change in the Nature of Warfare." *Naval Law Review* 60.

Jamnejad, M. and M. Wood. 2009. "The Principle of Non-intervention." *Leiden Journal of International Law* 22.

Jensen, E.T. 2013. "Cyber Attacks: Proportionality and Precautions in Attack." *International Law Studies* 89.

Joyner, C.C. and C. Lotrionte. 2001. "Information Warfare as International Coercion: Elements of a Legal Framework." *European Journal of International Law* 12.

Lin, H. 2010. "Offensive Cyber Operations and the Use of Force." *Journal of National Security Law and Policy* 4.

Lin, H. 2012. "Cyber Conflict and International Humanitarian Law." *International Review of the Red Cross* 94.

Lubell, N. 2013. "Lawful Targets in Cyber Operations: Does the Principle of Distinction Apply?" *International Law Studies* 89.

Moore, J.N. and R.F. Turner (eds). 1990. *National Security Law*. Durham, NC: Carolina Academic Press.

Parks, W.H. 1990. "The International Law of Intelligence Collection." *National Security Law*.

Pirker, Benedikt. 2013. "Territorial Sovereignty and Integrity and the Challenges of Cyberspace," in Katharina Ziolkowski (ed.), *Peacetime Regime for State Activities in Cyberspace; International Law, International Relations and Diplomacy*. CCDCOE: 189–216.

Randelzhofer, A. 2002. "Article 2 (4)," in B. Simma (ed.), *The Charter of the United Nations, A Commentary*. New York: Oxford University Press.

Robertson, H.B. Jr. 2002. "Self-Defense against Computer Network Attack under International Law." *International Law Studies* 76.

Roscini, M. 2010. "World Wide Warfare—Jus ad bellum and the Use of Cyber Force." *Max Planck Yearbook of United Nations Law* 14.

Schmitt, M.N. 1999. "Computer Network Attack and the Use of Force in International Law—Thoughts on a Normative Framework." *Columbia Journal of Transnational Law* 37.

Schmitt, M.N. 2010. "Cyber Operations and the Jus in Bello: Key Issues." *International Law Studies* 87.

Schmitt, M.N. 2011. "Cyber Operations and the Jus ad Bellum Revisited." *Villanova Law Review* 56.

Schmitt, M.N. (ed.). 2013. *The Tallinn Manual on the International Law applicable to Cyber Warfare*. New York: Cambridge University Press.

Shackelford, S.J. 2009. "From Nuclear War to Net War: Analogizing Cyber Attacks in International Law." *Berkeley Journal of International Law* 25.

Silver, D.B. 2002. "Computer Network Attack as a Use of Force under Article 2(4) of the United Nations Charter." *International Law Studies* 76.

Silver, D.B. 2005. "Intelligence and Counterintelligence," in J.N. Moore and R.F. Turner (eds), *National Security Law*. Durham, NC: Carolina Academic Press.

Stark, Holger. 2011. "Mossad's Miracle Weapon, Stuxnet Virus Opens New Era of Cyber War." *Der Spiegel*, August 8, at: www.spiegel.de/international/world/mossad-s-miracle-weapon-stuxnet-virus-opens-new-era-of-cyber-war-a-778912.html (accessed August 8, 2011).

Talbot, E. 2002. "Computer Attacks on Critical National Infrastructure: A Use of Force Invoking the Right of Self-Defense." *Stanford Journal of International Law* 38.

Turner R.F. *et al.* (eds). 2005. *National Security Law*. Durham, NC: Carolina Academic Press.

United Nations General Assembly (UNGA). 1981. *Declaration on the Inadmissibility of Intervention and Interference in the Internal Affairs of States.*

United Nations General Assembly (UNGA). 1970. *Declaration on Principles of International Law concerning Friendly Relations and Co-operation among States in accordance with the Charter of the United Nations.* October 24. *UN Doc A/RES/25/2625(XXV).*

Upadhyay, Dadan. 2013. *SCO Members to Cooperate in War on Cyber Terrorism.* Russia and India Report. April, at: http://in.rbth.com/world/2013/04/02/sco_members_to_cooperate_in_war_on_cyber_terrorism_23429.html (accessed December 3, 2015).

Ziolkowski, Katharina. 2013a. *Peacetime Regime for State Activities in Cyberspace; International Law, International Relations and Diplomacy*. CCDCOE.

Ziolkowski, Katharina. 2013b. "Peacetime Cyber Espionage—New Tendencies in Public International Law," in Katharina Ziolkowski (ed.), *Peacetime Regime for State Activities in Cyberspace; International Law, International Relations and Diplomacy.* CCDCOE: 425–64.

Wallace, D. and S.R. Reeves. 2013. "The Law of Armed Conflict's "Wicked" Problem: Levée in Masse in Cyber Warfare." *International Law Studies* 89.

Waxman, M.C. 2011. "Cyber-Attacks and the Use of Force: Back to the Future of Article 2(4)." *Yale Journal of International Law* 36: 425.

10 Cyber weapons

Oxymoron or a real world phenomenon to be regulated?

Bill Boothby

Introduction

At first glance the idea that one could properly describe a computer capability as a weapon is counter-intuitive. There is, indeed, all the difference in the world between the essentially peaceful activity of preparing word files, or Excel spreadsheets or, for that matter, the ubiquitous Powerpoint presentations, and the dropping of bombs, the firing of missiles or the shooting of rifles. The first purpose of this chapter is therefore to discuss whether the notion of cyber weapons makes practical and legal sense and, if so, whether this has implications for the applicability of international law rules. That is the task of the next Section. In Section 3, we consider what, in summary form, the applicable rules of weapons law consist of, noting how some of them would seem to apply to particular kinds of cyber weapon. In Section 4, the obligations of states legally to review new cyber weapons, means and methods of warfare are set forth, and the adjustments to normal processes and criteria that the legal review of cyber weapons seems likely to require are discussed. In Section 5 we seek to draw some conclusions, noting in particular why the application of weapons law to these capabilities is important.

Cyber weapons, sense or nonsense?

Practical and legal discussions of whether the very idea of cyber weapons is sensible converge, quite simply because there is no internationally agreed definition of the term "weapon." International law rules in this area refer, as we shall see, to "weapons, means and methods of warfare." Surprisingly, none of these terms is the subject of an internationally agreed definition. That does not of course mean that the terms have no meaning. A "weapon," when used in the context of an armed conflict, involves an offensive capability that can be applied to an adversary, for example to a military object or enemy combatant (Boothby 2009: 4; McClelland 2003),[1] and is critically linked to the use,[2] intended use[3] or design purpose[4] of the relevant capability. Often, that offensive capability will consist of an object, such as a rock, bullet, missile or bomb, but this is not necessarily so. A bacteriological toxin, used to spread infection and thus death or injury, while rendered illegal by customary law and the Biological Weapons Convention, is nevertheless a weapon notwithstanding that no kinetic use of force would necessarily be required. Similarly the release of asphyxiating gas would not necessarily require a kinetic activity but would widely be seen as involving the use of a weapon. A "weapon" can therefore be defined as an offensive capability that is applied, or that is intended or designed to be applied, to an adversary to cause death, injury or damage in connection with an armed conflict. So, while the damaging, injurious or fatal effect of a kinetic weapon will tend to result from physical impact of some sort, the offensive capability need not be kinetic. Accordingly, if computing technology is used to cause a destructive, damaging or injurious effect, there would seem to be every reason to regard the computer system, comprising hardware, software and the relevant data including malware as, taken together, a weapon system.

It follows from this that a cyber tool may be capable of causing damaging or injurious effects to military objects or to combatants with the result that it may be capable of constituting a weapon. That cyber tool only actually becomes a weapon, however, if it, or a system of which it is an integral part, is used, intended or designed to deliver an offensive capability against a military object or enemy combatant in the course of an armed conflict.[5] It is therefore logical that the Tallinn Manual defines cyber weapons as:

> cyber means of warfare that are by design, use or intended use capable of causing either (i) injury to, or death of, persons; or (ii) damage to, or destruction of, objects, that is, causing the consequences required for qualification of a cyber operation as an attack.
>
> (Tallinn Manual 2013: §2 Rule 41)

This link between the definition of cyber weapons and the definition of cyber attacks is significant. Concluding that certain cyber operations are cyber attacks justifies the application to those operations of the law of targeting rules in customary law and, inter alia, in Articles 48 to 67 of Additional Protocol I. Similarly, concluding that cyber capabilities that have the characteristics we have discussed are cyber weapons has the effect of rendering the law of weaponry applicable to those capabilities.

Before concluding this Section, we should note that "means of cyber warfare" are cyber weapons and their associated cyber systems (Tallinn Manual 2013: Rule 41a) while "methods of cyber warfare" are the cyber tactics, techniques and procedures by which hostilities are conducted (Tallinn Manual 2013, rule 41b).

Weapons law and its application to cyber weapons

The lawfulness of all weapons, including cyber weapons, is judged against the customary and treaty rules of weapons law. It is a well-recognized international law principle that the right of the parties to an armed conflict to choose methods and means of warfare is not unlimited.[6] So the rules that will be summarized below are the limitations that states have placed upon the weapons that may be used in armed conflict.

A customary principle, that therefore binds all states and that is reflected in Additional Protocol I, Article 35(2), provides that: "[i]t is prohibited to employ weapons, projectiles and material and methods of warfare of a nature to cause superfluous injury or unnecessary suffering" (Tallinn Manual: Rule 42[7]).

The author has in the past suggested that, applying this rule,

> [t]he legitimacy of a weapon, by reference to the superfluous injury and unnecessary suffering principle, must be determined by comparing the nature and scale of the generic military advantage to be anticipated from the weapon in the application for which it is designed to be used, with the pattern of injury and suffering associated with the normal intended use of the weapon.
>
> (Boothby 2009: Ch. 5 Sec. 5.2.2; Fenrick 1990; Cummings *et al.* 2006)[8]

If this formulation is correct, it follows that, if the designed or intended use of the cyber weapon will necessarily and inevitably give rise to greater injury or suffering without securing corresponding additional military utility, the rule will probably have been broken. The Tallinn Manual cites an example of a cyber operation that would potentially breach the rule, namely taking control of an Internet-addressable pacemaker device with built-in defibrillator fitted to an enemy commander with a view to stopping the target's heart and then reviving him multiple times before finally killing him.[9]

There is a second customary rule, which again therefore binds all states, prohibiting cyber weapons that are indiscriminate by nature. Weapons in general, and thus cyber weapons, are regarded as indiscriminate by nature if they employ a method or means of combat which cannot be directed at a specific military objective, or if they employ a method or means of combat the effects of which cannot be limited as required by the law of armed conflict and if as a result in each such case, they are of a nature to strike military objectives and civilians or civilian objects without distinction. An obvious example would be malware that inevitably, uncontrollably and harmfully spreads into civilian networks.[10]

In relation to the natural environment, customary law includes a general rule that binds all states, while treaty law prescribes two distinct rules that bind the states that are party to the relevant treaties. The first treaty rule addresses the use of the environment as a weapon, prohibiting states that are party to the UN Environmental Modification Convention 1976 from engaging in military or any other hostile use of environmental modification techniques having widespread, long-lasting or severe effects as the means of destruction, damage or injury to any other state party to that Convention (UN Environmental Modification Convention 1976: Article I). The customary law rule concerns collateral damage to the environment and requires all states to have due regard to the natural environment when procuring new weapons and weapon systems.[11] The second treaty law rule relates to collateral damage caused to the natural environment and goes rather further; it prohibits states that are party to Additional Protocol I to employ methods or means of warfare which are intended, or may be expected, to cause widespread, long-term and severe damage to the natural environment.[12] Significantly, all of the "widespread, long-term and severe" elements must be present for this Rule to be breached. These elements are not, however, defined in the treaty. It is, however, widely accepted that only the most serious damage will breach the rule.[13] A cyber attack, for example, on the computer system controlling the supply of coolant to the core of a nuclear electrical generating station with the intention that the flow of coolant will be switched off causing the core to explode and thereby occasion a "Fukoshima effect" would, likely, be regarded as breaching this rule.

In addition to these somewhat general rules, there are a series of specific weapons law rules that either prohibit or restrict the use of weapons or weapon technologies that are specified in the relevant rule. The majority of these rules are based on treaties, but some, for example the prohibition of poisons and poisoned weapons, were already customary in nature before they appeared in a treaty text. All states are bound by the customary rules, but only states that are party to the relevant treaty are bound by the rules it contains.

The detail of the ad hoc rules of weapons law lies outside the intended scope of the present chapter. The following list summarises some of the treaty sources in which these rules of weapons law can be found, namely:

- Hague Regulations 1899 and 1907 e.g., in relation to poison and poisoned weapons;[14]
- Hague Declaration 2 of 1899 and the Geneva Gas Protocol, 1925, in relation to asphyxiating gases and bacteriological weapons;
- Hague Declaration 3 of 1899 in relation to expanding bullets;
- St Petersburg Declaration 1868 and the associated customary law rule prohibiting exploding bullets designed for anti-personnel use;
- Protocol I to the Conventional Weapons Convention, as to non-detectable fragments;
- Protocol II and Amended Protocol II to the Conventional Weapons Convention, as to mines, booby-traps and other devices;
- Protocol III to the Conventional Weapons Convention, as to incendiary weapons;
- Protocol IV to the Conventional Weapons Convention as to blinding laser weapons;
- Chemical Weapons Convention 1993 as to chemical weapons, including riot control agents and asphyxiating gases;
- Biological Weapons Convention, 1972, in relation to biological and bacteriological weapons including toxins;
- Ottawa Convention, 1997 in relation to anti-personnel landmines;
- Cluster Munitions Convention, 2008, in relation to cluster munitions.

It is possible that a particular rule of weapons law will apply to a cyber capability because of the way in which that capability operates. Thus, the Tallinn

Manual notes that "it is forbidden to employ cyber booby-traps associated with certain objects specified in the law of armed conflict." For the purposes of Protocol II and Amended Protocol II to the Conventional Weapons Convention, a booby-trap is "any device or material which is designed, constructed or adapted to kill or injure, and which functions unexpectedly when a person disturbs or approaches an apparently harmless object or performs an apparently safe act."[15] So, if malware in the form of a kill switch were to be inserted into a targeted computer system that controls a life-critical system and if that kill switch is designed to be activated, say, when an enemy operator enters specified data into the computer, such a capability would be capable of amounting to a cyber booby-trap to which the rules in, for example, Amended Mines Protocol, Articles 3, 7, 9, 10 and 12 would apply.[16]

If by cyber means a state is able to take control of an enemy platform, such as a remotely piloted aircraft, with a view to using the weapon that the aircraft is carrying against the enemy, weapons law is likely to determine whether that weapon can in fact be used in this way. Imagine that the weapon is a cluster munition as defined in the Cluster Munitions Convention to which the state taking control of the aircraft is a state party. If that state takes control of the air-craft and fires the cluster munition knowing it is a cluster munition, it will breach its obligations under the Convention. If in similar circumstances, control is taken of a remotely-piloted aircraft carrying incendiary weapons, any subsequent use of such weapons would have to comply with Protocol III to the Conventional Weapons Convention, assuming the state taking control is a party to that treaty.

It is therefore important for states to realize that a cyber weapon may render ad hoc weapons law rules relevant if the cyber weapon is used to take control of weapons to which specific rules that bind the relevant state apply.

If future developments in cyber technology permit a state, having taken control of the enemy's weapon by cyber means, to redesign the weapon or the way in which it operates, there will be important legal implications. A number of weapons law treaties define the weapons they cover by reference to design purpose. If, therefore, cyber control were to be taken of a laser system originally designed as a range finder and if it is then by cyber means redesigned to have a combat function of causing permanent blindness to unenhanced vision, this would bring the weapon within Protocol IV to CCW, and a state party to that Protocol would be prohibited to use such a redesigned weapon. States planning to undertake such redesign operations by cyber means would therefore be advised to consider the weapons law provisions by which they are bound before embarking on such operations.

States' weapon review obligations in relation to cyber weapons

We shall now consider the legal obligation on states to review the lawfulness of the weapons they plan to produce or acquire, the criteria that are employed in undertaking such reviews, and how those criteria, and the processes associated with the legal review of weapons, are affected if it is a cyber capability that is being reviewed.

All states are bound by an implied requirement legally to review new weapons to determine whether their employment would in some or all circumstances breach the rules of international law applicable to the particular state.[17] States that are party to Additional Protocol I are required:

> [i]n the study, development, acquisition or adoption of a new weapon, means or method of warfare [...] to determine whether its employment would, in some or all circumstances, be prohibited by th[e] Protocol or by any other rule of international law applicable to the High Contracting Party.
>
> (Additional Protocol I 1977: Article 36)[18]

Accordingly, all states must legally review all new weapons and weapon systems, but states that are party to Additional Protocol I must also review new methods of warfare that they plan to employ. Moreover, the Additional Protocol I obligation applies to the study and development of weapons, means and methods, not just to acquisition or adoption. These requirements will also apply to cyber weapons (Tallinn Manual 2013: Rule 48a and 48b).

The rules summarized earlier in this chapter will constitute the criteria that must be applied when undertaking all legal reviews of new weapons. This is because the weapon review obligation specifies that it is the existing law of weaponry as it applies to the state conducting the weapon review that must be considered when determining whether the weapon, and its planned circumstances and manner of use, are lawful. Certain cyber technologies may, however, render additional criteria relevant. If, therefore, the cyber tool is designed to operate autonomously or with a significant degree of automation, the weapon review will also have to assess whether it can be used in accordance with targeting law rules. Of particular relevance are likely to be the detailed precautionary obligations in Article 57 of Additional Protocol I, which are largely customary in nature and thus bind all states. The person undertaking the review will have to determine whether, for example, the evaluative decision-making that is critically required in making proportionality assessments can be undertaken by a cyber tool that makes autonomous attack decisions. If it cannot and if there is no other way of complying with the precautionary rules in Article 57, the cyber weapon should not be procured or used. Complying with the hors de combat rule in Article 41 of Additional Protocol I may also present similarly complex challenges for such systems.

Procedures associated with weapon reviews may also be affected if it is a cyber weapon that is to be reviewed. Frequently, a cyber weapon will be developed with a particular attack in mind. The characteristics of the cyber weapon will be designed ad hoc so that it will reach the computer node or network that is the intended target and so that it will have a planned effect on it. It is therefore likely that the legal review of that new cyber weapon will have to be received by the Commander of the unit that will use it operationally and, logically, by the personnel who are involved in developing it. This is likely to constitute a departure from normal weapons review procedures, as when normal, non-cyber weapons are legally reviewed, the completed review document is normally addressed to the appropriate weapon procurement office within the Defense Ministry.

There is no international law obligation to conduct legal reviews of weapons that are to be used in situations that do not amount to armed conflict. When the security forces of a state are dealing with riots, civil disturbances, sporadic outbreaks of violence and similar circumstances that fall below the armed conflict threshold,[19] their actions in response to such situations are governed by applicable domestic law, which will differ from state to state, and by human rights law. It therefore follows that the security forces should be equipped with weapons that will enable them to comply with human rights law including the right to life. The human rights provisions that bind a particular state will depend on the the the human rights instruments to which that state is party. All States are bound by customary human rights norms.

Lethal force can only lawfully be used outside armed conflict situations if it is absolutely necessary, strictly proportionate (Harris *et al.* 2009: 62) to the achievement of its self-defense purpose (McCann *et al.* 1995: 21; Isayeva *et al.* 2005: §190, 191 and 200; Harris *et al.* 2009: 61–64), and if it is planned and undertaken with great care[20] taking into account the foreseeable consequences of a planned operation. Disproportionate use of force during an unplanned operation that gives rise to loss of life may well be judged a breach of the right to life.[21]

The security forces must therefore be equipped with a suitable range of response options so that lethal force can in practice be limited as the law requires. When likely to be confronted by riots, civil disturbances, etc., it would seem necessary that the available weaponry should include, for example, some or all of batons, truncheons or sticks, shields, CS or tear gas, water cannon, rubber bullets or similar non-lethal technologies.

It is worthy of note that some weapons that are prohibited during armed conflict are not specifically prohibited when used in situations that fall short of armed conflict. This applies to riot control agents and to expanding bullets, which may be necessary to deal effectively for example with certain dangerous hostage situations. It should be appreciated, however, that the human rights law requirements noted earlier as to proportionality, planning, absolute necessity and limitation and control of the use of force must be met.

Conclusion

It is important for all states, including small states, to appreciate that international law prohibits certain weapons and restricts the circumstances in which other weapons may lawfully be used. All states are obliged by treaty and/or customary law legally to review all new weapons they produce or acquire and should have an established procedure in place for this purpose. That requirement applies to new cyber weapons as to other, more conventional weapons types and, being a legal obligation, should be taken seriously by states, including small states. If a state fails legally to review new weapons, it risks acquiring weapons that are prohibited, or using them in a prohibited way and thus breaching international law (Lawand 2006).[22]

There is no requirement that states disclose their weapons reviews, either to other specific states or generally, so there is no necessity that the conduct of weapon reviews should have any adverse impact on national security. The law does not mandate that any particular system should be adopted for the conduct of such reviews. Indeed, it is preferable that each state should adopt the system that best suits its requirements, including its procurement processes.

Some will question whether it is satisfactory that such a significant element of enforcement of the law of weaponry is left in the hands of individual states.

There is, in the present author's view, a degree of inevitability about that. The purpose of such reviews, after all, is to seek to ensure that weapon systems supplied to armed forces in connection with armed conflicts comply with legal rules that states have either adopted in treaty form or developed by means of their practice as customary norms. It is national understandings of the law as it applies to the individual nation that must be applied, and national security considerations will preclude the disclosure to an outside body of the characteristics of weapons considered vital to the state's national security. If undertaken systematically, objectively and accurately, those whose task it is to use force can know that the weapons supplied to them comply with the law that applies to them. They will be informed in the weapon review of any limitations on the lawful use of the weapon, and this is a vital link in ensuring that the law is complied with.

Routinely complying with international law obligations such as these can only positively contribute to forming a habit of legal compliance. That is a habit which ought to be universally encouraged.

Notes

1 See W.H. Boothby, Weapons and the Law of Armed Conflict, (2009) at p. 4 and J. McClelland, The Review of Weapons in accordance with article 36 of Additional Protocol I (2003) 850 IRRC 397. Consider also the reference in the Harvard Manual on the International Law Applicable to Air and Missile Warfare (AMW Manual) to weapons as "a means of warfare used in combat operations, including a gun, missile, bomb or other munitions, that is capable of causing either (i) injury to, or death of, persons; or (ii) damage to, or destruction of, objects." AMW Manual, Rule 1(ff).
2 The decision, for example, to use a rock to cause injury to an adversary converts an inoffensive natural object into a weapon by virtue of use.
3 The collection of a number of rocks with the intention of using them in the future to cause injury to an adversary similarly converts those objects into weapons in advance of their actual use.
4 Designing an object so as to be used to cause injury or damage in the course of an armed conflict will render that object a weapon, for example when a flint is shaped into an arrowhead.
5 Consider for example Commentary to AMW Manual Rule 1(ff), at paragraph 1.
6 See for example API, Article 35(1).
7 For the suggested application of this rule in the cyber context, see Tallinn Manual, Rule 42.

8 W.H. Boothby, n. 1 at p. 63, and see W.J. Fenrick, "The Conventional Weapons Convention: A Modest But Useful Treaty," 279 IRRC 498 (1990), 500: "A weapon causes unnecessary suffering when in practice it inevitably causes injury or suffering disproportionate to its military effectiveness. In determining the military effectiveness of a weapon, one looks at the primary purpose for which it was designed." Consider also the formulation of the test for the purposes of the United States Department of Defense Weapons Review Directive, prepared by E.R. Cummings, W.A. Solf and H. Almond, given in W. Hays Parks, Means and Methods of Warfare, Symposium issued in Honour of Edward R. Cummings (2006), 38 GWILR 511 at n. 25.

9 Tallinn Manual, Commentary accompanying Rule 42, paragraph 6.

10 See Tallinn Manual, Rule 43, Additional Protocol I, Article 51(4)(b) and (c) and Tallinn Manual, Commentary accompanying Rule 43, paragraph 4.

11 The Tallinn Manual, at Rule 83a, notes that "[t]he natural environment is a civilian object and as such enjoys general protection from cyber attacks and their effects." Consider also AMW Manual, Rule 89.

12 Additional Protocol I, Articles 35(3) and 55.

13

> The time or duration required (i.e., long-term) was considered by some to be measured in decades. References to twenty or thirty years were made by some representatives as being a minimum. Others referred to battlefield destruction in France in the First World War as being outside the scope of the prohibition.... It appeared to be a widely shared assumption that battlefield damage incidental to conventional warfare would not normally be proscribed by this provision. What the article is primarily directed to is thus such damage as would be likely to prejudice, over a long term, the continued survival of the civilian population or would risk causing it major health problems.
>
> Rapporteur's Report CDDH/215/Rev.1 paragraph 27 reported in ICRC Commentary, paragraph 1454

14 Hague Regulations, 1907, Article 23(a).

15 See, for example, Amended Mines Protocol, 1996, Art. 2(4).

16 Whether the capability would amount to a device and thus a booby-trap would depend on how the relevant state interprets the language of the definition, and whether it is bound by the relevant rules will depend on whether the state is party to one of these treaties.

17 Note the 1868 St Petersburg Declaration, Article 1 of Hague Convention II of 1899 and of Hague Convention IV of 1907, which require States party to issue instructions to their armed land forces "in conformity with the Regulations" annexed to those instruments, and note "[t]he requirement that the legality of all new weapons, means and methods of warfare be systematically assessed is arguably one that applies to *all* States, regardless of whether or not they are party to Additional Protocol 1"; K. Lawand, *A Guide to the Legal Review of New Weapons, Means and Methods of Warfare: Measures to Implement Article 36 of Additional Protocol I of 1977*, ICRC (2006) at p. 4.

18 Additional Protocol I, Article 36.

19 Consider Additional Protocol II, 1977, Article 1(2).

20 As to the circumstances when a use of lethal force to disperse demonstrators was not found to be absolutely necessary, see Gülec vs Turkey, European Court of Human Rights, Application No 21593/93 Judgment of July 27, 1998. Note Gül vs Turkey, European Court of Human Rights, Application No 22676/93, Judgment of December 14, 2000.

21 Note the UN Basic Principles on the Use of Force and Firearms by Law Enforcement Officials adopted by the 9th UN Congress on the Prevention of Crime and Treatment of Offenders, Havana, August 27–September 7, 1990, UN Doc. A/CONF.144/28/Rev.1 at 112 (1990), Articles 9 and 10.

22 Regrettably, only relatively few states are known to have mechanisms or procedures for the conduct of weapons reviews, see K. Lawand, n. 17 at 5.

References

Additional Protocol I, 1977, Articles 35(3) and 55.

Amended Mines Protocol, 1996.

Boothby, W.H. 2009. *Weapons and the Law of Armed Conflict.* Oxford: Oxford University Press.

Fenrick, W.J. 1990. *The Conventional Weapons Convention: A Modest But Useful Treaty*, International Review of the Red Cross 279: 498, 500.

Gül vs Turkey, European Court of Human Rights, Application No 22676/93, Judgment of December 14, 2000.

Gülec vs Turkey, European Court of Human Rights, Application No 21593/93 Judgment of July 27, 1998.

Hague Regulations, 1907, Article 23(a).

Harris, D.J., M O'Boyle and C. Warbrick. 2009. *Law of the European Convention on Human Rights.* 2nd edition. Oxford: Oxford University Press.

HPCR. 2009. *AMW Manual*, Rule 89.

Isayeva, Yusupova and Bazayeva vs Russia 41 EHRR 847, 2005, Paragraphs 190, 191 and 200.

Lawand, K. 2006. *A Guide to the Legal Review of New Weapons, Means and Methods of Warfare: Measures to Implement Article 36 of Additional Protocol I of 1977.* ICRC.

McCann and others vs UK, *Application No 18984/91, Judgment of 27 September 1995.* 21 EHRR 97 paragraph 212.

Rapporteur's Report CDDH/215/Rev.1 paragraph 27 reported in ICRC Commentary, paragraph 1454.

Tallinn Manual on the International Law Applicable to Cyber Warfare. 2013. Commentary accompanying Rule 41, paragraph 2.

UN Basic Principles on the Use of Force and Firearms by Law Enforcement Officials adopted by the 9th UN Congress on the Prevention of Crime and Treatment of Offenders, Havana, August 27–September 7 1990. UN Doc. A/CONF.144/28/Rev.1 at 112 (1990), Articles 9 and 10.

UN Environmental Modification Convention, 1976, Article I.

The United States Department of Defense Weapons Review Directive. 2006. Prepared by E.R. Cummings, W.A. Solf and H. Almond. In *Means and Methods of Warfare* by W. Hays Parks. Symposium issue in Honour of Edward R Cummings, 38 GWILR 511 at note 25.

11 Law in the militarization of cyber space

Framing a critical research agenda

Kristin Bergtora Sandvik

Introduction

This chapter aims to set out some ideas and pointers for a further development of a research agenda on the role of law in the militarization of cyber space. Critical international relation and security studies scholars have given attention to the commercial and national security interests underpinning the academic and political framing of cyber war, on the basis that the cyber war discourse contributes to creating greater government and military control over civilian networks, leading to potential infringements of civil liberties (Dunn Cavelty 2008a, 2008b, 2012a, 2012b; Schneier 2010a, 2010b; Brito and Watkins 2011; Deibert and Rohozinski 2011; Lawson 2012a, 2012b). At the same time, critical legal thinking on cyber war remains an underdeveloped and fragmented endeavor (but see Henriksen this volume): international law scholars usually take the existence of cyber war at face value (see Boothby this volume), both with respect to the possibility that cyber attacks may cross threshold for armed attacks set out in the law of armed conflict and thus be labelled "cyber war" (though not war), and the appropriateness of applying this legal framework to the field of cyber security.

While slowly changing, the geographic bias in cyber war scholarship looms large (but Ebert and Maurer 2013). The writing on the legal regulation of cyber war continues to focus mostly on US military responses or the interpretation and application of the norms of the Laws of War in the USA national security context. Hence, the task for legal scholars is twofold: to respond critically to the US centric discourse on the role of law in the militarization of cyber space, but also to develop "local" or "regional" scholarly perspectives on the constitutive role of law with respect to cyber security. In the aftermath of the NSA mass surveillance revelations—and the exposure of a "Nine Eyes" inner circle (Denmark, Norway, France and Netherlands supplementing the "Five Eyes" consisting of the USA, Australia, Canada, New Zealand and the UK) engaging in a "focused cooperation" for intelligence exchange, including metadata (Moltke and Gjerding 2013), it seems pertinent for legal scholars outside the USA to provide a closer scrutiny of the role played by law and legal arguments in the process this chapter labels "the militarization of cyber space." To that end, this chapter aims to lay out a research agenda that both offers a theoretically and chronologically informed critical inventory of the role of law in the militarization of cyber space and proposes a set of substantive lines of inquiry.

Following the cyber attacks on Estonia in 2007, the task of providing an adequate international legal framework for cyber attacks has moved rapidly up the international political agenda, culminating with the publication of the *Tallinn Manual on the International Law Applicable to Cyber Warfare* in 2013 and the inclusion of cyber attacks under NATO Article 5. The chapter tries to show *how* law has operated in competing cyber war discourses over time; how cyber war as a concept has developed within the specific conversations of international law; and the symbolic and political role now allocated to law in grappling with the indeterminacy that is so pervasive when it comes to gauging the nature of insecurity.

The main argument is that legal arguments have functioned—and function— as a "workhorse" for the proponents of a cyber-insecurity-as-war. The chapter argues that the framing of cyber war as a topic for the law of armed conflict (broadly defined) and national security law to some degree is prognostic; it becomes about offering regulation of military solutions, and delineating the legal boundaries of the specific strategies, tactics, and objectives by which these solutions may be achieved. The general point put forward is that neither the emphasis on the law of armed conflict or the initiatives and doctrinal lenses through which it is interpreted are inevitable. Seeing cyber attacks through the lens of international law and international treaty making processes produces a particular kind of legitimate knowledge, and constructs a specific global social reality. The push to define cyber security in military terms, using metaphors of "war" and talking about cyber space as a "battle domain" engenders a particular set of implications with respect to the nature of cyber attacks, the motivations of the attacker, the potential political ramifications of the attack and the appropriate means, including law, to prevent, defend and repeal such attacks. While exercises of legal line drawing are important and useful, they are also strategic and political.

To contribute to a substantive agenda of resistance with both global and local purchase, this chapter offers a three-pronged mapping of the evolving legal discussions that could challenge the disciplines emphasis on "war" in the cyber-security context. The first concerns the so-called comprehensive legal approach to cyber security, the second relates to technology exports that fuels contemporary violent "grass-roots cyber wars" (where real people die as a consequence of surveillance by governments and armed actors) and the third pertains to the nascent cyber-peace agenda.

The chapter proceeds as follows: The first part lays out three background narratives on cyber insecurity in the critical political science literature broadly defined. The chapter looks at the role of cyber industrial–military complex and its lead entrepreneurs, and the so-called "China syndrome" in the framing of cyber war. Attention is then turned to the changing political conceptualizations of cyber security as it has shifted from crime to terror and espionage; to the internationalization of a cyber war concept; and finally toward the internationalization of cyber security. The second part discusses and critiques the evolving understandings of cyber war within international law, now firmly entrenched as a project of Northern international law through the Tallinn Manual. The third part outlines the counter narratives presented above. A brief conclusion follows.

The politics of cyber (in) security discourses

Changing notions of cyber security: crime, terror and espionage

The potential for cyber war, previously known through its early monikers "information war" or "netwar," has been on the radar of policymakers, security experts and military commanders since the inception of the Advanced Research Projects Agency Network (ARPANET), funded by the US Department of Defense in the 1960s. According to Myriam Dunn Cavelty, by the 1990s, there was a "rapid and considerable political impact of the widespread conceptualization of aspects of information technology as a security problem" (Dunn Cavelty 2007: 15–22). Since then, crime, espionage, terror and war have in turn been outfitted with the prefix "cyber" and framed as existential threats to national security.

Cyber crime started out as a very broad concept with various meanings, ranging from technology-enabled crimes to crimes committed against and for national security. Today, the codification of cyber crime in domestic jurisdictions as well as the widespread and transatlantic support for the 2001 European Convention on Cybercrime (into force in 2004) appear to have stabilized its content around a focus on criminal acts relating to the (mis)use of hardware and software, stealing and destruction of information for financial gain, to destroy competition or to gain a strategic advantage. Legal and policy attention to cyber crime has regularly been diverted by sudden public concern with cyber war, cyber terror or cyber espionage.

The cyber terror discourse has played out in the broader context of the global war on terror. Whereas the latter half of the 1990s saw an emergent interest in cyber war, this abruptly changed with 9/11. However, as no internationally agreed definition of terror exists in international law, talking about cyber terror has no defined focus, and as a result, in the absence of international events even broadly identified as cyber terror and in the context of the complicated international regulatory landscape, cyber terror has lost much of its traction as a perceived national security threat. This is also reflected in scholarly interest, which tapered off from the mid-2000s.

While seemingly not impinging much on the cyber war discourse, the Snowden revelations appear to have to the consequence that the cyber espionage gap—for a long time a type of legal void between the domain of cyber crime and cyber war—is disappearing as scholarly focus has turned toward the analysis of international legal frameworks for surveillance (Margulies 2014; Milanovic 2014). As noted by Deeks, international law has traditionally had little to say about foreign surveillance because "until recently, no court, treaty body, or government had suggested that international law, including basic privacy protections in human rights treaties, applied to purely foreign intelligence collection" (Deeks 2015: 291).

Unpacking the framing of cyber war: agendas, markets and ideologies

The attacks on Estonia in the wake of the relocation of the Bronze Soldier of Tallinn in 2007 and the Stuxnet attacks on Iran in 2010 have become the foundational myths of contemporary cyber war scholarship, repeated and rehearsed ad nauseam in academic work and popular reporting. Nevertheless, these events and the narratives spun around them are also considered game changers in global cyber security, with actual effects on policy and lawmaking.

Up until very recently, a dominant feature of popular cyber discourse has been the pervasiveness of what critical scholars have labeled "cyber doom scenarios" (Lawson 2012a). Labels such as "digital pearl harbor," "cyber 9/11," "eWMDs" or "cyber Katharina" are also used. The imprecise terminology for describing cyber conflict often leads to hyperbole.

As in political science scholarship, the legal literature brims with cyber war scenarios invoking imageries of mass casualties and large-scale destruction, such casualties have been notably absent in the three events commonly labeled as "cyber wars": in Estonia; Georgia (where kinetic force produced casualties) and with respect to the impact of the Stuxnet virus in Iran. Hailing from the USA but increasingly global in its reach, the cyber doom imagery conjures up scenarios where cyber attacks on electric grids, dams and military infrastructure leads to disastrous environmental and societal consequences, including mass civilian casualties. These scenarios contain vivid descriptions of the catastrophic effects of collapses in air traffic, mass deaths at hospitals without power, nuclear reactors out of control and colliding trains.

Important critical contributions have unpacked the crafting of these scenarios and the attendant linkages between cyber security and war by pointing to the importance of threat-framing, whereby government officials and experts use certain phrases and also certain types of stories to add urgency to their case (Dunn Cavelty 2007; Lawson 2012b). As noted by Myriam Dunn Cavelty, while often presented as an unquestionable and uncontested "truth," the link between cyber space and national security had to be forged, argued, and accepted in the (security) political process over the last two decades (Dunn Cavelty 2012a). This link has been forged by how particular agents develop specific interpretive schemas about what should be considered a threat or risk, how to respond to this threat, and who is responsible for it (Dunn Cavelty 2008a). The introduction of the "politics of fear" (Furedi 2005) into cyber politics is a contested development: As observed by Bruce Schneier "words have meaning, and metaphors matter ... if we accept the military's expansive cyberspace definition of 'war,' we feed our fears" (Schneier 2010a).

There are also important empirical criticism. Attention has been given to the possibility of bad outcomes: The tendency to focus on national security measures instead of economic and business solutions may detrimentally affect the overall level of security (Guitton 2013). There is a risk of crowding out effective prosecution of cyber crime—which poses the much bigger threat to cyber security—by diverting political attention and financial resources, leading to weak mandates and underfunding of cyber forensics (Schneier 2010b). Finally, the national security approach may simply be ineffective: due to the nature of critical infrastructure (in private hands) and the distribution of technology resources (also private), a further militarization of cyber space becomes "pointless" (Dunn Cavelty 2012b).

This militarization process has a deeply commercial aspect. Despite the ongoing financial crisis, governments continue to increase their spending on defensive and offensive cyber capabilities. While the USA cyber military–industrial complex is unique, it is also indicative of a rise of such military–industrial complexes worldwide (Brito and Watkins 2011). The continued growth of transnational IT firms such as Symantec and MacAfee is in part a consequence of the increase in cyber attacks, but it is also a direct outcome of the cyber threat assessments produced by IT companies looking for commercial opportunities. Commercial actors like Lockheed Martin, Boeing, and BAE Systems have all launched cyber-security divisions. Traditional defense contractors, such as Northrop Grumman, Raytheon, and ManTech International now invest heavily in information security products and services. Commentators compare this complex to the military-industrial complex of the Cold War and warn that it may serve to not only supply cyber-security solutions to governments, but also to drum up demand and secure spending on them (Deibert and Robozinski 2011; Brito and Watkins 2012).

Two categories of cyber-insecurity entrepreneurs (or less charitably, "cyber hawks") have emerged from this complex. When cyber attacks are framed as threats requiring military response, certain professional groups are designed as experts (Kessler and Werner 2013). Their expertise co-constitutes the reality which it is describing, including the allocation of resources (Leander and Aalberts 2013). The problem of revolving doors has been significant. High profile members of US presidential administrations, who have gone back and forth between government service and the private sector include Mike McConnell, formerly National Security Agency chief and Booz Allen Hamilton vice president, and Richard A. Clarke, formerly special advisor to several presidents on cyber security and currently the chairman of two corporate risk management firms. Together with Robert Knake, Clarke wrote the 2010 bestseller *Cyber War: The Next Threat to National Security and What to Do About it*. This book is often identified by more critical commentators as the archetypal harbinger of cyber doom imagery (for an example, see Lawson 2012a). As "experts" on the nature and origins of the Stuxnet virus, individual security specialists such as Ralph Langner and Eugene Kaspersky achieved worldwide fame. While these individuals have met with a critical reception in the security trade press, the mainstream media has enthusiastically embraced their messages.[1]

The cohort of external enemies essential to the cyber security and cyber war agenda have changed with geopolitical conjectures: in the late 1980s, the Soviets were the main information war adversary for Western governments (Metcalfe 1988). From the mid-1990s, there has been a growing but inconsistent focus on China as the chief foe in a future cyber war (Yoshihara 2001), reaching a high point in spring 2013 (Sanger *et al.* 2013) before subsiding markedly from the onset of the Snowden revelations and then returning with the indictment of five Chinese hackers for cyber espionage in 2014 (Nakashima 2014). In reports and scholarly contributions, Chinese cyber espionage has been framed as a one-sided (until the NSA-leaks), serious and credible threat to national security. Scenarios of future (but not too distant) cyber wars with China are prominently featured. Examples include the thirty or so pages dedicated to the issue by Clarke and Knake in their 2010 bestseller; *Blown to Bits China's War in Cyberspace* by Christopher Bronk (2011) and the industry provider Northrop Grumman's 2012 report prepared for the USA–China Economic and Security Review Commission entitled "Occupying the Information High Ground: Chinese Capabilities for Computer Network Operations and Cyber Espionage" (Northrop Grumman 2012). In the eyes of the European public, the Snowden revelations seem to have put US cyber aggression only very temporarily on par with the perceived Chinese cyber threat. On a broader European level, the exposé of the NSA surveillance increased distrust between NATO allies, complicating the task of agreeing on what capabilities might be provided to NATO members experiencing cyber attacks.

The internationalization of cyber security

While the UN Security Council did not mention the cyber aspect in its resolution on Georgia in 2008, and no resolutions were passed after the attacks on Estonia and Iran, the UN has for some time seen an "astonishing rate of norm emergence in cyber-space relative to typical international relations timelines" (Maurer 2011). The two principal streams of negotiations regarding cyber security are an economic stream focusing on cyber crime[2] and a politico-military stream focusing on cyber warfare.[3] Since 1998, Russia has been particularly vocal in calling for a set of international rules. The US perception has been that Russia would remain a haven for cyber crime, while wanting a cyber treaty to compensate for national security cyber vulnerabilities. The US refusal to engage with this effort has been explained as a rejection of Russia's discursive shift from cyber crime to cyber war (Gjelten 2010). Only in 2010 did the USA agree to co-sponsor a draft resolution on cyber security in the UN General Assembly (Maurer 2011).

Cyber security also continues to be tied up with the broader regulatory question of internet governance and freedom of expression (Mueller 2002; Mueller 2010). Indicative here is the cold Northern reception of the international norm-making efforts of the Shanghai Cooperation Organization (SCO). The SCO is an intergovernmental mutual-security organization founded in 2001 by China, Russia, Kazakhstan, Kyrgyzstan, Tajikistan and Uzbekistan. An SCO-accord adopted in 2009 defined "information war" in part, as an effort by a state to undermine another's "political, economic, and social systems." The SCO proposed that the dissemination of information "harmful to the spiritual, moral and cultural spheres of other states" should be considered a security threat (Gjelten 2010). In 2011, the SCO presented an international code of conduct for information security to the 66th UN General Assembly. The proposal, which included the principle that "policy authority for Internet-related public issues is the sovereign right of states" was rejected (Mueller 2011).

During the 2012 World Conference on international Telecommunications, held under the auspices of the International Telecommunications Union (ITU), a coalition of 55 member states including the USA refused to sign a new treaty promoted by SCO and like-minded states revising ITUs telecommunications regulations, allegedly because one of the conferences resolutions would allow the Internet to be placed under government control. At the same time

The historical US dominance over ICANN, the private sector, international organization managing key features of the Internet such as the domain name system and Internet Protocol (IP) addressing was only altered in early 2014 (Kruger 2015).[4]

Shaping cyber conflict through legal interpretation

The politics of legal classification

The conceptual and doctrinal link between legal scholarship, information technology and warfare is not new, neither is the concern with defining cyber war: As noted by Richard Aldrich: "how the law of war and international treaties proscribe the scope and use of information war hinges largely on how it is defined" (Aldrich 1996). The early debates on of information warfare were connected to the literatures on *Revolution in military affairs* and the dawning of the information age (Tilford 1995; Toffler and Toffler 2004). Prolific conceptual attention was given to fleshing out more nuanced understandings of the nature of the threat, and what was "new" about war in an era of information technology.[5]

The initial debate on the need for an international response and the need to provide international legal regulation of information war emerged in the mid-1990s, as the empirical evidence of the possible impact of information war began to surface, and as computer crime and espionage became increasingly prevalent. Scholars focused on known information war techniques and the international legal implications of their use. While the scholarship on computer crime was already well established, considerable attention was given to the task of providing an analytical separation between information war, and cyber crime and cyber espionage (Greenberg *et al.* 1998). Previewing later debates, some early commentators argued that information warfare needed an international legal response, but that international law was geared toward "antiquated" forms of war, unable to keep up with technological developments (Kanuck 1996: 272). Others saw the existing international legal framework as adequate (Zengel 1996; Grove *et al.* 2003; Joyner and Lotrionte 2001). Reflecting on this classic schism, a commentator noted that "the introduction of new means and methods of warfare has often been accompanied by the claim that technological developments are taking place in a legal vacuum and, consequently, demand a new legal paradigm" (Haslam 2000: 158).

In the latter part of the 1990s, the availability and affordability of information technology became more widespread, and the number of cyber attacks more prevalent. Gradually, the legal analysis moved from more general concerns with treaty interpretation issues, the validity of Article 2(4) as a norm in international law, and its applicability to cyber attacks, to become more cyber specific. The term "cyber war" began to replace information war (and other terms). While agreeing on the applicability of the laws of war to cyber attacks, a notion that these attacks would *not* constitute an illegal use of force or an armed attack under international law gained significant traction. As mentioned above, whereas 9/11 directed the attention of legal scholars toward the issue of cyber terror, events in Estonia (2007) and Georgia (2009) led to a doctrinal return to the preoccupation with cyber attacks as "armed conflict."

In the contemporary cyber doom imagery, NATO, the USA and Western countries more generally are depicted as inadequately prepared for a looming cyber war against China, North Korea, Russia and other adversaries. Key to the unpreparedness argument is a narrative of lack. A central motif is the notion of national security as being *under threat*, due to inadequate infrastructure, funding, manpower, domestic policy and national and international legal frameworks (see for example, Clarke and Knake 2010). More specifically, a perceived *lack* of legal regulation of interstate conduct as well as the lack of legal obligations on the part of private companies, international organizations, and government bureaucracies to provide cyber security, is seen as creating vulnerabilities and constituting a threat to national security and to a peaceful world order. Today, calls for the application of the law of armed conflict; or more precisely, a new and cyber-specific LOAC instrument; is frequently voiced as part of the demand for tougher government action on adversaries, more comprehensive institutionalization of cyber war in the national security infrastructure and more spending on both defensive and offensive cyber capabilities

A second position rejects the militarization of cyber space represented by the cyber doom agenda. Critics (most famously Rid 2012) have argued that not only have the proponents of this agenda changed the story about who threatens what, how, and with what potential impact over time, but they have done so with very little evidence provided to support the claims being made. Hence, the laws of warfare do not and should not apply.

A third position partially accepts the framing of certain cyber events as national security threats. It holds that regardless of labels, cyber threats are real and that various cyber tools and techniques are becoming increasingly important in international conflict. This position focuses on the necessity of protecting critical information infrastructure. According to this perspective, resilience is the best strategy to maintain national security and avoid escalation of international cyber conflicts. Resilience is achieved by using both humans and technologies to resist some attacks, absorb and mitigate others, and reach out to anticipate and stop other attacks (Demchak 2011). While this middle-of-the-road approach appears less critically attuned to the militarization agenda, the type of comprehensive legal approach that accompanies it may over time gain stronger purchase in challenging the rhetorical concern with "war" than the position arguing against the application of the laws of armed conflict as such. It holds that while international law offers a regulatory framework for a crucial but small part of the cyber-security challenge, inadequate protection of critical information infrastructure and unsatisfactory coordination of domestic legal regimes remain insufficiently addressed by policymakers in most jurisdictions. What is needed is a "comprehensive" legal approach capable of addressing the full spectrum of cyber-security issues.

Legal models

While legal arguments function as a resource in the general cyber war debate, doctrinal legal interpretation also molds political conceptualizations of cyber war, particularly with respect to threshold questions and their place on the political agenda. Whether a cyber attack constitutes a weapon of war depends on the scale, target, objective and outcome of the attack. Yet, the lexicon for describing cyber conflict is imprecise and highly malleable (Lewis 2009; Sharma 2010). In the context of international law, there is no politically agreed-upon definition of cyber war, and there is deep disagreement about which attacks might amount to a cyber war: how it starts, how it ends or how it should be conducted, as well as the potential legal ramifications (Goldsmith 2013). At the same time, the availability of legal remedies hinges on the ability to identify who is behind the attack, what their intention is, what damage is incurred and whether causality between the attack and its consequences can be established. Too narrow and too broad definitions create challenges with respect to divisions of labor between civil and military domains; between the government and the private sector; and between national governments and international entities.

Three positions have so far dominated the doctrinal legal debate on how the international community should regulate cyber war. The first perspective sees cyber war as difficult or impossible to regulate at the international level. The second position calls for new legal instruments while the third position mainly sees cyber war as a problem of applying the law of armed conflict. This approach has now been codified through the Manual on International Law Applicable to Cyber Warfare. While avoiding the pitfalls of embarking on a treaty making process, the project of creating authoritative restatements has its own legitimacy challenges. Hence there is a value to tracing the uses of legal arguments and the moves within legal debate prior to the Manual.

According to the first perspective, the perceived inability of law to deal with the Internet and information technology is often held up as a barrier against effective regulation, concerning the rapid development of technology and the cross-border nature of the Internet (Tikk 2011). Cyber attacks will often be too ambiguous, or too different from the categories of classic kinetic warfare to fall under the law of war framework (Lewis 2010). Furthermore, the regulatory task is perceived as extremely complex: an international framework for cyber war must address the multidimensional nature of cyber war, taking the strong civil/ military, national/international and private/public dimensions into account. The difficult challenge of harmonizing cyber-security norms at the national, bilateral and international level is further hampered by the clash of interest between governments and the private sector (Goldsmith 2010). Moreover, an international agreement is difficult to achieve because the distribution of emerging cyber capabilities and vulnerabilities is unlikely to correspond to the status quo distribution of power built on traditional measures including military and economic might (Waxman 2011). Even if a broad agreement could be reached, the challenges belonging to the well-known inventory of regime choices characteristic of such ventures persist. Stakeholders need to agree on who should make the new law, what form the rules should take, the role of institutions in overseeing the implementation and enforcement of the new law as well as the actual content and dynamism of the substantive norms (Hollis 2007).

The proponents of the second standpoint engage in an activity familiar to historians of military law: Faced with new military technology, legal scholars and practitioners habitually call for new legal instruments. Contemporary proponents of a new treaty hold that while cyber warfare can be regulated by law, it represents a qualitative change in the meaning and nature of warfare, and a new international treaty regime dealing exclusively with cyber security and its status in international law should be developed. The scholars calling for a new treaty mostly focus on norms for jus in bello (Barkham 2001; Brown 2006; Shackelford 2009). Related propositions are to apply other legal instruments by analogy (Silver 2002) or the adoption of self-governing rules or non-legally binding norms (codes of conduct, rules of engagement) with the expectation that international legal rules will emerge from them in time (Hollis 2007). The emphasis on an international treaty is based on the assumptions that a treaty limits and controls state action in the cyber realm, imposes responsibility for the behavior of private actors, establishes mechanisms of interstate cooperation, clarifies definitions and creates an international organization to facilitate cooperation and monitoring (or a dispute referral mechanism, such as ICJ or the ICC [Ophardt 2010]). The new treaty-approach has been criticized for having *idealized a multilateral treaty akin to the Geneva Conventions*, which would neither be able to obtain sufficient state participation or be flexible enough to accommodate technological developments (Hollis 2007: 18).

The proponents of the third perspective—which over time has come to dominate the legal debate on cyber war—argue that cyber attacks may fall under the law of armed conflict and that the interpretation and application of the existing law of war framework is sufficient (Dinstein 2002). At the political level, whether an attack is classified as an economic or political–military issue by the government and the military will depend on the scale, sophistication and motivation of the attack, but also on the geopolitical and strategic resources of the country under attack, and the (attributed) identity of the attacker. Not unique to the case of cyber war, the interpretation of norms is generally characterized by the different strategic logics and unequal power relationships between nations. Moreover, national approaches largely reflect those strategic positions generally taken on the use of force, the permissibility of self-defense and the means and methods of warfare (for a discussion, see Henriksen this volume).

The power of threshold discussions, the Tallinn Manual and NATO Article 5

As a matter of disciplinary practice, legal scholars spend much of their energy on threshold discussions. The visibility and importance of this activity situates the threshold issue as a central topic for cyber war scholarship, with reverse effects for the range of topics that fall outside this sphere of interpretive activity. The key discussions in the jus ad bellum (of relevance for NATO Article 5) concern the use of force under the Charter of the United Nations. While the political science community continues to be embroiled in a debate over defini-tional issues and the possibility of cyber war, legal scholars have largely aban-doned the erstwhile stance that cyber attacks could not constitute a use of force or an armed attack and agree that a cyber attack *may* represent a prohibited use of force under Art. 2(4). Nevertheless, the threshold levels for *when* a cyber attack constitutes a use of force or an armed attack remain highly contested. These are important debates, because the higher the threshold for considering a cyber attack to be a prohibited use of force, the higher the threshold at which cyber attacks contribute to the instigation or escalation of a conflict. Moreover, the higher the threshold for permitting armed self-defense (under Article 51), the lower is the likelihood of escalating a conflict. As law talk takes center stage in the cyber war discourse, legalistic threshold discussions will steadily accrue more influence. As of 2013, the Tallinn Cyber Warfare Manual became the focal point for such discussions.

The Manual on International Law Applicable to Cyber Warfare was a three-year project sponsored by NATO CCD COE and spearheaded by Professor Michael Schmitt, the most influential cyber war scholar in international law. The objective of this Manual is to develop authoritative reference on the international law applicable to cyber conflict. The Manual is divided into "black letter rules" and accompanying "commentary." Prior to the publication of the Tallinn Manual, it was obvious that many questions concerning cyber attacks remained unresolved; but not necessarily that the international laws of force and armed conflict were the exclusive bodies of law to apply. This latter debate is now largely closed. With respect to the first debate, for a number of reasons discussed below; the Manual may have institutionalized rather than eliminated uncertainty.

The Manual is modeled after the 1995 San Remo Manual on International Law Applicable to Armed Conflicts at Sea and the 2010 HPCR Manual on Inter-national Law Applicable to Air and Missile Warfare. Like these manuals, the Tallinn Manual project draws on a "world-class international law and law of armed conflict experts" who consist exclusively of European and US American scholars. The composition of the group of experts was "crucial to the credibility of the final product" (p. 9) and "sought to capture all reasonable positions for inclusion" in the Manual's commentary (p. 6).[6] At the presentation of the Manual at the 2011 NATO Coe conference in Tallinn, this author listen to a participant from "the Global South" voice his concerns about the composition of the expert group, an unease reflected by Dieter Fleck, who notes that: "cyber security deserves and receives a wide-reaching interest at global scale and there are already relevant policy documents of the European Union and at least 25 states including the Russian Federation" (Fleck 2013: 331–51).

According to the logic of legal interpretation espoused by the Manual, the group of experts will by following the sources of international law have arrived at doctrinally correct result. Nevertheless, there appears to be a propensity to rely on Schmitt's previous influential work as the correct solution to cyber threshold questions while the Manual deals lightly with the criticisms levied against these legal positions in the period between 1999 and 2013 (Boer 2013).

While the Manual self-presents as a work based on the formally enumerated sources of international law, it substantively draws on the military manuals of Canada, Germany, the UK and the USA—manuals considered "especially useful" (p. 8). Schmitt has also argued that "the relative congruency" between the views outlined in the September 2012 speech of State Department Legal Adviser Harold Koh on the US positions on how international law applies to cyber space and those of the International Group of Experts "is striking." Schmitt has suggested that: "This confluence of a state's expression of opinio juris with a work constituting the teachings of the most highly qualified publicists of the various nations' significantly enhances the persuasiveness of common conclusions" (Schmitt 2012).

It is clearly possible to see things differently, and in future work on the Manual, Northern legal scholars should carefully consider its global legitimacy. Moreover, Tallinn 2.0 will soon be upon us. To be published in 2016, it is designed to expand the scope of the Manual to encompass "cyber operations of lesser gravity." Tallinn 2.0 will incorporate discussions on the law of the sea, international telecommunications law, space law, diplomatic and consular law and human rights law, as well as principles of international law as they relate to sovereignty and the prohibition of intervention. Tallinn 2.0 is being developed by four of the original experts under Schmitt's leadership and with the assistance of a team of legal and technical experts from the NATO Defense Centre of Excellence. While the Manual will "continue to solely represent the views of its authors," it will no doubt also yield influential pronouncements—this time on the much broader field of cyber security.

Finally, in 2014, NATO adopted a new cyber defense policy whereby cyber attacks that amount to armed attacks may activate the collective defense clause under Article 5 of the NATO charter (Cheng 2014). As evident from the Wales Summit Declaration (2014), the policy's indeterminacy and open-endedness whereby the threshold for triggering the application for Article 5 will be determined on a case-by-case basis further heightens the political importance of clarifying how the rules of armed conflict govern cyber hostilities—and it heightens the legitimacy and political currency of legal interpretation (Sandvik 2014).

Counter narratives

The comprehensive legal approach

The chapter now moves to identify three lines of legal inquiry that might provide starting points for scholarly resistance to the militarization of the cyber-security agenda. The first concerns the so-called "comprehensive legal approach."

Key sectors of modern society rely on a spectrum of highly interdependent national and international software-based control systems for their smooth, reliable, and continuous operation (Dunn Cavelty 2005). In addition to the World Wide Web, cyber space includes all networked digital activities, such as separate military defense networks, private sector networks and academic networks, as well as SCADA (supervisory control and data acquisition) systems. Together, these networks constitute society's *critical information infrastructure.* Critical information infrastructure is in general regarded as inherently insecure. Most of the components are developed in the private sector, where profit motifs and competition, not security, drives system design: hence, computer and network vulnerabilities should be expected (Dunn Cavelty 2007). At the same time, these systems are seen as vulnerable because they constitute attractive targets. Hence, in recent years, "the comprehensive security model" has emerged, emphasizing extensive coordination of legal approaches. While this model integrates the cyber war component, it considers a broader spectrum of threats to national and international security, as it links the danger of cyber conflict to cyber threats to critical infrastructure. This approach is based on the notion that the obstacles to a better cyber security are not technical, but policy based on outdated analysis (Lewis 2011). The need for such an approach has been acknowledged on the international level only in the past few years, while national calls for a broad approach to cyber security date back almost a decade (Tikk 2011). It has received renewed relevance as critics have questioned the effectiveness of the NATO Article 5 incorporation on the account that too many NATO members still lack cyber strategies and tools, and have not sufficiently engaged with general low cost "cyber hygiene" measures that can increase cyber security for critical information infrastructure.[7]

Under the "comprehensive approach" proposed by Enneken Tikk (2011), law is seen as a required element for cyber security. While cyber security is not understood as a new domain, it is seen as a new strategic issue, posing new challenges and complex issues. In this context, the problem is identified as gaps in regulation and legal practice; the gaps in themselves create vulnerabilities. Moreover, it is emphasized that legal interpretation must be more cognizant of technology as well as its social use. Similarly, there is a need to clarify legal authority, and coordinate it between private stakeholders, national CERT-teams

(Computer Emergency Response Teams), law enforcement and the military: today's fragmented mandates engender opportunities for malicious activity.

The need for a comprehensive approach derives both from architecture of Internet and emerging cyber-security threats and incidents. The architecture of the Internet and the set-up of the information society mean that no country or organization can come up with an all-encompassing solution. The critical information structure on which government, military and information society rely, is mostly privately owned. These are systems with security standards developed in peace time and within a commercial frame. Emerging security challenges require management from a number of stakeholders—information technology experts, national policymakers, diplomats, military commanders and intelligence communities.

In short, what is needed is a substantive framework for addressing the *full* spectrum of cyber security: an approach combining considerations of threat, deterrence and response from different areas of authority and responsibility, thereby aiming at eliminating gaps between different aspects of cyber incident prevention, detection, response and recovery. Such an approach requires a systematic development, interpretation and application of legal areas and instruments in a number of legal fields, including information society and telecommunications, cyber crime, national security and armed conflict. This would involve expertise across legal, policy and technological boundaries. This might or might not entail the need for *special* regulation of cyber warfare: a comprehensive approach will in any event be a necessary interim step for determining which aspects of cyber security would require additional international regulation (Tikk 2011).

Too much law, too little justice: giving scrutiny to domestic cyber industry

A different perspective holds that there is no lack of law. Cyber-security issues are governed by a plethora of national and international legal regimes, including computer law; criminal law; security law; human rights, the law of armed conflict—and by an increasingly thickening international framework of cyber-specific norms. According to this perspective, there is *too much* law and too much regulation, stifling both innovation and freedom of expression. Commentators have long argued that as governments and commercial providers intensify their quest for a "reform" of the Internet, this will effectively mean the "end of Internet" because control and excessive regulation will stifle innovation (Zittrain 2008). There has been a technical transformation of the "endless information highway" of the 1990s into the walled social media gardens of the present decade (Denning 2001). Internet is no longer "lawless" or "without borders." Alternative "bordered" Internets have emerged through national changes of the Internet's architecture (following national laws and technological developments), thus enabling the implementation of certain policies (Wu and Goldsmith 2008). Authoritarian *and* democratic governments have moved rapidly to obtain tighter regulation and more advanced technological means for control over the Internet and the filtering, denial (the so-called "kill switch") and control of access is becoming widespread as a governance practice (Deibert 2008a; Deibert *et al.* 2010, 2011).

Since the late 1990s, information technology has become accessible across the globe. The long-held notion that the "virtual" world is a different social space than the "real world" is finally giving way to the understanding that there is one social world which contains both traditional and technologically advanced modes of communication and sites of social activity (Garcia *et al.* 2009). This development has accelerated with the rise of social media: the humanization of technology coupled with the increasing human *dependence* on technology is profoundly changing concepts of identity and citizenship, as well as the ways in which we are governed—or accept to be governed. It has also become clear that technology implicates the human agent in a life and death grass-roots cyber war. Since 2011, the optimistic early analysis of the emancipatory potential of social media in the Arab spring, and previously in the Iranian 2009 Green revolution has been countered by contributions emphasizing Internet as a tool of oppression (Shirky 2011; Morozov 2012). So far, legal commentators have been seeking out a middle position (Anupam 2012; Joseph 2012).

This chapter argues that legal scholars should seize opportunities to do more: through a number of important publications, organizations which Deibert (2008b) calls "contrary forces" for good, such as Citizenlab, the Electronic Frontier Foundation and Human Rights First, have exposed how Internet service and information technology providers in the West have assisted authoritarian regimes in persecuting human rights defenders and social movements leaders. The coalition against unlawful surveillance exports was launched in April 2014.[8] However, very limited legal attention has so far been given to the legal role and responsibilities of vendors and regulatory authorities in the West under domestic or international human rights law. In a report titled "Some Devices Wander by Mistake: Planet Blue Coat Redux" (2013), Citizenlab raised questions around the sale of "dual-use" communication technologies to national jurisdictions (such as Syria, Iran and Sudan) where the implementation of such technology has not been publicly debated or shaped by the rule of law, and where the technology is used for crackdowns on dissidents (Marquis-Boire *et al.* 2013). A number of NGOs have pointed attention to inadequate human rights due diligence processes in the companies that produce this information technology and their investors. As noted by Human Rights First, there are "excuses, excuses" (Roggensack and Walters 2011). The absence of rigorous legal analyzes of these practices, particularly seen in the context of an almost obsessive doctrinal concern with determining the thresholds of cyber war, should be a concern.

The cyber-peace agenda: is law missing in action?

Lastly, "cyber peace" is an obvious antidote to cyber war rhetoric. Yet, cyber peace remains a surprisingly immature concept, legally and otherwise. As observed by Shackelford, to date, the attempts to define "cyber peace" have so far been underwhelming (Shackelford 2013). Previous initiatives did not make significant impact, such as the International Telecommunication Union (ITU) cyber-peace initiative (compromised by its previous association with former Egyptian presidential wife, Suzanne Mubarak), which attempted to "delegitimize cyberwar through reversing the perspective offering a counter-narrative in a debate that tends to be dominated by terms like cyber attack, cyber war, or electronic Pearl Harbor" (Wegener 2011).

Inside the legal debate, some scholars have put forward the argument that cyber war makes war more humane, and that international law should adapt to and promote cyber war as an alternative to traditional warfare (Kelsey 2008). This chapter disagrees and asks how scholars can contribute to the development of a legally sound *and* diplomatically palatable international "cyber-peace" agenda. As the threshold discussions outlined above should indicate, it would be a stretch to recast the extensive doctrinal efforts to clarify the norms of the law of armed conflict as substantive contributions to a "cyber peace": In the context of the law of war, the considerations that support expanded or restrictive interpretations of "use of force" or "armed attack" will be strategic and linked to national interest. Cyber peace could be promoted by delinking cyber-security issues from armed force and by imposing a high legal threshold for treating them as equivalent. An opportunity for critical engagement has arisen with the development of Tallinn 2.0, which will deal with cyber operations that do not rise to the level of armed attack as well as the relationship to peacetime international law (Vihul 2013).

At the same time, cyber peace should not be defined only in the negative: attention must be given to the role of international law in the development of a substantive cyber-peace agenda. Scott Shackelford's proposal for a "bottom-up governance framework" promoting self-organization and networking regulations to address collective action problems, is a welcome contribution but skirts the global perspective (Shackelford 2013). While ideas for "cyber warfare peace-keeping" were voiced more than a decade ago (Cahill *et al.* 2003), the first substantive contribution has been offered by Jann Kleffner and Heather Dinniss (2013) whose starting point is the observation that as a result of the deployment of complex peace operations and the increasing prevalence of cyber components in contemporary conflicts, the utility of engaging in cyber operations will increase for peacekeepers (Kleffner and Dinnis 2013). Nevertheless, none of these contributions take up the challenge of conceptualizing the parameters of "cyber peace" through a legal lens. Contributing to the clearer articulation of a cyber-peace agenda should be a priority for scholars.

Conclusion

This chapter has attempted to unpack the role of law in the decades-old drive to move cyber-security issues into the domain of warfare, culminating with the incorporation of cyber war into NATO Article 5. From the publication of "Cyberwar is coming!" in 1993 to the 2013 Tallinn Manual, cyber war has become an institutionalized fact in political discourse, military organizations and international law. It has also become institutionalized as a manifestation of Northern international law. Legal scholars have played an active and often uncritical role in this development, while the international legal academic community has given little attention to ways of resisting this conceptual transformation of cyber security. Perhaps, part of the explanation lies in the nature of the problem: much of the research on cyber attacks is classified and thus inaccessible. At the same time, legal scholars lack scientific and technical skills to analyze available information about technological developments, and to develop realistic scenarios. This often leads to the uncritical adoption of partial accounts of actual events or generic future doomsday scenarios. The Tallinn Manual reinforces this bias, and makes a truly global conversation on cyber security and international law more difficult. It is in this landscape that critical legal scholars must take the opportunity to unpack dominant narratives and develop situated analysis of domestic regulation and legal discourse.

Notes

1 For example the *New York Times* describing how "Ralph Langner, an independent computer security expert, 'solved Stuxnet'" (Broad, Markoff and Sanger 2011) or "Anti-Virus Pioneer Evgeny Kaspersky: 'I Fear the Net Will Soon Become a War Zone'" (*Spiegel* 2011).

2 For the economic stream, the central UN agencies are UNDOC (United Nations office on Drugs and Crime) and the ITU (the International Telecoms union). At the European level, ENISA (the European network and information security agency) was set up in 2004 to enhance the capability of the European Union, the EU Member States and the business community to prevent, address and respond to network and information security problems.

3 In response to the 2007 cyber attacks on Estonia, NATO set up the Cooperative Cyber defense center of excellence in Tallinn. The Lisbon Summit Declaration and NATO's 2010 Strategic Concept emphasized cyber defense as a crucial aspect of the security of NATO, its member states, and its partner states. NATOs first official cyber-defense policy was presented in June 2011.

4 In tandem with official norm making efforts, in recent years significant focus has been turned toward so-called "confidence building measures" (CBM) (Bendiek and Porter 2013; Ziolowski 2013; Healey *et al.* 2013). For example, a diplomatic effort incorporating three confidence building measures on cyber security between the USA and Russia from 2013 was "designed to increase transparency and reduce the possibility that a misunderstood cyber incident could create instability or a crisis in our bilateral relationship" (White House 2013).

5 In a pioneering contribution, John Arquilla and David Ronfeldt offered a distinction between what they called "netwar," by which they meant societal-level ideational conflicts waged in part through communication technology, and "cyber war" at the military level (Arquilla and Ronfeldt 1993). In an influential analysis, Martin Libicki (1995) distinguished between seven different forms of information warfare, including command-and-control warfare; intelligence-based warfare; electronic warfare; psychological warfare; hacker warfare; economic information warfare; and cyber warfare (Libicki 1995). Adding to the conceptual richness, Aldrich (1996) included info war, informations operation, netwar, command and control counter war (C2W), third wave war, knowledge war and cyber war.

6 The Manual on International Law Applicable to Cyber Warfare.
7 The argument is that deterrence and retaliation may be less effective than trying to mitigate the harmful consequences in the physical world (Smith 2014; Wolff 2014).
8 The campaigns members are Privacy International, Amnesty International, Digitale Gesellschaft, FIDH, Human Rights Watch, Reporters without Borders, and the New America Foundation's Open Technology Institute. *See* www.globalcause.net/ (accessed December 1, 2015).

References

Aldrich, Richard W. 1996. "The International Legal Implications of Information Warfare." *INSS Occasional Paper* 9. Information Warfare Series, US Air Force Academy, Colorado.

Anupam, Chander. 2012. "Jasmine Revolutions." *Cornell Law Review* 97.

Arquilla, John and David Ronfeldt. 1993. "Cyberwar is coming!" *Comparative Strategy* 12 (2): 141–65.

Barkham, Jason. 2001. "Information Warfare and International Law on the Use of Force." *New York University Journal of International Law and Politics* 34.

Bendiek, Annegret and Andrew L. Porter. 2013. "European Cyber Security Policy within a Global Multistakeholder Structure." *European Foreign Affairs Review* 18 (2).

Boer, Lianne J.M. 2013. "Restating the Law 'As It Is': On the Tallinn Manual and the Use of Force in Cyberspace." *Amsterdam Law Forum* 5: 3.

Brito, Jerry and Ted Watkins. 2011. "The Cybersecurity-Industrial Complex." *Reason*, August/September 2011 issue, at: http://reason.com/archives/2011/07/25/the-cybersecurity-industrial-c/2 (accessed December 1, 2015).

Brito, Jerry and Ted Watkins. 2012. "Loving the Cyber Bomb? The Dangers of Threat Inflation in Cybersecurity Policy." *Harvard National Security Journal* 3.

Broad, William J., John Markoff and David E. Sanger. 2011. "Israeli Test on Worm Called Crucial in Iran Nuclear Delay." *New York Times*, January 15, at: www.nytimes.com/2011/01/16/world/middleeast/16stuxnet.html?pagewanted=all&_r=0 (accessed December 1, 2015).

Bronk, Christopher. 2011. *Blown to Bits China's War in Cyberspace, August–September 2020.* Strategic Studies Quarterly.

Brown, Davis. 2006. "A Proposal for an International Convention to Regulate the Use of Information Systems in Armed Conflict." *Harvard International Law Journal* 47.

Cahill, Thomas, Konstantin Rozinov and Christopher Mule. 2003. *Cyber warfare peacekeeping.* Information Assurance Workshop, IEEE Systems, Man and Cybernetics Society.

Cheng, Joey. 2014. *Raising the Stakes: NATO says a cyber attack on one is an attack on all.* September 8, at: http://defensesystems.com/Articles/2014/09/08/NATO-cyber-attack-collective-response.aspx (accessed December 1, 2015).

Clarke, Richard A. and Robert Knake. 2010. *Cyber War: The Next Threat to National Security and What to Do About It.* Ecco Reprint Edition.

Deeks, Ashley. 2015. "An International Legal Framework for Surveillance." *Virginia Journal of International Law* 55.

Deibert, Ron. 2008a. *Access Denied: The Practice and Policy of Global Internet Filtering.* Cambridge, MA: The MIT Press.

Deibert, Ron. 2008b. "Black Code Redux: Censorship, Surveillance, and the Militarization of Cyberspace," in M. Boler (ed.), *Digital Media and Democracy: Tactics in Hard Times.* Cambridge, MA: The MIT Press, 137–64.

Deibert, Ron, John Palfrey, Rafal Rohozinski, Jonathan Zittrain and M. Harazti. 2010. *Access Controlled: The Shaping of Power, Rights, and Rule in Cyberspace*. Cambridge, MA: The MIT Press.

Deibert, Ron, John Palfrey, Rafal Rohozinski and Jonathan Zittrain. 2011. *Access Contested: Security, Identity and Resistance in Asian Cyberspace*. Cambridge, MA: The MIT Press.

Deibert, Ron and Rafal Rohozinski. 2011. *The "New Cyber Military-Industrial Complex."* Munk School of Global Affairs, University of Toronto, at: http://citizenlab. org/2011/03/deibert-and-rohozinski-the-new-cyber-military-industrial-complex/ (accessed December 1, 2015).

Demchak, Chris. 2011. *Conflicting Policy Presumptions about Cybersecurity: Cyber–Prophets,—Priests,—Detectives, and—Designers, and Strategies for a Cybered World*. Atlantic Council Issue Brief.

Denning, Dorothy E. 2001. "Activism, Hacktivism, and Cyberterrorism: The Internet as a Tool for Influencing Foreign Policy," in J. Arquilla and D. Ronfeldt (eds), *Networks and Netwars: The Future of Terror, Crime, and Militancy*. RAND.

Dinstein, Yoram. 2002. "Computer Network Attacks and Self-Defense." *INT'L L. STUD* 76.

Dunn Cavelty, Myriam. 2005. *The Socio-Political Dimensions of Critical Information Infrastructure Protection (CIIP)*. 1 Int. J. Critical Infrastructures 2/3.

Dunn Cavelty, Myriam. 2007. *Critical Information Infrastructure: Vulnerabilities, Threats and Responses*. 3 Disarmament Forum ICTs and International Security.

Dunn Cavelty, Myriam. 2008a. *Cyber-Security and Threat Politics: US Efforts to Secure the Information Age*. Routledge, London.

Dunn Cavelty, Myriam. 2008b. "Cyber-terror—Looming Threat or Ohantom Menace? The Framing of the US Cyber-Threat Debate." *Journal of Information Technology and Politics* 4 (1).

Dunn Cavelty, Myriam. 2012a. "From Cyber-Bombs to Political Fallout: Threat Representations with an Impact in the Cyber-Security Discourse." *International Studies Review* 15 (1).

Dunn Cavelty, Myriam. 2012b. *The Militarisation of Cyberspace: Why Less may be Better*, in C. Czosseck, R. Ottis and K. Ziolkowski (eds), 2012 4th international conference on cyber conflict.

Ebert, Hannes and Tim Maurer. 2013. "Contested Cyberspace and Rising Powers." *Third World Quarterly* 34 (6): 1054–74.

EFF. 2012. "Human Rights and Technology Sales." *Electronic Frontier Foundation*, at: https://we.riseup.net/assets/92532/human-rights-technology-sales.pdf (accessed December 1, 2015).

Fleck, Dieter. 2013. "Searching for International Rules Applicable to Cyber Warfare—A Critical First Assessment of the New Tallinn Manual." *Journal of Conflict and Security Law* 18 (2).

Furedi, Frank. 2005. *Culture of Fear Revisited*. London: Continuum Press.

Garcia, Angela C., Alecea I. Standlee, Jennifer Bechhoff and Yan Cui. 2009. "Ethnographic Approaches to the Internet and Computer-Mediated Communication." *Journal of Contemporary Ethnography* 38.

Gjelten, Tom. 2010. "Shadow Wars: Debating Cyber 'Disarmament'." *World Affairs Journal*, at: www.worldaffairsjournal.org/article/shadow-wars-debating-cyber-disarmament (accessed December 1, 2015).

Goldsmith, Jack. 2010. "The New Vulnerability." *The New Republic*, at: www.tnr.com/article/books-and-arts/75262/the-new-vulnerability (accessed December 1, 2015).

194   *K.B. Sandvik*

Goldsmith, Jack. 2013. "How Cyber Changes the Laws of War." *European Journal of International Law* 24.

Greenberg, L.T., S.E. Goodman and K.J. Soo Hoo. 1998. *Information Warfare and International Law.*

Grove, G., S. Goodman and S. Lukasik. 2000. "Cyber-attacks and International Law." *Survival: Global Politics and Strategy* 42.

Guitton, Clement. 2013. "Cyber Insecurity as a National Threat: Overreaction from Germany, France and the UK?" *European Security* 22.

Haslam, Emily. 2000. "Information Warfare, Technological Challenges and International Warfare." *Journal of Conflict and Security Law* 5.

Healey, Jason, John C. Mallery, Klara Tothova Jordan and Nathaniel V. Youd. 2013. *Confidence-Building Measures in Cyberspace A Multistakeholder Approach for Stability and Security.* Atlantic Council.

Hollis, David M. 2007. "Why States Need an International Law for Information Operations." *Lewis & Clark Law Review* 11.

Joseph, Sarah. 2012. "Social Media, Political Change, and Human Rights." *Boston College International and Comparative Law Review* 35.

Joyner, Christopher and Cathrine Lotrionte. 2001. "Information Warfare as International Coercion: Elements of a Legal Framework." *European Journal of International Law* 12.

Kanuck, Sean. 1996. "Recent Development, Information Warfare: New Challenges for Public International Law." *Harvard International Law Journal* 37.

Kelsey, Jeffrey. 2008. "Hacking into International Humanitarian Law: The Principles of Distinction and Neutrality in the Age of Cyber Warfare." *Michigan Law Review* 106.

Kessler, Oliver and Wouter Werner. 2013. "Expertise, Uncertainty, and International Law: A Study of the Tallinn Manual on Cyberwarfare." *Leiden Journal of International Law* 26 (04): 793–810.

Kleffner, Jann K. and Heather Dinniss. 2013. "Keeping the Cyber Peace: International Legal Aspects of Cyber Activities in Peace Operations." *INT'L L. STUD.* 89.

Kruger, Lennard. 2015. *Internet Governance and the Domain Name System: Issues for Congress. CRS,* at: www.fas.org/sgp/crs/misc/R42351.pdf (accessed December 1, 2015).

Lawson, Sean. 2012a. "Beyond Cyber-Doom: Cyberattack Scenarios and the Evidence of History," in Paul Ducheine, Frans Osinga, and Joseph Soeters (eds), *Cyber Warfare: Critical Perspectives.* The Hague: Asser Press, 276–307.

Lawson, Sean. 2012b. "Putting the "War" in Cyberwar: Metaphor, Analogy, and Cybersecurity Discourse in the United States." *First Monday,* at: http://firstmonday.org/ojs/index.php/fm/article/view/3848/3270 (accessed December 1, 2015).

Leander, Anna and Tanya Aalberts. 2013. "The Co-Constitution of Legal Expertise and International Security." *Leiden Journal of International Law.*

Lewis, James A. 2009. "Cyberwarfare and its Impact on International Security." *UNODA Occasional Papers* 19.

Lewis, James A. 2010. "A Note on the Laws of War in Cyberspace." *CSIS,* at: http://csis.org/files/publication/100425_Laws%20of%20War%20Applicable%20to%20Cyber%20Conflict.pdf (accessed December 1, 2015).

Lewis, James A. 2011. *Rethinking Cybersecurity—A Comprehensive Approach.* Speech at Sasakawa Peace Foundation, Tokyo, September 12, 2011, at: http://csis.org/files/publication/110920_Japan_speech_2011.pdf (accessed December 1, 2015).

Libicki, Martin C. 1995 *What is Information Warfare?* National Defense University Washington DC inst. Strategic Studies.

Margulies, Peter. 2014. "The NSA in Global Perspective: Surveillance, Human Rights, and International Counterterrorism." *Fordham Law Review* 82 (5).

Marquis-Boire, Morgane, Jakub Dalek, John Scott-Railton and Sarah McKune. 2013. *Some Devices Wander by Mistake: Planet Blue Coat Redux*. Munk School of Global Affairs, at: https://citizenlab.org/2013/07/planet-blue-coat-redux/ (accessed December 1, 2015).

Maurer, Tim. 2011. "Cyber norm emergence at the United Nations—An Analysis of the Activities at the UN Regarding Cyber-security." *Explorations in Cyber International Relations Discussion Paper Series*, at: http://belfercenter.ksg.harvard.edu/files/maurer-cyber-norm-dp-2011-11-final.pdf (accessed December 1, 2015).

Metcalfe, Robyn S. 1988. *The New Wizard War: How The Soviets Steal U.S. High Technology—and How We Give It Away*. Foreword S.D. Bryen. Redmond, WA: Microsoft Press.

Milanovic, Marko. 2015. "Human Rights Treaties and Foreign Surveillance: Privacy in the Digital Age." *Harvard International Law Journal* 56: 1.

Moltke, Henrik and Sebastian Gjerding. 2013. "Denmark Part of NSA Inner Circle." *Information*, November 4, at: www.information.dk/477405 (accessed December 1, 2015).

Morozov, Evgeny. 2012. *The Net Delusion: The Dark Side of Internet Freedom*. New York: PublicAffairs.

Mueller, Milton. 2002. *Ruling the Root: Internet Governance and the Taming of Cyberspace*. Boston, MA: MIT Press.

Mueller, Milton. 2010. *Networks and States: The Global Politics of Internet Governance*. Boston, MA: MIT Press.

Mueller, Milton. 2011. "Russia & China propose UN General Assembly Resolution on 'information security'," at: http://blog.internetgovernance.org/blog/_archives/2011/9/20/4903371.html?utm_source=feedburner&utm_medium=feed&utm_campaign=Feed%3A+IGPBlog+%28IGP+Blog+Main%29 (accessed December 1, 2015).

Nakashima, Ellen. 2014. "Indictment of PLA Hackers is Part of Broad U.S. Strategy to Curb Chinese Cyberspying." May 22. *Washington Post*, at: www.washingtonpost.com/world/national-security/indictment-of-pla-hackers-is-part-of-broad-us-strategy-to-curb-chinese-cyberspying/2014/05/22/a66cf26a-e1b4-11e3-9743-bb9b59cde7b9_story.html (accessed December 1, 2015).

Northrop Grumman Corp. 2012. "Occupying the Information High Ground: Chinese Capabilities for Computer Network Operations and Cyber Espionage." Report prepared for the U.S.-China Economic and Security Review Commission.

Ophardt, Jonathan. 2010. "Cyber Warfare and the Crime of Aggression: The Need for Individual Accountability on Tomorrow's Battlefield." *Duke Law and Tech. Review* 3.

Rid, Thomas. 2012. "Cyber War Will Not Take Place." *Journal of Strategic Studies* 35 (1): 5–32.

Roggensack, Meg and Betsy Walters. 2011. *Excuses, Excuses: Surveillance Technology and Oppressive Regimes*, at: www.humanrightsfirst.org/2011/11/18/excuses-excuses-surveillance-technology-and-oppressive-regimes/ (accessed December 1, 2015).

Sandvik, Kristin B. 2014. "New NATO Cyber Defense Policy: Unclear on Key Issues." October 14, at: www.ui.se/eng/blog/blog/2014/10/14/new-nato-cyber-defense-policy-unclear-on-key-issues.aspx (accessed December 1, 2015).

Sanger, David, David Barboza and Nicole Perlroth. 2013. "Chinese Army Unit Is Seen as Tied to Hacking Against U.S." *New York Times*, at: www.nytimes.com/2013/02/19/technology/chinas-army-is-seen-as-tied-to-hacking-against-us.html?pagewanted=all (accessed December 1, 2015).

Shackelford, Scott J. 2009. "Nuclear War to Net War: Analogizing Cyber Attacks in International Law." *Berkeley Journal of International Law* 25.

Shackelford, Scott J. 2013. "Toward Cyberpeace: Managing Cyberattacks through Polycentric Governance." In *America the Virtual: Security, Privacy, and Interoperability in an Interconnected World.* American University Law Review 62.

Sharma, Amit. 2010. "Cyber Wars: A Paradigm Shift from Means to Ends." *Strategic Analysis* 34 (1).

Schmitt, Michael N. 2012. "International Law in Cyberspace: The Koh Speech and Tallinn Manual Juxtaposed." *Harvard International Law Journal Online* 54 (13), at: www.harvardilj.org/2012/12/online-articles-online_54_schmitt/ at 15 (accessed December 1, 2015).

Schneier, Bruce. 2010a. *The Threat of Cyberwar has been Grossly Exaggerated*, at: www.schneier.com/blog/archives/2010/07/the_threat_of_c.html (accessed December 1, 2015).

Schneier, Bruce. 2010b. *Threat of "Cyberwar" Has Been Hugely Hyped*, at: http://edition.cnn.com/2010/OPINION/07/07/schneier.cyberwar.hyped/ (accessed December 1, 2015).

Shirky, Clay. 2011. "Political Power of Social Media—Technology, the Public Sphere Sphere, and Political Change." *Foreign Affairs* 90 (28).

Silver, Daniel. 2002. "Computer Network Attack as a Use of Force Under Article 2(4) of the United Nations Charter." *INT'L L. STUD.* 76.

Smith, Julianne. 2014. *NATO Must Get More Serious on Cyber Security.* February 6, at: www.atlanticcouncil.org/en/blogs/natosource/nato-must-get-more-serious-on-cyber-security (accessed December 1, 2015).

Spiegel. 2011. "Anti-Virus Pioneer Evgeny Kaspersky: 'I Fear the Net Will Soon Become a War Zone," at: www.spiegel.de/international/world/anti-virus-pioneer-evgeny-kaspersky-i-fear-the-net-will-soon-become-a-war-zone-a-770191.html (accessed December 1, 2015).

Tikk, Enneken. T. 2011. *Comprehensive Legal Approach to Cyber Security.* PhD dissertation on file, Tartu University Press.

Tilford, E.H. 1995. *The Revolution in Military Affairs: Prospects and Cautions.* U.S. Army War College Strategic Studies Institute.

Toffler, A. and H. Toffler. 2004. *War and Anti-War: Survival at the Dawn of the 21st Century.* Boston, MA: Little Brown.

Vihul, Liss. 2013. *The Talling Manual on the International Law Applicable to Cyber Warfare.* April 15, at: www.ejiltalk.org/the-tallinn-manual-on-the-international-law-applicable-to-cyber-warfare/ (accessed December 1, 2015).

Waxman, Max C. 2011. "Cyber-Attacks and the Use of Force: Back to the Future of Article 2(4)." *Yale Journal of International Law* 36.

Wegener, Henning. 2011. *The Quest for Cyber Peace.* International Telecommunication Union and World Federation of Scientists.

White House. 2013. *FACT SHEET: U.S.-Russian Cooperation on Information and Communications Technology Security.* June 17, at: www.whitehouse.gov/the-press-office/2013/06/17/fact-sheet-us-russian-cooperation-information-and-communications-technol (accessed December 1, 2015).

Wolff, Josephine. 2014. *NATO's Empty Cybersecurity Gesture*, at: www.slate.com/articles/technology/future_tense/2014/09/nato_s_statement_on_cyberattacks_misses_some_fundamental_points.html (accessed December 1, 2015).

Wu, Tim and Jack Goldsmith. 2008. *Who Controls the Internet—Illusions of a Borderless World.* New York: Oxford University Press.

Yoshihara, T. 2001. *Chinese Information Warfare: A Phantom Menace or Emerging Threat?* DIANE publishing.

Zengel, Patricia. 1996. *Responding with Force to Information Warfare: Legal Perspectives.* Newport, RI: Naval War College.

Ziolowski, Katharina. 2013. *Confidence Building Measures for Cyberspace—Legal Implications.* NATO Cooperative Cyber Defence Centre of Exellence, Tallin, Estonia.

Zittrain, Jonathan. 2008. *The Future of the Internet: And How to Stop It.* New Haven, CT: Yale University Press.

Index

Page numbers in *italics* denote tables, those in **bold** denote figures.